The Night Is Dark
and I Am Far from Home

7/14/10

Andrea,

A Book
To REMEMBER.

The Night Is Dark and I Am Far from Home

Jonathan Kozol

CONTINUUM · New York

1980
The Continuum Publishing Corporation
815 Second Avenue, New York, NY 10017

Printed in the United States of America

Library of Congress Catalog Card Number: 79-27504
ISBN: 0-8264-0008-6
Previously ISBN: 0-8164-9011-2

Portions of this book have appeared, as work in
progress, in *The Teacher Paper, Fellowship, The
Boston Phoenix, Social Policy, Saturday Review, New
Schools Exchange, The Harvard Crimson, The
Newsletter of the Teacher Drop-Out Center,
Ramparts, The B.U. News, The New York Times* and
The Boston Globe. An early version of the manuscript
was published in a limited edition as a CIDOC
CUADERNO (No. 88), Cuernavaca, Mexico, 1974.
The title of this book is borrowed from an essay by the
dramatist and critic Eric Bentley; its origin is the hymn
"Lead, Kindly Light."

"In this life we prepare for things, for moments and events and situations . . . . We worry about wrongs, think about injustices, read what Tolstoi or Ruskin . . . has to say . . . Then, all of a sudden, the issue is not whether we agree with what we have heard and read and studied . . . The issue is *us,* and what we have become."

— ROBERT COLES

PREFACE TO THE THIRD EDITION

The panic signals are out again, and the parents of the nation are unanimous in stating their concern about the seeming failure of the public schools to teach their children how to read and write. It is, admittedly, a real and present problem. In my own view, however, it is not the ultimate problem. It is a "screen issue" which disguises a number of deeper reasons for alarm.

The ultimate issue is not the failure of some, most, or all of our schools to teach our children basic skills. It is our hesitation or refusal to ask remorseless, penetrating questions concerning the intended or potential *uses* of those skills.

Until the question of the use and application of hard skills receives some serious attention, we may very well manage to teach a few more million children how to read and write; but we will not have solved the overarching problem of a technological competence gone wild, a scientific expertise gone mad, an intellectual excellence that does not even dare to state or specify what master it will serve.

This last point is the key to all the rest.

There is no such thing as a "neutral" skill, nor is there "neutral education." Children can learn to read in order to understand instructions, dictates, and commands. Or else they can read in order to grasp the subtle devices of their own manipulation—the methods and means by which a people may be subjugated and controlled.

We live in a land of managed wants and skillfully created needs. To learn to read—but not to learn, at the same time, the leverage and sophistication by which to separate the truth from the distortion, the fabrication from the fact—to learn this much, but no more, is to learn to lose our soul even as we gain the competence to win a kingdom.

The parents of the children now attending public school—much like people at a party "calling out" for pizza or for Chinese food—want to be sure that schools "deliver" the familiar skills that they expect. They do not think it worth their while to ask for critical consciousness or for an ethical "cutting edge" at the same time.

In the wake of the decade that began with Kent State, Watergate, and My Lai and ended with a series of unprecedented technological and aeronautical deceptions and disasters, this is no trivial omission.

A story is told, of J. Robert Oppenheimer, that is perhaps an ideal illustration of the problem we confront.

Pressed by his fellow physicists, during 1945, as to the moral implications of their work—Oppenheimer was, at that time, working on the final stages of development of the atom bomb—Oppenheimer and his co-worker Fermi replied that they were "without special competence on the moral question."

In retrospect, and with all reverence for the man that Oppenheimer was, or sought to be, it is difficult not to be troubled by this curious response. Any person, we might feel prompted to reply, who has the shrewdness and sophistication to help contrive a weapon that has power to destroy all life upon the earth, had damn well better have some "special competence" concerning the ethical implications of his work.

If he cannot, or does not feel the right and power—the expertise—to do so, then he is in a gruesome situation, by my own belief; but this is not nearly so gruesome as the place in which he leaves the rest of us. It is a kind of tangled "Nagasaki of the Soul."

Parents continue to cry, teachers to cringe, because of the purported "disaster" of a drop in reading-scores. If they must cry and cringe at all, at least it would be a blessing in our times if they were able to cry about the *real* disaster.

There was no lack of basic skills among the scientists who built and who now operate the plant at Three Mile Island, but there was an almost total lack of effort, competence, or will to stop and think about the ethical implications of the work at hand. It is this, not basic skills but basic competence for basic ethical inquiry and indignation, which is most dangerously absent in our schools and our society today.

It is this, too, which we must do our best somehow to repossess as we step, with no small doubt and trepidation, out of the present tense and move, with measured pace, into the 1980s.

Boston
January 1980

TO THE READER

MOST OF THIS BOOK is autobiographical in character. In general, therefore, I speak of the child as a boy and of the adult as a man. The one exception is the situation of the first three grades of school. Here, the teacher is most often female. I keep the female noun-form for these early years.

In spite of suggestions from some readers, I have decided not to speak here of the Watergate disaster. I do not think that it calls for additional discussion now. It is perhaps just one more piece of evidence that we do not have free choice in elections any more than in our public schools. If Watergate represents some sort of an exception to the norm, it is such only by its tawdry details and, above all, by the fact that it was brought to light. In other respects — the crime itself, the cancellation of the democratic pretense which it represents and, in particular, the circus atmosphere, followed by numbness on the part of nine tenths of the population — Watergate is not new matter. Teachers will handle it as they have done with every previous revelation of this kind. It is "an aberration." Already I hear children speaking of the matter in these terms.

CONTENTS

FOREWORD

WHEN I WAS SIXTEEN years of age, in 1952, my closest friend and only rival, in a secondary school not far from Boston, went up into the attic of his father's house and hanged himself from one of the huge rafters. It was the night before the first day of our junior year.

I do not know, of course, exactly how my classmates felt. I know, for my part, that it was a time of icelike horror. First days, then weeks, then a whole month had glided by, before I started to come back to something like a state of calm perception. The next clear memory I have is of a day in late November when the skating-pond froze over and the hockey team began to practice for its winter season.

In the past few months, I have found a number of the details of that year returning to me when I try to sleep. I look back with sadness, sometimes with desperation, on the hours and afternoons when he and I used to "skip out," in only the most uncertain and most tentative rebellion, from the routine obligations of our academic lives, in order to talk with one another of our hopes and plans for all the years ahead. We used to go and sit up high against a hillside that looked down upon a river that ran through the woods and meadows of our school.

I remember the physical elevation of the spot, the power that it held for both of us. In class, they talked of common matters, ordinary goals: Betsy Ross, the Panama Canal, Theodore Roosevelt ("carry a big stick!"). Up on the hill, we told each other of our deepest dreams.

He told me that he planned to be a priest, as well as artist, and a parish worker. He told me also that he planned to live his life among poor people. He told me that the model of his life had been, and would forever be, Saint Francis of Assisi. I did not know then who Saint Francis was; but it seemed wonderful to me that he had found his life's vocation when he was just sixteen years old. Later, he asked me what I hoped to do with my career. I told him that I hoped I could become a writer.

I remember those times. I remember also how we always had to hurry back to class in order to do whatever it might be that we were scheduled for. All of the hours that mattered most to us, in terms of passion, high stakes, daydreams and ideals of justice: all of those hours were times "sneaked-in," "unlicensed," "unpermitted." We got no credit-hours for them.

He died: I lived. So did my classmates, with exception of one boy who died of cancer two years later. Each death allowed us pause. Then we went back to lockstep labor, texts and homework, "requisite sports," then College Boards, then college, then (for most) a graduate school, then something which was later described to me as my adult life.

Now I am here: He isn't.

I think back often on those afternoons, when we were both fifteen. Then, only then, were we the *subjects*, strong and active, of our own existence. I remember especially how we told each other what we planned to do with our own lives when they returned to us some day. He was trustful, never satirical, about my plan to be a writer. I remember his kind eyes.

Now I look back, and I do not feel bitter for the way in which we were compelled to spend those years. Nor do I dream of saying that my teachers would have wished me or my friend to undergo that sense of terror, loss of blood and loss of life. I just think of it as of a time when all of us, teachers and pupils — for some reason that we never would be told — had been condemned to live in prison. We made a couple of jail-breaks, as it were, out to the high grass and the hill above the stream. For the rest, we sat alone within our cells and did the work that we were told to do.

I have a yearning to go back there now, to the same place and to the same hour, when we were students in our sixteenth year — and "start all over." We can't though: each for a unique but quite implacable set of reasons. My friend was named James G. MacDonald. If he had lived, he would, like me, be thirty-nine years old today. This book is dedicated to his memory.

I. DECEPTIONS OF THE NINETEEN SIXTIES

U.S. EDUCATION is by no means an inept, disordered miscon-
struction. It is an ice-cold and superb machine. It does the job: not
mine, not yours perhaps, but that for which it was originally con-
ceived. It is only if we try to lie and tell ourselves that the true
purpose of a school is to inspire ethics, to provoke irreverence or
to stimulate a sense of outrage at injustice and despair, that we are
able to evade the fact that public school is a spectacular device,
flawed beyond question but effective beyond dreams. The problem
is not that public schools do *not* work well, but that they *do*.

The first goal and primary function of the U.S. public school is not
to educate good people, but good citizens. It is the function which
we call — in enemy nations — "state indoctrination." In speaking
of the U.S.S.R., for example, we feel little hesitation to apply this
term. In the U.S., in the double talk of Schools of Education, we
employ more elegant expressions like "the socializing function."

The words are different. The function is the same: twelve years
of mandatory self-dehumanization, self-debilitation, blood-loss.
The use of a term like "socialization" may temporarily dignify and,
in some ways, complexify the process. It does not, however, make
that process either less debilitating or less brutal in its impact on our
children.

Three points seem essential to establish before going on:

(1) There is, to start with, a familiar liberal defense. "Don't we
need some sort of social 'glue' to hold us all together in one land?"
This is a naïve and, in certain situations, consciously diversionary
question. It is, of course, the truth that *every* social order finds
some ways to socialize young people. The fact becomes important,
and the question of the power of the school becomes intense and
urgent only if we feel that there is something, in particular, destructive, evil or dehumanizing in *this brand* of socialization or, on

another level, in the kind of life defined as normal in this nation.

I am not opposed to the idea of adult "imposition" on the minds of children. Indeed, I am convinced there is no way by which to overcome such imposition. The Afro-Indian scholar, Joao Coutinho, has established the transparent truth of this in writing published in The Harvard Educational Review five years ago.* "There is no neutral education," he observed. "Education is either for domestication or for freedom." I know very well that I can spare myself objections in some liberal readers if I will agree to blur this point and to adopt instead the customary code-words of romantic child-adulation: "Kids are neat. Why don't we let them be, to grow, and blossom, and explore, according to their own organic and spontaneous needs?" To me, this statement strains all credibility. "Spontaneous Growth" does not exist within a nation governed by stage-managed views. There is either the uncontested bias of the state or else — in those combative situations which I seek at every chance to bring about — a number of forms of counter-imposition, competition, provocation, dialectic. Whether we choose this loaded label ("dialectic") or one of the less intimidating terms, the point at this stage can be summarized in few words: I am not in political or pedagogic opposition to the risk of adult imposition on a child's mind. I am in strongest possible opposition to the present social order of the U.S. and, for this reason only, to the lies which are inevitably purveyed by schools which stand in service to its flag and anthem.

(2) There is a viewpoint, popularized by many authors now, that schools may be "a good deal less decisive" in the evolution of a child's life, or ideology, or income, than was previously believed. This point of view, which has some merit in specific subject-areas, is not relevant to this book. The question here is not if school is (or is not) the one, most potent and effective means of ideological and ethical manipulation in the land. It is enough that schools do exercise a devastating impact in the realm of moral values and political indoctrination. Whether the root-cause lies in "the whole economic system," in homes, in neighborhoods, in T.V. studios or in the boardrooms of large corporations, the bias of the school itself is clearly anti-ethical

---

* For this, and for all subsequent items of quotation, documentation or statistic, see Notes, beginning on page 198.

and anti-human. If certain evils (hard self-interest, for example) do not start within the public school, then it is clear at least that they are deepened and authenticated there. It is pointless, therefore, to debate the possible degree to which we now confront, in public school, a "prime mover" or a law-mandated ally of the murderous values which prevail within the nation as a whole.

Words like these should not astonish us. School historians point out that, from the first, school indoctrination was not unintended but one open, clear-cut and consistent function of the public schools. Horace Mann, addressing himself primarily to business interests during 1844, made the argument for public school as agent of indoctrination and class stratification in straightforward terms: "Finally, in regard to those who possess the largest shares in the stock of worldly goods, could there, in your opinion, be any police so vigilant and effective, for the protection of all the rights of person, property and character, as such a sound and comprehensive education and training as our system of common schools could be made to impart . . . Would not the payment of a sufficient tax to make such training universal, be the cheapest means of self-protection and insurance?"

It is apparent to us all that there are many other forms of self-protection for the ruling class. Wherever else, however, there is ideological bias in the field of forces that surround a child as he grows up in this land, all but school are random, casual and inconsistent. Only public school presents a law-mandated, certified, non-optional realm of childhood-indoctrination. For those who are the children of the very rich, in prep schools governed by Trustees instead of School Boards, there is a parallel version of indoctrination. Somewhat more subtle, it is also more effective. The bias of both, however, is the same.

(3) Teachers often speak today, and at great length, of wishing to see the public school less rigid, less oppressive in its operation, more "free," more "democratic" and the like. Yet they are not willing to confront, at the same time, *the one, exclusive and historic function* of a system that runs counter to these goals. It is not even the benevolent case of "getting done some bits of good right here and now in pleasant, non-subversive ways," as wistful teachers often say, "even if we have to wait to deal with larger issues until

later on." If it were this, the willingness to get down on the floor with kids and loosen up the mood and have some fun, it would, from a kindly point of view, be unassailable.

I am convinced, however, that, far from real liberation, such a process, if divorced from larger goals, does the reverse. It does not break the bars, but fashions them more strong while rendering them less visible. It does not undermine the basic function of the school, but helps to save it from important condemnation by the introduction of bright-colored paint, soft cushions, gerbil cages.

"School," Jules Henry has written, "is an institution for drilling children . . . The early schooling process is not successful unless it has accomplished in the child an acquiescence in its criteria, unless the child *wants* to think the way the school has taught him to think."

The lip service paid today to words like "open education," out of keeping with that pretense of free options that has long been useful to the process of indoctrination, must not delude us as to the real goals for which our schools exist. Rather, it should serve as a reminder that indoctrination, in a nation dedicated to the idea of free conscience, must be far more subtle than in nations that are openly totalitarian. In a social order such as ours, Galbraith has said, people need to think themselves unmanaged, independent, free, if they are to be controlled with maximum success.

This point seems of special import in the present decade, when so many people are expending vast amounts of time to make the school *appear* less binding than before. I do not believe that many of these women and these men are grateful to be told exactly what it is that they are really doing. What that is, in my own view, is to assist the process, well-described by Galbraith and Jules Henry, of enabling the imprisoned to feel free and the crippled to interpret their toe-movements as real ambulation.

Schools that have evolved the most sophisticated pretenses of freedom are often those whose pupils are least free, and educators who devise the most intriguing methods of "free learning" are today the most effective narcotizers that we have. "Educationists," Jules Henry has observed, "have attempted to free the school from drill . . . always choosing the most obvious 'enemy' to attack . . . With every enemy destroyed, new ones are installed . . . Educators think that when they have made arithmetic or spelling into a game; made it unnecessary for children to 'sit up straight'; defined the relationship between teacher and children as democratic; and introduced plants, fish, and hamsters into schoolrooms, they have settled the problem of drill. They are mistaken.''

The statement is true. It is for this reason that I find some of the most intriguing work of those of my colleagues I admire most, so dangerous. Their greatest contributions stand today in the same relationship to freedom as those of Einstein did to the preservation of life. Bruner's discoveries about how people acquire information and remember it, John Holt's views on how our children fail and how they learn, are now being used by corporations such as I.B.M., Xerox and E.D.C. in order to develop the most clever methods ever known for teaching children how to phantasize a sense of freedom that does not exist. Scott Foresman, and my old schoolteacher with her foolish list of "favorable modifiers," seem innocent indeed beside the skillful methodologies of this new age of Innovative Bondage.

To put on blinders, and pretend we do not see this point, is too much like the willingness to co-exist with knowledge of an operable cancer. If we are to live our lives as honest people, we cannot work with teachers and develop classroom methods and materials for their use unless we simultaneously set out to introduce specific strategies for raising consciousness about the function which those teachers are compelled to carry out — *and then assist them in the struggle to transform that function.* We cannot play the disingenuous game of trying to participate in trivial and non-substantial innovation, while hoping to "slip in a little hint of ethics now and then, when nobody is looking." We cannot do this if, in fact, we know that schools do not exist with these ideals in mind and that even those state-authorized "alternatives" which School Boards now and then allow will be permitted only if they serve priorities that are not ours. To cruise along, make prettier classrooms and less candidly manipulative tools, if at the same time we perceive the prime indoctrinational purpose of the schools and are not willing to engage in realistic tactics to confront this goal, is to decorate the evil we perceive with charm, and to invalidate our own worth.

In my belief, few books on education published in the past ten years are ethical books. They are not ethical because they are not invocations to lived visions. They *tell* of challenges, *refer* to agonies, *comment* on difficulties. They do not ask an answer in the form of action from the reader. Their power begins and ends within the world of words and paragraphs alone.

If the present book does not compel transformed behavior, in the life of its own author and in that of its authentic reader too, then it does not merit the expense of labor which it now commands and has commanded for the past five years; nor can it justify the pain and anguish I would wish it to provoke within the conscience of an undefended reader.

People who are looking for "a lot of interesting ideas," and hope to dabble here for little more, offend the author and degrade themselves. They would do well to stop right now. Those who read in order to take action on their consequent beliefs — these are the only readers I respect or look for. Atrocities, real and repeated, proliferate within this social order. The deepest of all lies in our will not to respond to what we see before us. When we declare that we are troubled by the lockstep life that has been charted for us by the men and women who now govern and control our public schools, what we are doing is to state our disavowal of an evil and unwanted patrimony. We are not living in an ordinary time, but in an hour of intense and unrelenting pain for many human beings. It is not good enough to favor justice in high literary flourish and to feel compassion for the victims of the very system that sustains our privileged position. We must be able to disown and disavow that privileged position. If we cannot we are not ethical men and women, and do not lead lives worth living.

II. STRAIGHTFORWARD LIES

> "There is good reason to believe that the average Chinese is
> not getting enough food to keep healthy, and in many cases
> even to keep alive . . . The communes are a failure . . ."
> — Xerox Publications (1971)

CHILDREN ask us: "Why do I have to go to school?"

We act as if it were a foolish question and we answer: "It is for your own good."

It isn't a foolish question, though; and the answer that we give is far from honest. Children do not go to school "for their own good." They go to school for something that is called "their nation's good." They go to school to learn how *not* to interrupt the evil patterns that they see before them, how *not* to question and how *not* to doubt: to learn to vote with reasonable regularity, to kill on orders and to sleep eight hours without grief. They go to school to learn to be proficient at mechanical procedures, docile in the presence of all processes they do not understand, acquiescent in the presence of a seeming barbarism. It is not so much that they learn to be "cruel" people. Rather it is, they learn it is not needful to be urgent in compassion or importunate in justice. Not positive desolation, but a genial capability for well-behaved abstention in the presence of despair: this is the innocence we teach our children.

For ten years, most of the books on school reform have been either (1) technical, (2) mischievous, (3) therapeutic. They speak a great deal of the "decency" of "kids," the "stupidity" of schools, the "mindlessness" of the school systems: seldom, however, of the efficacious action of a school in training up the kind of citizen this nation needs. They speak of "process" (a luxurious term because it sidesteps politics and ethics both in an explicit form) and cast the stigma of "the obvious" upon the glaring fact that poison *content* is today, as it has been for something like one hundred years, the single, most identifiable and damaging ingredient of that consumer fraud which is a public school. The situation is a great deal too much like that of the Emperor's Clothes.

Process counts. It counts enormously, and in some vicious ways that liberal reformers do not like to say; yet it is naïve, if it is not just dishonest, to pretend that content does not have its devastating power too. The Gifted Evasion of the Central Point (a well-paid skill in the U.S. today) leads in-house school reformers to address themselves instead to "how we structure, learn, relate to teacher and to peers." It nicely steers away from loaded matters like the Flag Pledge or a course of study which is nine-tenths lies.

I do not pretend that I have come upon a point which has not been discussed by others. It is a point, however, that has not been taken up by many others as a matter *basic to the issue*. This omission could not go unnoticed in the work of serious thinkers in the Third World. Again and again, the shadow of a Cold War concept ("End of Ideology") hangs over the discussion. Few school reformers wish to recognize their own enslavement to three decades of indoctrination on this score. The presence, moreover, *in their own work,* of an ideology that they will not confess — in form of loyalty, for instance, to the white and well-to-do whose cold self-interest they adorn with harmless innovation — is hidden behind the mask of value-free reform and non-political intentions. The facile application of such words as "beautiful" (for kids), "mindless" (for schools), "crazy" (for school systems) builds a basis wholly of aesthetic or else humanistic reference for the subsequent discussion.

By this device, the language of debate obscures the point that something like life-struggle might now be at stake: a struggle which concerns quite realistic and intensely dangerous self-interests, ideologies and competitions. Education writers, in large numbers, hold their disputations in the inoffensive framework of a decent nation, of a democratic culture, of (at worst) an inept, unwise, but benign and well-intending corporate structure. Indoctrination is regarded by these critics as so trivial that it does not warrant our consideration, or else so obvious that no one subtle and sophisticated needs to speak of it at all. At the least, this is a sweeping oversight. At the most, it is a vicious and self-serving definition of "sophistication."

The containment of youth, which lies at the heart of school indoctrination, depends upon the demolition of a child's ideological and ethical perceptions quite as much as psychological obliteration, tedium and torpor. The child who perceives his own enclave-existence as a form of individual oppression in a closed room of political restraints, begins in that perception a procession of ideas which cannot fail but lead to active intervention in those processes which he identifies and comprehends. All of school indoctrination is contrived to fend off just such recognitions.

The first objective and the most consistent consequence of public school is the perpetration of a U.S. value system: one that dominates both how we think and how we feel about those people who do *not* live in this land, or else who *do*, but live here in those Third World colonies which are the non-white ghettos. The goal is self-protection in the face of activating guilt and shame. Texts for years have trained us to believe in the benign relationship in which we stand beside those people who are still described, with more than optimism, as "Our Friends in Other Lands." The surfeit, over-fullness, over-richness we enjoy, exist somehow upon a plateau of untouched and non-malignant privilege.

Seldom is a profit motive worked into those cheerful passages on North American incursions into Chile or Bolivia or Brazil. We go to foreign nations, every time, to bring "new methods," "modern technology" or financial aid. Nobody tells the children, in plain fact, that we are there (1) to make money, (2) to operate a missile base, (3) to put down social revolution. Galbraith speaks of consumer-manipulation by means of press and T.V. as "organized public bamboozlement." Nationalistic education is a special brand of such bamboozlement; patriotic mindlessness is the product being sold. Most children buy it, unresistingly.

"When Richard Nixon was a little boy, he said, 'I want to be a lawyer, an honest lawyer who doesn't cheat people but helps them.'" This is an excerpt from a book in recent use within the Cambridge Public Schools. "Dick had to work hard at jobs all the time he was at school, but graduation day finally came. He opened a law office. Then, a few years later, some men asked Dick to run for Congress. He won. Later he became the Vice-President and, in

1968, he was elected to be President. He always remembered what his mother had told him. 'You must try to be good at everything.' "

Lies of this kind — ideological deception of overt or else sophisti-cated form, identification of "the good" with U.S. interests, of "the bad" with Eastern, Marxist-Leninist direction — these are the vis-ible portion of the iceberg of indoctrinational control. There are many days, in many schools, when children never get to science, math or reading. There are very few days, in very few schools in the United States, when children do not stand before the teacher, place hand on heart, raise eyes to flag and ritualistically incant a pledge of prior, absolute allegiance to the power and the interests which that banner signifies.

Teachers often try to make light of the pledge: "The kids don't know the words . . . It doesn't work . . . We never sing the anthem anyway . . ." It is a nervous effort to ward off a sense of dangerous self-accusation for participation in a ritual of unforgivable deceit. The Flag Pledge "works," no matter how we smile, fudge its syl-lables or talk about its "meaning" with the children. A child cannot swear an absolute allegiance to a single viewpoint, bias, goal or interest, and then proceed into a day or year of honest inquiry and of unbiased disputation.

School serves the state. The interests of *this* state are not compat-ible with private ethics or unmanageable dissent. The stars and stripes are not above the door for decoration. They tell us, in the clearest possible terms, the name and motives of the owner of the structure that our learning shall inhabit. Teachers who try to obvi-ate this fact are lying, not just to themselves, but to the children in their power.

Nationalistic self-deceit, however, is by no means a sufficient definition of the major function of the public schools. The goal is less specific and less factual: more surgical and more invidious. The space in which the public classroom stands is, in this sense, much like the atmosphere within a diplomatic compound, business outpost or high-rise hotel, walled carefully with glass and steel and stone, and guarded well against the rage of desperate people in impover-ished lands.

The message that gets through is one of calm, benevolent and untumultuous assurance. The world is nice and people are okay.

Poverty, pain and desperation are not real, or, if real, then at least they are not realizable in normal school-imaginations. It is a "filtered" message: one the C.I.A. might label "sanitized." The world exists with "serious problems," "difficult dilemmas" and a certain number of admissible imperfections — never, however, with ordeals or agonies, or with indecencies or terrors. It is a world that might require, at most, some modest alterations: not, however, one which calls for dangerous upheaval. It is a world which might use somebody like Nehru, but not Gandhi, one which might show gratitude for Emerson, but will not be looking for Thoreau.

To the extent that certain situations may be labeled as "unjust," they are, in almost every case, those which can be met by handsome men and square-jawed boys like those who smile out, as after lobotomy, from milk and health-care posters. To the extent that the U.S. is culpable at all, it is never a case of "doing wrong" but only of *not doing enough "good" fast enough.* The world's sorrows, defined in public school, are "problems" to be "tackled" by the use of combine harvesters, crop rotation, U.S. doctors, Ford cars, "schools like this one," Point Four, Alliance For Progress, War On Poverty, "modern management methods . . ."

Few evils are accepted that will not admit of technological correction. The blind of India are relieved of cataracts by Indian doctors trained in Cleveland and Los Angeles; the starving children of North Africa and Asia receive their daily glass of powdered milk out of a carton bearing English words. All of it works, in concert, to create for us a sense of calm, of manageable pain and undeserved serenity. School is the ether of our lives by now: the first emaciation along the surgical road that qualifies the young to be effective citizens, alert to need but tempered as to passion, cognizant of horror but well-inoculated against vigorous response.

The way the schools define a term such as "the use of force" provides a good example of the undisguised indoctrination I have now in mind. Schools distinguish between two kinds of force. One (that of the tortured and rebellious victim) is condemned without remorse. The second (that of the relaxed and genteel victimizer) is condoned on grounds of its non-visible and, too often, technological expression. Violence serving U.S. geographical expansion or industrial investment somehow wins an ethical exemption. It does not "count." It does not seem illegal, violent, unjust. Nor does the quiet violence of malnutrition, mass-starvation, medical despair. Forty thousand poor-white, black and Spanish-speaking children who die each year in the U.S., for lack of pediatric and pre-natal and obstetric care, are — from an objective point of view — the victims of mass murder by neglect. This, however, is not designated as a form of violent action in the texts and lessons of the U.S. schools. Reaction to such brutal life-conditions — in the sudden, clear and visible upheaval of a Third World Revolution or a U.S. ghetto population — this is the only form of violence and force which public education trains us to abhor.

This kind of lie (by fact or by omission) is not a mindless or an unexpected outcome of the educating process. Education of this kind makes perfect sense within a nation such as ours: one that is today, more than at any time before, harassed by the proliferation and exposure of unprecedented exploitation on all sides — much of it, as we know, to our own profit — and when we are now surrounded by a world of people in revolt who do not trust us. Just children are a formidable danger to an unjust nation unless they can be etherized successfully when they are still young. It is the major function of the public schools to offer us that ether.

It must be self-evident, by this stage, that most statements I am making here are far less relevant to schools that serve poor children than to those that serve the children of the rich. My concern within this book (unlike my last two books) is a great deal less with the destructive education of the victim, more with the desensitizing education of the victimizer; less with the well-documented *agon* of the ghetto inmate, more with the dehumanizing anaesthesia of his future boss, employer and oppressor; less with the domestication of the slumlord's tenant, more with the "initiation" of the slumlord's children.

It is essential, though, once having stated emphasis like this, to make it clear that I am not concerned with school reform which helps to rescue children of rich people from the turbulence of guilt and shame — in name of "joy" or "therapy" or "self-respect" — but solely with those issues that enable us to understand exactly how it is that serious children are, or can be, ethically defused, within the walls of hard, impermeable self-interest, prior to their tenth, fifteenth or twentieth year. It is bitter that so large a portion of the education of rich children is not beautiful, and not ecstatic, and devoid of peace and joy. It is more than bitter, however — it is tragic, evil and immoral — that public schools which serve the children of the rich also mass-produce so many murderers, or else soul-broken automatons, for an unjust social order: one that is perpetuated to advance the few at direct cost to many millions.

The question here is not yet the much larger and more solemn question of the possible role that rebel-children in an unjust nation can, or cannot, seize, sustain, uphold within a serious period of upheaval. The question is not even whether rebel-children of the rich can ever be looked upon to further social revolutions which are calculated to subvert their own well-padded lives. For now, the question is just this: To what degree is it within our power to confront, either within or from outside the confines of the U.S. public school, the uncomplex and overt evil of perpetuation of a well-trained, highly skilled but numb, and therefore brutal, ruling class? To what degree can we pin down the myths, the ideologies and lies, of which the present air-tent of dehumanized technology is built?

An ethical child might, or might not, grow up to be poet, saint or revolutionary. For the larger numbers of rich children, we are still ten thousand light-years distant from such burning consummations. The question here is *not* if they might someday constitute an adult population of effective rebels. The point is: They *do* represent right now a student population of prospective pilots, Pentagon planners, doctors, lawyers, landlords, owners and oppressors.

This, to me, is one clear instance of the need for uncomplex priorities. Some things are sad. Others are tragic. Others are grotesque. The brand of school indoctrination I describe within this book is evil *not* because it bores or wearies children, nor even because it turns out dull and broken and exhausted human beings. The evil part is that we grow up "ethical incompetents" within a time of torment. It is the willingness to make distinctions of this kind that public schools do all within their power to kill off within the conscience of the rich.

Those who like to think it does not work would do very well to look at the behavior of well-educated U.S. citizens when traveling in foreign lands, but in particular within a Third World nation. There is a quality of grotesque disaffiliation in our ceaseless search for ventilated satisfactions. From streamlined jet and glass-protected airport, we drive in rented car on modern roads, walled with a thin line of decorative shrubs, bordered with sculpted trees, into the cool and glass-protected lobby of the best hotel. From hotel-balcony or hotel-window we look out on the fresh and water-drenched expanse of hotel-garden and of hotel-fountains. When we go out into the city, and return all damp and weary from our day's experience, the wrinkled clothes we wear go down to hotel-laundry and are found outside our hotel-bedroom the next morning in a pretty hotel-basket. When we are ready to depart this city ten days later, we will not even need to drive back in a rented car, but will be taken to the airport gate within an air-conditioned hotel-limousine.

The body and the conscience of the U.S. citizen alike are taught to live within an ethical quarantine: one that is transported with us to whatever places we may visit and wherever we may wish to go. It is made of steel, clean air and plastic credit card. It is made of lies, twelve years of school, large, boring, fresh-ink-smelling textbooks, teachers with dangerous nails and blue-dyed hair. It is well-ventilated. It does not ask for upkeep. It is guilt-free.

Whether it comes to view in course of travel in a Third World nation, or in the ordinary details of our day-to-day existence here at home, the capability for cold and self-awarded amnesty from pain, and disaffiliation from self-accusation, is now a standard outcome of the public schools. It is not "odd." It must no longer be described to us as "mindless" or "bizarre." It is our lot to live within a world of pain. Much of that pain is now the economic bedrock of our own material advantage. It is essential to perpetuation of this disproportion that we do not recognize the evil that we live by. If we do, it is essential that we come upon the moment of discovery from a posture of capitulation.

If we did not, if we could all at once be shaken from our dreams, we might grow up to understand we do not *need* to race and run forever, buy without cease and borrow without thought, living forever on the tail-end of the debt incurred last week or mortgage taken up last year. We might grow up instead to feel enraged about sick people, dead black infants, napalm, war-machines. We might grow up to wonder just what kind of land it is we really live in: what kind of government it is to which we hold allegiance.

Most of all, we might grow up without the shell, the casement, the surrounding lacquer that protects us from acute perceptions of those things we understand, or visible action on those evils we perceive. We might grow up to be brave and subversive human beings. It is against this ever-present danger that twelve years in public school protect us.

III. SAYING NO

"There is a constant increase, a stupendously rapid increase, in the number of obedient, docile men."

— Georges Bernanos

IN THE PUBLIC SCHOOLS of Boston, as in many other cities, there is a verse which, for long decades, was recited by all children in the course of character instruction: "Every day, in every way it is our duty to obey." Those who do not learn this verse today learn others like it. Those who do not learn it from a verse, learn it in other ways. *But all young men and women who submit to schooling learn it, somehow.*

Like every other form of public school indoctrination, the bias not to SAY NO takes on both preposterous and grim proportions. Jules Henry offers us a vivid instance of the former kind. "Generation upon generation of American children," he observes, "have been enthusiastically taught by teachers that a peninsula is a body of land surrounded on three sides by water." One wonders, he says: "(a) what is the reason for the enthusiasm over *this* relatively unimportant fact? . . . (b) of what importance is it to know what a peninsula is?"

The significance, as Henry demonstrates, is not to test our acquisition of a single, odd and useless piece of mediocre information. Instead, like many other exercises, questions, regulations in the U.S. school, its sole significance consists in this: It tests the readiness, on part of children, to give up reservations in the face of all established categories of school-expectation. Stated more simply: Its one serious objective is to test the child's willingness not to SAY NO.

I introduce this relatively harmless case-example, out of any number of such possibilities, only to reveal what I would call the visible portion of the iceberg of indoctrination in self-abnegation. Trivial and even foolish in itself, it is a clear-cut evidence of something which takes on more subtle and pernicious forms in more sophisticated schools.

Less blatant, but far more effective, forms of education-in-self-abnegation are those I witness in the wealthy neighborhoods and in the "innovative" schools. Here, it is a matter not so much of stupefaction by hypnosis, rhyme or admonition, but rather of lifted eyebrows, hesitant smiles and "constructive" emphasis on "cheerful" ways of looking at disturbing subject-areas. In either situation, whether by old-time definitions of peninsulas or by new, liberal, all-comprehending methods of domestication and intimidation, the action of denunciation is described to children as unwholesome. Negative criticism ("unconstructive commentary") is the classroom euphemism for a dangerous foray into uncredentialized rebellion on the part of pint-sized people.

The bias is not just to "go along with things," but in particular to go along with anything that is already set in motion when we get there. Since almost everything appears in operation (buildings rising, factories humming, planes flying, government functioning) at the time the child arrives, the teacher is in fact endorsing the political and moral status quo; but he does not wish to state it in this way. Instead, he offers only a good-natured and, it seems, unbiased point of view. It is a good thing to be "positive." It is not a good thing to be "negative."

In application, this involves both child and teacher right away in the "positive" affirmation of a large and murderous Industry of War, an ongoing situation of starvation, malnutrition, retardation of poor children, medical havoc in the Northern ghettos and the rural South, a simulation of democratic options by the ritual of meaningless election-choices between candidates of virtually identical position. The point is that it asks no courage, no conviction, no decision, to say yes to processes like these. They are already in existence. In effect, then, what the school approves as an "affirmative" approach is pretty much the sort of thing that we can do quite well while we are sleeping.

The symmetrical opposite — the "negative" approach — is

viewed by public school as either reckless or uncivilized: "Let's not be negative and hostile. Let's not indulge in unconstructive criticism. Let's try to find the good points in the story . . ."

From this, it is a short step to a more important and more dangerous idea. This is the idea that we not only *should* not, but do not possess the moral *right* to break down any structure, system or machine, until we are ourselves in a position to construct a working model of our own conception:

"It isn't right to knock things down," the teacher says, "unless we are prepared to put up new things in their place . . ."

"It doesn't take much courage to attack what other people do or say. The hard thing is for us to offer something better . . ."

"A great many people have worked for a very long time to write these stories for us, Susan, and to draw these illustrations, and to print this book. It is very easy for you to criticize their work without suggesting an alternative."

The truth is that it is *not* easy. The prejudice against effective criticism in a grade school classroom is so serious and so hypnotic and so frequently repeated that a little girl or boy must often be a minor prodigy of close-packed intellectual explosives even to discover adjectives sufficiently pejorative to bear their meaning. It is, very often, an act of consummate imagination, an achievement of considerable moral force and intellectual bravado, to introduce a moment of pure demolition into the bland process of the normal school day. "It doesn't take much skill to say what's bad," the teacher says. The opposite, in fact, is more the case. It takes a child of near-genius.

It is, of course, intolerable to tell a child that he does not have the right to criticize what he cannot immediately replace. A patient in surgery has an unquestioned right to protest with all fury at the use of rusty or unsterile instruments, even if he cannot claim to do the surgery himself; and a child who cannot conceive, compose, publish and distribute a professional Fourth Grade text must not, for that reason, be denied the right to question one that seems to be inept or evil.

The admonition that we do not have the right to criticize or to attack a system or an apparatus that we cannot instantly replace carries with it a whole set of overloaded implications which the child has no way to disavow. The teacher says we must not dare to break down something which we cannot instantly replace with "something better." The intricate deception in this kind of statement lies in the idea that there has got to *be* a "something better" every time. It is the notion that there is, or has to be, a special place within the world for *just this kind of structure*. The fact that something now is standing on that spot of land, or in that space of sky, leads children to believe that there was never any time when you might walk across that space and look at the horizon: "Take it as it is, or find a workable alternative." From this day on, we are too much involved in looking for the expertise by which to build that workable alternative to find the time to ask ourselves if this is something that we could not do *without*.

Then, too, the teacher is not being absolutely candid when he says to children that their detailed protest calls for a specific plan of reconstruction. This is seldom the real point. The child protests at a stupid and archaic ritual such as the use of something called a "Basic Reader" in the Fourth Grade program of the Language Arts. The teacher introduces a false issue when he asks the child if he is prepared to write a "better" reader. The real negation, on the child's part, is of the whole *idea* of "Basic Readers" — indeed the whole idea of formalizing love and of rigidifying fiction, myth and verse in something known as "Language Arts." The thing that he rejects is larger than the teacher is prepared to recognize. It is the same with many other forms of protest and denunciation. When college students SAID NO to the use of napalm, to the defoliation of the fields and to the incineration of the children of Vietnam, they did not have in mind "some other method" of conducting an illegal war; they demanded that the war itself should be arrested. The insistence upon "constructive criticism" in a situation of this sort was to pretend to miss the real point of the protest.

In refusal to accept the range and value of the child's symbol of non-supplication, the school sets out to take the metaphor at its literal and lowest level. The same routine takes place when we protest against the present level of health service in the slums. Boston City Hospital is one of the few institutions in the Western world where supervision is so inept that people die of asthma. When we protest with rage and tears against the barbarism of this situation, it is an evil form of intellectual diversion to ask us to stop, go back and say it once again "in more constructive terms." Somebody in all of Boston, someone out of all of those skilled and prosperous physicians in the medical schools of Harvard, Tufts and Boston University, knows what to do, and how to do it, by what stages, at what pace and with what blueprint. A student says all that he can, and no more than he must, when he gets up in class and cries, in trembling and tears: *"This can't go on!"*

The point is that the school creates its own complexities and builds its own walls. Within those terms, and inside the restriction of those walls, the action of denunciation is continually devalued into something of less serious dimensions. Since the system, once we are within it, seems almost entirely self-contained, it is not often possible to recognize the moment of our own capitulation. The ultimate lesson that the school conveys, no matter by what words it may be phrased, is the clear and simple lesson of unquestioned acquiescence: It is safe to say okay. It is extremely risky to SAY NO.

School defines the act of SAYING NO, in general, as unsound and unwholesome; but SAYING NO to school itself is treason. If moderate terror and a certain modest level of contamination are attached to any child who attempts to question the Scott Foresman Reader, Language Arts, the definition of "peninsula" and such, a far more dangerous level of contamination is attached to those who dare to undermine the larger, twelve-year interlock of school-credential and reward.

Acquiescence in the face of *sequence* in and of itself — this is the final and the most remorseless means by which we demonstrate our willingness to forgo reservations and withhold dissent. No matter what we do, or say, in individual classes or in isolated moments *during* those twelve years, the fact that we have stuck it out in relative silence for one sixth of our entire life, this in itself is primary evidence, for those who need to know, that we have been correctly trained to permanent abnegation of our own beliefs.

This is no accidental end-result of public school. The child who learns to acquiesce without denunciation in the loss of his own soul, can in all likelihood be counted on, as well, not to resist the loss of life in those who will, in few years, be his victims, servants or officially appointed enemies. Stated differently: Those who are content to undergo their intellectual suicide without remorse can probably be counted on, as well, to look upon the murder of their brothers and their sisters also in an untumultuous state of mind. Which of us· dares to fight to resurrect for others what we do not feel it worth our while to salvage for ourselves?

It may well be there have been other times, or other lands, in which the stakes were low to start with and in which, therefore, these kinds of issues did not seem to greatly matter. In times like these, it might not seem of great importance to be able to burn documents in public places, withhold a tax, march to the public square, stand up in school before the blackboard, and beneath the flag, and withhold our assent to all the things that flag and blackboard represent. In situations or in social orders of that kind, the acquiescent labor of a class of thoughtful children learning to draw blueprints might appear to us to be a worthwhile form of education: at least a form that would not do a vast amount of harm to other human beings. There are other times and other places where a well-placed bomb is worth a thousand blueprints.

Several million Jews and gypsies, Russian, French and Belgian, Dutch and other European people, would in all likelihood be alive today if Albert Speer — that brilliant and, in certain terrifying ways, attractive German counterpart to so many of our own most skillful social engineers and planners and advisers — had only once walked into Hitler's office with a time bomb, instead of a blueprint, in his briefcase. The inability of a reflective, literate, well-educated architect like Albert Speer to SAY NO in the face of the ongoing operations of the German military and industrial apparatus of the Nineteen Thirties, *and to offer to provide no positive alternative,* is one of the awesome tragedies of World War II. For millions of young people in Great Britain, France, the U.S., the U.S.S.R. and a number of the other large and rich and skillful nations of the present decade, the engines are already in motion when the child arrives, the wheels are turning and the gears are meshing to perfection. It would be a lifetime's enterprise to comprehend the operation of the engine, let alone to build another, but it would be an act of grace to stop the wheels from turning.

Summer 1966: A million people read, within the pages of The New York Times, a vivid and disturbing narrative of life as it is lived by migrant workers, just two hours' drive from New York City. "At one farm . . . Negroes have been crowded into chicken coops. In another, they cook, drink and bathe from a foul water tap that has been grossly polluted by a nearby privy . . . In every camp, flies swarm over the garbage-strewn dust, the young children and the cooking grits and stolen vegetables that migrants usually live on.

"At night in the camps as many as six or more children are stacked like cordwood onto one roach-infested bed . . . Many children have distended navels, indicating malnutrition, and many also [are] ridden with lice and ticks. Worm-infested infants, left unattended in camps for hours by their mothers in the fields, are sometimes bitten by rats."

We ask ourselves direct, uncomfortable questions: *What is the capacity of a well-fed and well-indoctrinated population to respond in word or action to the moral havoc of these syllables?* The Times reports the prevalence of chicken coops in New York and New Jersey. The chicken coops, we come to understand, are now inhabited by migrant laborers, poisonous rats, malarial mosquitoes, lice-ridden, worm-infested, tick-infected, unattended, cordwood-piled, navel-distended infants. Witnesses tell the nation of starvation in the Deep South: "We see malnourished babies a year old weighing seven pounds. We see the results . . . in mental retardation . . . I have seen children . . . three, four, and five years old, who weighed only twenty pounds."

If we did not first *know* about these things, if we did not have at hand the means of total and immediate relief, if there were not doctors living comfortably in good hundred-thousand-dollar homes in Great Neck, Greenwich and Grosse Point, if there were not milk and meat and medication and good comfortable warm clothes, if there were no roads or railroads to transport the personnel and produce, if it all were complex, intricate, secret and unknown, then perhaps we might explain it somehow as a riddle to be worked out by sophisticated technocrats and experts who can better understand these things than simple people like ourselves. It is not complex, however; it is not sophisticated. It is not intricate or undiscovered, secret or unknown. It is a clear and simple matter of the inability of intellectually asphyxiated people to summon up the courage for an overwhelming and resistless instant of denunciation. *We do not possess the sense of moral leverage to rise up and to denounce the evil now committed in our name.*

There is a woman I know in Roxbury. She is now thirty-five years old. With four children, ages two months to thirteen years, she lives on $2800 in a year: "Jonathan, I never have bought a new coat in my life. I never have gone to the store in these thirteen years but I have had to take home just one piece of clothes: the mittens or the boots or underwear for Sylvia. I never could buy all that she needed in one time. I gave up waiting in the line for welfare food last year because they shame you so. I had some money extra from the year before when I was doing housework; but that near to drove me crazy with my own kids here at home, plaster falling out of the walls, the rats we got, and they be waiting to get into bed there with the children. 'You know, Elizabeth, you mean as Hell,' that lady said to me one time. I said to her: 'Lady, Hell is mean.' She look at me a minute, like she don't know who I am or what I said."

Regarding the plaster: It is covered with sweet and sticky lead paint that poor children eat or chew as it flakes off the wall. The lead paint poisons the brain-cells of infants. Children die, are paralyzed, sometimes go blind, if they eat it and chew it over a long period of time.

The landlords of Roxbury live in the beautiful country west of Boston. They send their children to the Montessori Schools and little schools modeled upon Summerhill. They have their yachts in Falmouth Harbor. Buildings at universities are erected with the money donated by the landlords of Roxbury, and the names of the landlords of Roxbury are carved in handsome letters of New Hampshire granite upon the lintels of the doorways of the libraries and the dormitories that they pay for. The law does not compel a landlord to replace, repaint, or cover over the sweet, sticky plaster that paralyzes children. The law does allow a landlord to take action to evict a woman like Elizabeth who misses one rent-payment by as much as fifteen days.

This month, 1970, in the winter, a child dies in Roxbury. The doctor's statement indicates the cause is lead-paint poison. It does not make the front page of The Boston Globe because it is on the same day that the U.S. Air Force has renewed the bombing of Vietnam.

"How I like to go into a real good store down there on Newbury Street and put down forty dollars and bring home a new coat for me to wear. A brand new coat: pay forty dollars. Buy it new, and bring it home that day; not buy it on time-payment."

It is not difficult for me to get hold of the cash. The next day, I put it in an envelope with a brief note, embarrassed. I go to visit a month later. She says: "Sylvia, come on out, let Jonathan see you in your new coat." I say: "Elizabeth, you didn't get yourself the coat." She says: "No, wait. I tell you just what happened if you promise not to get mad. I went downtown to all the nice stores. It was just about two weeks ahead of Christmas, so I took the children with me. They don't say nothing; but I keep on seeing Sylvia look back into the windows of the stores. She don't say nothing but I see her keep on looking. I see that look and I know she be wanting something nice and pretty for herself to wear to school, but she want me to have mine first . . . She be so good, Jonathan, I near to cry. She didn't want me to give up the coat I planned on for so long . . ."

She stops; then she calls out once more into the back room: "Sylvia, you come right in, let me and Jonathan see you in your new coat . . ."

One night she tells me a story: how they collect money at the local school "for children of the poor." It seems a little strange, but she explains it to me this way: "It used to be a white school, up to maybe five years back. Now it's all black, or maybe with some Portuguese or Puerto Rican too. Some of the teachers keep on doing just the same things like they used to do. They don't stop and look *hard* at the children that they got. So every year around Thanksgiving time they ask the children to contribute money to the poor. They give a speech about the kids who don't have things like we got here in this country . . . all these nice things like we got . . . so all the children bring in dimes and quarters.

"Sylvia say to me: 'Mama, I got to bring in money for poor

children. They don't get nothing good for Christmas if we don't help out.'

" 'How you know that?' I say.

"She say: 'I know it from my teacher 'cause she say so.'

"So I say: 'God bless the teacher — here's a dime. You tell her we be sorry not to give a little more but we be kind of short ourselves this year . . .'

"Sylvia, she be real pleased, and she take the dime in to her teacher and the teacher say she be a real good girl."

Two or three times in every year, there is a reason for me to visit with a family that I know in Lexington, a suburb twenty minutes out of Boston. There are many beautiful homes out there in Lexington, and it is very easy to relax while you are in this setting, and not to think of crazy things like lead paint or ruined brain-cells while you are surrounded with exquisite silver, beautiful furnishings and sloping gardens.

Every so often, however, my head begins to do arithmetic. I add up the value of the things that I am sitting on or things that I can touch. The sofa that I am on, covered with silk from Shanghai from before the war, is worth at least two thousand dollars; the lamps at either end must cost four hundred dollars each. The rug my shoes are soiling costs at least three thousand dollars. The lady before me is no brighter than Elizabeth, no more profound or brave or clever, kind or earnest, decent, humane, yearning or desirous. She is a nice lady, liberal and well-educated, who was sent to Foxcroft in Virginia as a young girl, later married a man who went to Milton, and now lives in Lexington. Her carpet, her two lamps and her sofa, sold at auction, would bring in at least five thousand dollars. It is a little insane, but I keep on thinking of this figure. I ask myself how much the house itself is worth and I decide: about one hundred thousand dollars. It occurs to me, as I am sitting here, that this would make a nice school . . . a good, removed and isolated rest-house for narcotics addicts . . . a wonderful location for intensive, residential health care for malnourished, worm-infested, tick-infected, navel-distended infants.

If we could SAY NO to this — to disproportion on this scale — if we could say it not just once, not just in private and not only in a situation that relieves our conscience and consoles our grief, but many times, in numerous ways, with powerful allies and with perceptive recognitions of the larger context and causation of our rage, then perhaps we might be able to SAY YES as well to the first stages of a deep and solemn form of economic and political rebellion. The bias against a disencumbered statement of denunciation does not stand alone within the lexicon of school-mandated instruments of child-debilitation. It is just one of many ways in which school serves the flag it flies and labors to defend the inequalities and disproportions it exists to foster.

IV. NO CONNECTIONS

"Politics is your concern; mine is the education of young children. If it is only children of rich people who can choose for schools like this, it is my own decision nonetheless. I choose to lead a stable, rational existence; I do not choose to deal with politics, racism and class-exploitation."

— teacher in an upper-class school
of Cambridge, Massachusetts

THE IDEA stated in these grotesque but familiar words — that it remains for anyone to choose or not to choose to be involved in someone else's desperation — depends upon the prior myth that he is not involved already in its *proceeds*.

Self-deception of this kind would not be possible if we had not been trained in school to undergo the infinite fullness of the world through patterns of disjunction, segmentation, separation. School is not the only place where segmentation is purveyed to children. I wonder, however, if it does not represent the first place in the lives of many children where clean divisions and what will prove much later on to be quite brutal separations have been given an official ratification from an outside source.

Prior to the classroom, outside of the school, most things flow into each other, one thing blends into another; many things certainly at any single moment are residing simultaneously within a child's mind. Suddenly in kindergarten, then more clearly in the First and Second Grades, the day begins to lose its complex wholeness and turns into separate items known as "periods." Imagination, diffuse as in reality it is, begins to be divided into items known as "subject matter." Intellect itself gets split up two ways into "reason" and "emotion." The day and the week and the season and the year are turned into two items known as "school" and "real world";

and the future is transformed into twelve evenly divided, but distinct and isolable, items known as "school years" — separated by invisible connectives called "promotions."

The point is not that teachers find it useful to teach subjects separately. It is the fact that we should need to separate each item with such clean *division*. One thing must not "bleed" into another. It is as if the teacher had been handed a cold Sheffield blade when he came in to teach the class and took, as his first job, the task of carving up each life into so many marketable pieces. Educators used to speak of something known as "the whole child"; yet, in certain ways, the teacher's job is less one of amalgamation than skilled surgery. In most cases, he has first applied the same divisions to his own sense of experience. If not, it has been done *for* him by *his* teachers: so that he does not sense the surgical function, nor feel the sharpness of the blade he wields. Yet even the ordinary language of his daily use reveals the underlying process.

Words like "division," "period," "section," "unit," "grade," "assignment," "chapter," "topic" and "sub-topic," "term," "semester," "credit-hour," "area of concentration" are far more common in the public schools than words that speak of continuity or wholeness. I have in my mind a kindly teacher I once knew who used to ask the class, at certain moments, to "put on our thinking-caps." Once they were "on," often enacted by a bit of ritual, she would, in most cases, pose a thoughtful question to which it was made clear that she expected thoughtful answers. Surely she did not mean that we might not have been thinking earlier than that moment — or that we might not keep right on thinking later. Still, there was the definite and intriguing sense that "thinking" as a high-priority action began with putting on the "thinking-cap" and ended with its symbolized removal. To me, this seems an apt, if innocent, example of the whole idea of carving up our intellectual experience into discrete and separate pieces. The child puts on, or takes off, his "thinking-cap." In much the same way, adults put on, or take off, their feelings of compassion, their recognition of delight, their instinct for rebellion or their inclination to self-interest.

A fine discrimination along lines of time and place assists the process. We deal with certain things in their close presence only, severing the bond of love, or chain of obligation, the instant we have

moved away in time and situation. The ghetto teacher, who lives
outside the city, cares a lot about his young black pupils and senses
a wave of strong compassion every day as he drives in along the
highway to their neighborhood: compassion which does not "dis-
solve" — but loses strength, persistence, credibility, each night —
as he drives back along the opposite side of the same highway to the
segregated suburb where he has his home. The doctor comes into
the City Hospital each morning for a year of clinical instruction in a
special field — neurology, perhaps, or pediatrics — experiences a
sense of strong involvement and disturbing confrontation with the
bitter life of those within the ghetto neighborhood who are his clients
and, sometimes, his friends: a sense of confrontation and involvement which do not cease to "exist" so much as they cease to "obtain," to "feel believable," once he is back at night within the
pleasant neighborhood of trees and lawns and flagstone walks and
nightlamp-lighted terraces, and foliage-protected porches and illumi-
nated pools, in which he has his home and leads his life with his
three children and young wife.

I lead, as I believe, a too-divided life myself. Often, therefore, I
meet such men and women at both ends of their careers. The contrast between the daytime mood of absolute immersion and commitment — and the other mood, or kingdom, or condition of entire
absolution, distance and relief — is so remarkable, so sweeping and
so deep, that it is like meeting a new person, a new section or sub-
section, a new continent as it were, of the old person, once night
comes down and scenery is shifted and the plywood windows and
the neon designations are replaced by linen tablecloths and lighted
candles and the gentle ripplings of Vivaldi or of Boccherini.

It is not easy to approach this point without the implication that
the people that I have in mind are in some manner consciously
corrupt. This is not what I feel. It is much more like a knife-blade
coming down on memory than like a cruel dismissal of remembered
pain. In the day the scarred child, snot on nostril, no warm stockings,
coat missing its third button, open sore on swollen wrist, is altogether
vivid and believable. By night, in the ample acreage of Westwood,
or out amid the cold stone of Lexington and Concord, that little
kid is *just no longer there;* nor is the sense of passion and conviction
that she has inspired in the mind and the perception of her would-be

benefactor. The high mood, the glib and giddy humor, the elegance of silver, the delicious sense of beautiful companionship and of adept and clever conversation: all testify to the falling of the blade, to the coldness of the metal, to the efficient cleanness of the steel.

Like the falling tree in the wood we do not hear, so too the desperation, lead-paint poison, ruined brain-cell, horror of the blinded child and of the mother's havoc-ridden cry, the siren's scream and blue light spinning in the neon sky are just not credible to us when they are not "there" in the sense of being validated, comprehended and authenticated by our vision. The rich man carves his beefsteak with impunity because he first applies the knife-blade to his brain. The liberal scholar finds it possible to stretch out, to relax, to savor his unhurried and enjoyable career, within an insular and well-rewarded circle of New Haven, Palo Alto or Pough-keepsie, because — *while he is in that circle* — several million starving souls of Harlem, Roxbury or Mississippi cease to be. Most of us look with terror on the knife-blade of the archetypal neurosurgeon; yet each, in our well-tailored way, has been quite tactfully loboto-mized. The wires do not meet. The messages from one part no longer seem to reach the other. The brain, like the new school-structure, is divided into "modular units" and our lives, like school-days, are segregated into subject-areas that never meet.

The twelve-year exercise in psychological and moral dis-connection takes on a specific form when we must deal with matters which involve direct and clear-cut lines of economic exploitation. Few concepts threaten to disturb rich students quite so much as the explicit recognition that they may have gained their own good health, T.V. or twelve-gear bike at the direct expense of someone else. School administrations pander to this fear by ruling out all narratives of straightforward economic exploitation.

Little by little, year by year, a wall of separation is constructed in the child's mind to offer self-protection in the face of realistic guilt at unearned privilege and inherited excess. Poor people exist — so also do the rich — but there are no identifiable connections. One side does not live well *because* another side must live in pain and fear. It is a matter, rather of two things that happen to occur at the same time: and side by side. The slumlord's daughter, therefore, is not forced to be unsettled, and still less tormented, by the fact that there are black and Puerto Rican families two miles distant who must pay the rent to make her luxuries conceivable. The general's children do not need to know their father's hands are steeped within the blood of innocent people in far-distant lands. The bank-director's child, the foreign-investment analyst's son, do not need to know the price in pain their privilege, their peace and their unprecedented economic strength are built upon.

In most instances in Northern cities now, the line between two sides is virtually impossible to find. Topographical divisions on the grid of U.S. urban architecture and design function well to reinforce the economic fictions offered in the public school. Exploitation, therefore, does not seem believable. Misery, hunger or starvation is perceived as if it were, in every case, a situation of uncaused ordeal, "benign misfortune," technological or biological mistake. There is no underlined affiliation between people who must live in grim slum-areas on one side of town and those who are invited to enjoy the art collection and the penthouse garden of the slumlord on the other. "Too little" can be said of food or of resources that belong to some — but not "too much." To say "too little" and "too much" within the same phrase is to speak of victims. In psychological terms there *are* no victims in the world-view of the U.S. public schools. To believe in victims is to believe, as well, in victimizers. It is to be forced to come into the presence of the whole idea that there must be *oppressors* in the world for there to be *oppressed*. It is to be forced, as well, to feel, and understand, that bad results too often have bad causes, that evil acts don't just "occur" — like mushrooms after rain — but have most often been initiated by the will of those who stand to profit from them.

The recognition of direct, explicit and not accidental causes and connections of this kind portends enormous danger for the conscience of the children of rich people. It is of great importance for the children of the ruling class, in a divided social order such as this, to be allowed to think of fear, starvation, sickness, in the terms of social accident or technological mistake; to think of hunger, for example, or the lack of medical care, like a season with too little rainfall, or a river that did not come up as high as usual this year. It is not comfortable to understand that the reason rivers do not rise as high as usual some years is that they have been diverted to the fields and irrigation ditches of another person in the upper meadow. It is even more disturbing to be forced to understand that oftentimes that other person is no stranger, but our friend, our next-door neighbor or our father.

Tolstoi was tormented by the implications of this self-deceit. "Men have long been living a life which is contrary to their consciousness," he wrote. "If it were not for hypocrisy, they would not be able to live this life." In *The Kingdom of God Is Within You,* published in 1905, Tolstoi speaks about the way we train ourselves not to believe in causative connections, not to believe that our advancement rests upon the soil of someone else's deprivation. "It would seem to be impossible to deny that which is so obvious," he writes, in direct reference to the causative connections which exist between great desperation and immense excess, "yet it is precisely what is being done."

He then says this: "The men of the ruling classes — the honest, good, clever men among them — cannot help but suffer from these internal contradictions . . . We cannot pretend that we do not see the policeman who walks in front of the windows with a loaded revolver, defending us, while we eat our savoury dinner or view a new performance . . . We certainly know that if we shall finish eating our dinner, or seeing the latest drama, or having our fun at a ball, at the Christmas tree, at the skating, at the races, or at the chase, we do so only thanks to the bullet in the policeman's revolver and in the soldier's gun . . ."

In evident anguish for his own sense of immersion in the self-deception he describes, Tolstoi directs his words to those of his own class: "All these men and those who live on them, their wives, teachers, children, cooks, actors, jockeys, and so forth, live by the blood which in one way or another, by one class of leeches or by another, is sucked out of the working people; thus they live, devouring each day for their pleasures hundreds and thousands of workdays of the exhausted labourers. . . They see the privations and sufferings of these labourers, of their children, old men, women, sick people; they know of the penalties to which the violators of this established spoliation are subjected . . . They not only do not diminish their luxury, do not conceal it, but impudently display before these oppressed labourers . . . their parks, castles, theatres, chases, races . . ." At the same time, he says, they also "assure themselves and one another that they are all very much concerned about the good of the masses . . ." On Sundays they dress up and drive in expensive carriages to church, "houses especially built for the purpose of making fun of Christianity." There, they listen to men, "especially trained" in pacification, "who in every manner possible, in vestments and without vestments, in white neckties, preach to one another the love of men" — all of which they "deny with their whole lives."

Tolstoi is unsparing when he talks about the willed oblivion by which rich people, in his day, as ours, contrive their own self-exculpation: "Men who own large tracts of land or have large capitals, or who receive large salaries, which are collected from the working people, who are in need of the simplest necessities . . . are fond of believing that those prerogatives which they enjoy are not due to violence, but to an absolutely free and regular exchange of services . . ." They like to think that "these prerogatives are not only not the result of assault upon people, and the murder of them . . . but have even *no connection whatsoever with these cases . . .*"*

These people, Tolstoi says, try to pretend that all those privileges which they enjoy "exist in themselves." This, to me, is the essential point. There is the myth, potent in its early implantation, cancerous and irresistible in its later growth, that the lives of children of the white and well-to-do within a land like ours exist upon a plateau of relaxed and innocent intent: one which turns at times, if we so wish, to passages of benefaction, at other times to academic labors, string quartets or summer garden parties, yet one which is at all times disaffiliated from the exploitation that it rests on, uncontaminated by the blood that nourishes its soil.

The high school senior, college freshman, university professor needs to believe his own career exists "in vacuo." He cannot dare to understand that he is there at the expense of someone else. The private patient in a pastel-painted air-conditioned room within the high-rise hospital along the river here in Boston, Massachusetts, cannot bear to know that he is there at the direct expense of those

* My emphasis.

who wait five, six or seven hours on a long and steamy summer afternoon within the basement of a ghetto hospital far over on the other side of town, before a hectic and unpracticed intern offers ten, twelve, fifteen minutes out of his long siege of eighteen desperate hours before he sends them up into a hot, unsupervised and often-times unsterile hospital ward — or else back to the fever-ridden streets they came from. No one believes that he exploits someone else. It is more like this: "the one thing here, the other over there." It is, indeed, a pity that the two things must reside together in one city. The one, however, does not "bleed" into the other. Each exists in its own private realm and separate universe. Clean steel edges: hard, explicit separations: No Connections.

There is today, in Boston, one particularly vivid instance of this surgical determination. Brandeis University, highly respected and increasingly prestigious, stands outside the city limits in suburban Boston. One of the most impressive buildings on this campus bears the name of one of the most hated slumlords in the Boston area. For many years, the man was so despised within the Boston ghetto that Jewish agencies did all they could to counteract, disown or modulate his predatory acts. The ethics of priest, rabbi, minister alike never were equal to the influence of this man or his immense reserve of cash with which to buy prestige and sidestep condemnation. There is no mystery about his methods, about his reputation or his manner of exploitation. The only mystery lies in the means by which the Trustees of this institution, as well as those who labor in its libraries and labs, are able to pretend that they do not directly profit from the desperation of a slumlord's victims.

The tall stone structure stands today upon the green and sloping hills of this expensive university: financed with misery, nourished with injustice and erected on despair. No one stands outside, with forehead bare and eyes on fire, shakes his fist and asks of one and all who come and go, enter or leave, just how much pain and how much desperation it requires in order that a structure such as this may rise and stand, in order that such luxuries as these may now accrue to those who are the children of the men whose names appear in carven words above the door. Nobody asks. If someone does, it is the type of question we dispatch with labels such as "excess rage," "innocence of the world," or else the more familiar designation:

"poor taste." In the universities and in the cocktail parties and in the dinner parties of the children of the rich, it is inevitably in the worst of taste to try to tell each other where the money comes from.

In a series of conversations held with Daniel Berrigan in 1972, Robert Coles explores this point in words which bring back to my mind the atmosphere in which I lived, and studied, and advanced my own career, when I was still a Harvard student back in 1958. The candor with which Coles discusses his own fears is brought forth by a question posed by Berrigan. The question asks if he believes that he is free, in his work as a doctor, to pursue his own ideals. Coles begins by saying that he doubts that many doctors, or professionals of any kind, ever dare to ask themselves such questions: "where their money comes from, who pays them, who rewards them . . . whom they never get to represent . . ." His deeper answer is contained, however, in these words: "When I was at Harvard . . . I never questioned the fact that the university not only had its own police force, but was buying up property . . . only in certain areas of Cambridge and not buying up property where the professors lived or where the wealthier people . . . lived . . . I never questioned that, I just thought it was part of the legitimate needs of a university — to have land, to put buildings on that land, so that people like me could learn . . . I never asked . . . what people are being educated . . . for what reason, by whom . . . at whose expense?"

This question, and the danger it conveys, does not "obtain," is not "allowed," within the U.S. public schools. The ruling principle is: No Connections. The primary action is the action of the surgical division. The myth of prior disaffiliation constitutes our "document" of diplomatic passage. It becomes our "paper of safe transit" in closed cars across the continents of fear. If it were not for powerful and persuasive fictions of this kind, much of our foreign travel would, I think, be finished in one hour. Planes would not fly, and steamships would not sail. People would stop frozen in the tracks of intellectual perseverance or within the lockstep of professional careers. The five-ten from Grand Central to New Canaan would roll slowly to a stop some place in Harlem. The air-conditioner would not work. Ice in cocktail glasses would melt. Seersucker would wilt. Tall men with exquisite manners and fine fingers would begin to tremble. They would throw away their pipes and thin cigars. It does not happen. It is not by chance.

There is one city in North Africa I know which never has found its way into the textbooks issued to the children in the U.S. schools. It is a city that has, for several decades, been a diplomatic colony — almost a military outpost — of the U.S. government. Each morning, U.S. diplomats and businessmen and military attachés, their wives and children come out from the hotel doorway and proceed across the city square. Outside the hotel, in a long, long line of silence, patience and despair, are dozens of very old and often crippled people, wrapped all in white, the women in white veils as well, and often with a quite small child standing at the side of mother or grandfather.

At eight A.M., as the sun comes up above the city square, the oldest people will be standing straight with palm outstretched before them, the other hand resting gently on the child's head, the child's palm outstretched as well. By twelve o'clock, the oldest people start to bend somewhat, forehead declined beneath the heat of noon, eyes closing slightly. By night, the old, old people are asleep, or half-asleep, asleep in pain, in fixed and frightening immobility there against the long white silence of the wall beneath the evening heat.

The Americans pass, and pass again, as they go to and fro in crisp bright jackets, seersucker and cord, attractive people, clever and adept, graceful and well-tailored in the modulation of their own compassionate reactions. Children at times will pull their mother's or their father's arm, or cry, or shudder, or in other ways react to what they see. Mother is cool and calm, well-bred and cleanly limbed and neatly dressed for travel. Father is concerned about his government assignment or his business plans.

At midnight often, when the hotel guests return from various places they have been, voices shrill and bright with good delight and memory of fine colonial service in some French or British club, the old blind beggars have fallen down the full length of the wall, unspeaking, uncomplaining and, but for the slow decline along that wall, unmoving since the dawn. Crouched, huddled now, stooped-over, bent in one white triangle of silence, anaesthesia and oblivion, the beggar slumbers at the bottom of the day's long journey downward, while infant, borrowed companion or grandchild sleeps as well, curled up against the older person's side, sores on forehead, scars and scabs and growths all over legs and arms, feet filthy, small toes bare, but hand still open, outstretched still, with palm still pleading even in the sleep of midnight on this silent street, where only the attractive young Americans from New York or from San Francisco might still chance to come by once, and shudder once, then to move on to customary and appropriate places of refined and air-conditioned slumber.

The child, unsophisticated, cries or questions. His parents, better instructed in the disciplines of North American adulthood, know well by now how to control their sense of unrest and to keep on with the evening's pleasure. If they ever stop to think about this street of misery at all, it might be only to persuade themselves that what they see before them is, in some way, spurious or inauthentic: a trick to fool the heart or to subvert the mind. In any event, they can assure themselves that grief and pain of this variety and on this scale are unrelated to the world of glass and steel in which they work and dwell.

At worst, it is a matter of a marginally perceived despair that is permitted to exist somehow within the same world as seersucker and fresh linen. Connections there are none: causations there are not any. They are Americans: rich, fortunate, well-educated, skillful. These others in the white veils are, admittedly, real people, but not rich, or fortunate, well-educated, skillful. Clean steel edges in the secret places of the well-indoctrinated brain have drawn explicit demarcations. Things break down into acceptable divisions. They are, indeed, well-educated: trained and schooled to logical postures of oblivion and acceptable self-interest. They live in one world: the starving beggars and their desperate children in another. It is a property of reason, of good sense and civilized adulthood, both to respect and understand the space that stands between.

V. PROGRESS

THE MYTH OF PROGRESS is today a basic item in the world view of the social studies text. It is, for most young men and women, a familiar myth: the sense of self-awarded respite from concern for those who *are* in trouble on the part of those who *aren't*.

The palpable illusion of inevitable progress up and onward to a place that waits for us at all times just beyond the line of sky is so pervasive now in the machinery of phrase and title, heading and sub-heading, text and illustrative photo, that a child ceases soon to notice any longer that it is a bedrock premise for the whole narration: Our Nation's Rise to Greatness . . . Building a Highway to the Latin Nations . . . Learning to Harness the Majestic Rivers . . . Conquering Space . . . We Start to Tackle Social Problems . . .

Human process, from the first, is narrated to children like the story of Horatio Alger — only with months replaced by centuries, and years by "ages" or by "civilizations." History begins, in almost every school, with a tedious study of the Fertile Crescent: images of sand and stone, and one tall, lone Egyptian walking sideways across time, his eye misplaced somehow halfway between his forehead and his ear. Each subsequent age is studied, not for anguish, passion or for moral evolution, but for "Major Contributions." The contributions of the Fertile Crescent are: the pyramid, the use of irrigation-ditches and what generally is labeled as "Discovery of Only Two Gods." The Hebrew civilization carries things a little further by "discovery" of one God. The Christians (in the Catholic texts, at any rate) consolidate the progress of the Jews, but carry things one better and identify the "right" God. Thus, as textbooks grow from page to page, and unit to sub-heading, each civilization leaves its mark on time and makes its "Major Contribution."

During the time between the Fall of Rome until the early Thirteenth Century, it might appear to some of us that nothing much is "going on," that progress has "slowed down." Instead, however, in most texts, there is the sense, not that the world has "given up" but that good people are just "resting." The period is studied, not as a negation of the myth, but rather as a quiet, yet significant, time when lots of decent folk are getting set for "something big." Suddenly, with the efflorescence of the Renaissance and Reformation, progress comes into its own once more. Martin Luther hammers out his message on the church door. Dozens of talented but childlike men (as schools imply) rush about northern Italy, painting frescoes every place that they can find a little niche above the door. Then, too — and this turns out to be a crucial point for the U.S. — transportation joins the march of progress. "Boats" become "ships." Queens become generous. Kings become competitive. Admirals grow audacious and head west to set foot on "The New World."

Henceforth, progress picks up speed and moves at rates undreamed-of in the previous four thousand years. Whereas, before, it seemed to take place every hundred years, or in each generation, now it takes place pretty much by four-year intervals. Tedious, or retrogressive, episodes such as the presidential terms of Pierce or Fillmore, or the murder of one hundred thousand souls at Hiroshima, are transcended or somehow romanticized. High points are emphasized; and every "high point" seems, by definition, a bit "higher" than the one before. Auschwitz, Selma, My Lai, Kent State are ignored or treated as historic aberrations. From this point on, the Myth of Progress seems inexorable. We cease to notice any longer how profoundly it affects the tone of press, of text, of teacher's voice, or even of our own discussion of ongoing issues. Kids, in their term papers, pick up much the same delusion:

"Drug addiction is a very important problem in this nation. It must not be imagined that the use of heavy drugs is limited to the urban areas. High incidence of drug abuse is known throughout the country and throughout all areas of the social spectrum. Many national commissions have been set in operation in the past few years . . . The Surgeon General's Report of 1965 said such and so . . . The Combined Committee of State and Federal Agencies has made a number of suggestions. It is accepted that addiction cannot flourish without serious corruption at the lower levels of the various municipal agencies. The Mayor of San Francisco has released the following directives . . . The Commission on Children and Youth has called for a discussion to deal with this problem during early summer of next year . . .

"Now that the wheels of state and Federal government are turning, we can expect to see significant changes and, we hope, statistical amelioration in this area. We cannot, of course, afford to be too optimistic. Those who sell narcotics will not hesitate to prey upon the moral fiber of the young. Nor can the problem of police corruption, when it does occur, be solved within a single month or single year. Indeed, a basic item in the democratic process that has made this nation strong is just precisely our preparedness to work through proper channels and to place our confidence in sober legislation, in coordination with executive determination and the backing of enlightened citizens . . ."

The tone is false. The facts are wrong. The theme is fatuous. The moment of North American perfection — safe cities, decent schools, clean rivers, highways to Montevideo, powdered milk for starving peons in Peru — is eternally before us; but the evil little secret in the center of the Myth of Progress is the lie that it will come about without us, without the price of payment offered, pain exacted, vow accepted, loneliness incurred. In a letter Gandhi sent to an important leader whom he scarcely knew in 1894, he wrote these words: "A word for myself and for what I have done . . . I am the only available person who can handle the question." It is not possible, however, for a man to speak in words like these if he has already been assured that anything of great importance will take place without him anyway, that human transformations do not call for his participation, that he is superfluous to pain and marginal to love, that he is forever on the outside of the circle that effectiveness and decency inhabit.

Schools attempt to cover their own tracks by offering us a half-believed and insincere narration. They speak of something known as "active citizenship," "concerned participation" in what is often labeled, mechanistically, "the workings" of our government. I say that it is insincere for just this reason: that, while we hear about the need to vote, to run for Town Committee and for School Board and the like, school simultaneously awards to each of us an individually engraved certificate of moral and political self-abdication. Things that are tangential, trivial and unimportant, we will be allowed to deal with. Things that matter deeply to the world go on eternally without us.

Textbooks tell us in considerable detail about the operation of the little levers in the voting booth, and show us photographs of people wrapped in woolly hats and cumbersome mittens in Leningrad or Moscow to convince us of how fortunate we are to have the right to tamper with these levers in the closed booth of our constitutional effectiveness. It is perhaps the only leverage we shall ever know. Education takes away from children, as unjust nations take away the labor of the poor, the leverage of our own inherent sense of moral potency, and then invites us to come down and exercise our impotence within the voting booth. The secret message, though it is one that has been written in no text or lesson-plan, is the message that all things that count will come about without us anyway.

This is the neighborhood in which I came to live in 1965: Twenty thousand people live here. With the exception of two redeveloped and well-demarcated sections of the district, most of the residents are Puerto Rican, black, poor-white, Chinese or Lebanese. In one direction or another, it encompasses approximately fifty square blocks. Many buildings have been boarded up; some are still partly occupied, one or two families camping out in partly heated rooms. There are many broken-down rooming houses, crumbling brownstones, urine-smelling city welfare-projects. In the alleyways and on the fringes of this neighborhood there are large numbers of poor derelicts: solitary men and penniless old women, dozens of whom die along the sidewalks or between the cars each winter, two thousand heroin addicts and four thousand homeless men, many of them alcoholics who live on the cheapest brand of sweet wine. The largest numbers, though, are neither derelicts nor alcoholics. They are the poor, the black, the undefended.

I do not know all of the houses and the buildings in these fifty blocks; I know perhaps fifteen or twenty houses in about ten sections. I have a picture, then, of what life might be like for many people I do *not* know. In the kitchen, faucets keep on dripping, water leaking also underneath the sink and in the bath. Heat is often choking and cannot be turned down; yet, in some of the buildings, there is just no heat at all and children keep on outside coats all day. Potato-chip bags, part-empty, get kicked under kitchen tables. Cold food hardens on the plates inside the sink, while mother is sick, or working nights, and the oldest child is an eleven-year-old girl who cannot cope with all the needs and voices, appetites and tempers of the younger ones. In the choking heat, one large blue light, the huge T.V., is never shut off but keeps pumping out the sound, like an extra and maniacal presence in the room, of an endless series of romantic episodes, doctor programs, kiddies' cartoons, advertisements for racing tracks and miniature cars, for plastic gar-bage-bags and for fruit-flavored wines to go with candlelight and dinner. There are some books in the living room, but many are torn up, lost or scattered among underpants and sofas. Homework papers are also torn up, shredded, lost or scattered among the lamps and clothes, some of the pages spilled with milk out in the kitchen. If I had to describe the total experience of these children with a single phrase, I think that I would speak of it as a life of stifling slowly among dirty underclothes, millions of roaches and the endless hypnotism of one large blue light.

I go downstairs and walk out onto Shawmut Avenue.

Standing here, I ask myself, like someone who attempts to take his own pulse: What, then, do I think about these children? I find that what I think, what I experience and feel and live with, is that everything is getting better all the time, that change is somehow on the way, that time is on the side of children such as these, that next year cannot be the same as this year. School will be happier. Mother will come home all better from the hospital. The children will eat real meals. Their teeth will stop rotting. Someone will fix the drip under the sink.

It is like mental illness. There is no basis for this optimism. I go back next year, and things are no better. The children are settled only a little deeper into squalor and despair, dying amid potato-chip bags and nonstop television. Two years later, I go back once more.

They are in a new apartment in another section now: new objects, junk commodities piled, torn and ruined on the bathroom floor, underneath the T.V. and beside the door. The sink works; but plaster falls out of the ceiling, and the whole place stinks of urine and of unwashed diapers. There is a new baby. The oldest child is her mother.

Things did not get better. They grew worse. Twisted, contorted lives grew only more intricately twisted. Still, the voice within me, granting amnesty from rage, and respite from upheaval, says to me again what it has always said before: Things are getting better. Time heals all things, slowly. It is as if I were, by my own longing for centrifugal release, eternally transformed out of the status of committed agent, into the passive, tranquil and invulnerable observer of the scene of pain. Once I can feel this way, there is no longer any mandate for my own participation. Then I no longer have to think of anything so painful and disturbing as the need to place *my* body on the line for something I believe.

I walk often in my neighborhood at night. In the streets are children I have known for years. When we are together, we have fun and feel at ease with one another. We fool around. We do things that are silly. Later, in the quiet of my own apartment, I find that I am thinking once again of a particular child by the name of Peter. I knew Peter for a year, thinking him to be about eight or nine before I learned he was fourteen. I wrote that off to malnutrition. We could feed him, my girlfriend and I, when he came by for supper, or else we could go over to his place and make sure he'd had his supper. So we'd go there, or he'd be here, and we'd cook something good, spaghetti with hamburger, or good lamb chops, something like that, make him eat, sit down and eat with him: "Come on, let's eat it all up, Peter!"

At night sometimes, as late as twelve, my doorbell rings and Peter's down there: hungry. He has known, by now, at least six different white men and white women, just like me, cadging his meals and shirts and shoes and short-term love. Now most of them are gone but Peter makes the rounds. I find myself afraid to go out nights for fear that he'll be sitting on the stoop in front when I get home.

So we do good, as we believe we ought to, and for a year or more we tell ourselves that he needs fattening. And he has trouble learning in the school. But we say he's just hungry in the mornings. A year has come, a year has gone. One day, I am forced to recognize that Peter is no longer growing at a normal rate. I go into a panic, and the world falls into pieces. We have tests made: a psychological exam. Peter is examined by a specialist on growth and on the nervous system. The word he brings into our life is this: "microcephalic." It is a term that has to do with brain development. Brain growth was impeded prior to birth or else in infancy; he will not grow up to normal size. We protest to the doctor, whom we do not know: "He is only the size of a small child."

The doctor is firm in his professional decision: *"This young man will not grow up to normal size."* He can learn. He can be educated; but there will be limits. We ask if this is common and we ask, as well, what causes something of this sort. Pre-natal care. The mother is ill, or poor, or underfed. Often there is no obstetric treatment. Sometimes, too, it is a case of malnutrition in the first few weeks of life. We look at one another in a state of grim unwillingness to credit what we hear. Peter's mother *was,* in fact, extremely ill. Peter was born six weeks or eight weeks premature. His infancy was lived in almost unabated hunger.

The doctor goes on: "With proper facilities and with the right health programs, and with the proper care, we'd deal with this when the mother first came in to visit at the clinic . . . or even when she first came in to ask for contraceptive pills. With the right kind of care, this could be totally eliminated." He goes on for a while in his almost optimistic frame of mind: "It hardly ever happens in white neighborhoods anymore. It's a problem of the poor, of rural slums and of impacted sections in the cities. Someday, of course, we ought to have facilities to deal with this."

Someday, but we are alive on this day. And Peter will not be born someday, will not be crippled one day. He is sitting here, right outside the office *this* day. Peter is not a child who might perhaps come in for an examination someday, whom we might meet or think of, deal with, one day in a statistician's future. He is a real boy, in the real world, with a real curse.

There is a moment when I tell myself that this curse ought to doom the city that I live in. Then that rewarding instinct for the

Apocalypse subsides. I have been given assurance, after all, that medical services will one day be provided for poor people such as Peter and his mother. And someday there will be pre-natal clinics, out-patient departments for expectant mothers, a treatment center for the child who is not born exactly whole or with entirely proper brain-development. Someday, but not *this* day. Some place, but not in *this* place. For some child, but not for *this* child. This child, this one real child, this one thin boy right here, aged fourteen, by the name of Peter, is alive today. He will not profit from the research and evaluation of the next ten decades. He will not be born again in 1980 or in 1985. He will not get a second run-through on the hour of his imperfect birth by the goodness of the U.S. Congress or of the assembled leaders of the A.M.A. He is alive right now. It will be too late for him the next time.

We thank the doctor and we go outside and head out to the door, and pick up Peter, and we come back home to have some dinner with him, and to watch T.V., then to talk and fool around about his girls, and friends, and racing cars, and things like that, which do not matter but which seem familiar to us. At eleven o'clock, I walk him home and stop by at the store to get the milk and cream and come back home, and we sit up a while and talk and try to think how we can tell this to his father.

The doctor tells himself that things will not be like this too much longer. In actual fact, medical treatment for poor people has deteriorated somewhat in these neighborhoods during the past ten years. There is *less* good treatment for poor people now in Northern cities than there was in 1965. More of these children grow up on deficient diets. Hunger and malnutrition in these sections of the nation are more, and not less, critical today than ten years back. All of this constitutes a painful body of reality for North Americans to live with. That we *do* live with it, and do so moreover with a fair amount of ease and skill, and even with a certain amount of self-congratulation on the reasonable nature of our own response, is just one index of the real success of mass indoctrination in this land.

To me, most bitter evidence once more of real effectiveness on part of public school is the response of certain halfway rebels: those, above all, who work for certain hours, or for certain days, to forge a lever of specific ethical rebellion, who therefore know of pain and exploitation and perceive the most intense and obvious forms of devastation, have on their desks the tapes and "T-graphs," data and statistics to confirm and document it all — yet still, once at a distance, can cool off their conscience and abate their discontent by telling themselves of "ongoing areas of technological and governmental, socio-political amelioration . . ."

There is a brutal self-deception here: *Silence and the passage of five years are evidence that Peter is not dying.* It is the more cold, the more evil, when it comes from those who are so well-informed and cannot help but recognize that they are lying to themselves about this child whom they used to know in those remarkable days of blue jeans and bare feet, but now in settled adulthood, with an infant of their own, cannot remember. If I should remind them of these kinds of things, if I should say that there are now, not less, but more poor children in this city in attendance at the old and antiquated public schools, I would not tell them anything they do not know. If I should say that there are now more kids on heroin but less space in the hospitals and clinics that exist to serve them, if I should say the kids that they nostalgically recall are no less bitter, no less thin and no less hungry now than they were back in 1965, if I should say this and then look them straight-on in the eyes, and ask them how it was with them last year on their sabbatical in France, and in the year before since I have seen them last, what will they say and where then will our conversation lead us after that? What will we do and how then will we be able to converse in the sad space that will be left behind after the tide has gone back down the shore across the Myth of Progress that we used to live by?

There is more in this than self-deceit. There is plain cruelty too. If I should hear this kind of statement now, and if I find the will *not* to be silent and respectful, as I have too often been before, but if instead I say — what is, of course, within my mind — that all these torments, devastations, "deprivations" are not "somewhat better," and have not "remained the same," but are, in certain ways, a good deal worse now than they were in 1965, there is an almost "backward-stepping" look within their eyes, and not just backward-stepping either but quite often with a flash of visible irritation too. It is as if I am committing cultural treason in their point of view if I will not join them in corroboration of the lie they live with. It is as if they think that, by their *faith* in progress, they have made a real investment of their lives in the life-struggle of those kids whom they once knew but now cannot remember by their real names anymore.

In every other realm of national existence, these people are prepared to understand that nothing is gotten for nothing and that end-results are tied directly to the nature of the contribution. If we intend to send some people to the moon, then we cut back on health care or on highway spending. If we intend to build more military aircraft, then we cut back in other areas: naval expenses possibly, or in civilian programs. In every other area, we can accept this truth. Yet it is notable to see how easily large numbers of well-educated people have been trained to make exception when it comes to matters that afflict the public conscience. Here alone do we pretend that serious changes can occur within the lives of those who live nearby, in pain and need, without the need for *our* lives to be altered too.

It is a myth; but myths, of course, are made and propagated in this nation by the people who have cash and power. It is not surprising, then, that we adhere with so much willing self-deceit to habits of thought which are, above all, styles of self-protection. The stakes are high. Far back in memory and mind we know that we have the advantage of the hour, that we have had it best in areas in which it counts the most, and that we are intensely threatened by the thought of losing any part of that advantage which we now enjoy. We fight for it skillfully, not with tooth and nail but with our ideologies and lies. The Myth of Progress — progress without danger, progress without sacrifice or pain — is one of the most important ways in which we do this. Things get better. The poor get richer. The lame walk and the sick will soon be healed. Those all-day lines of pain and waiting in poor people's hospitals around the land will soon be gone, and in their place will be a new regime of swift, efficient service. In the meantime, politicians and executives can have their private rooms at Doctors Hospital, the rich can check into the Mayo Clinic and the poor can sweat it out in crowded corridors of stucco shacks called "Health Dispensaries" outside of Tucson. Pain goes away without us.

Soft rains of change and silent benefaction fall upon the earth while we are watching T.V., or away in Normandy on a Federal grant. Silently brooding, secretly breeding in the heat that lies beneath the blanket of neglect, progress comes to the earth while we are sleeping. It does not ask of us. It does not call to us. It does not issue to us an invocation. It will take place while we are working on a research paper; or it will take place while we are getting our degree in sociology at Stanford or Ann Arbor; or it will take place while we are building our own home, and settling down, and planning our own lives, attending to our needs and to those of our own children.

It is, as we are told in school when we are young — and more than willing to believe — another remarkable characteristic of our unexampled economic system. If it is not that, it is a product at the very least of one of the most efficient and reliable machineries of self-deceit and of self-pacification that a nation in danger has ever yet devised to still a turbulent conscience or to resurrect a fragile and endangered sense of grace.

TEN YEARS: Friends from old times, from 1964 and 1965. I go out sometimes into rural sections west of Boston where they have their homes. We sit whole nights and reminisce and talk. Many are friends I knew from S.N.C.C. or CORE. They ask these questions: "What's been going on in the South End? Is the Head Start center going well at Orchard Park? What is the impact of the Federal funds?"

The questions fall out in familiar patterns. It is not *whether* things have gotten better, only (1) how much? (2) in what ways? The more I talk with old friends from that time, the more I sense the permanent portion of the sequence. The eyes of one well-educated, white and competent American seek in another's eyes the confirmation of the myth that both men live by. Jet planes do not fly backward. Nor, in our belief, does U.S. energy expend itself in motion retrograde.

"What was the name of that little boy who always used to wear the Red Sox baseball jersey — the one who always used to look so thin and hungry?" His name was Peter. His name is *still* Peter. He was hungry then. He is *still* hungry today. You are right that he was thin. He is a little *more* thin now. He does not have the Red Sox baseball jersey any longer . . .

I am here, in the secluded home of two warm, old and trusted friends. In their quiet eyes, and in the peaceful settlement that they appear to have been able to arrive at in the silent places of their own minds, I become aware I am afraid that I will see the life that I too soon may undertake: nostalgia for those old remembered days in Roxbury, in S.N.C.C. or CORE, or something of that kind, old records of the Mississippi Freedom Movement and Peter Seeger, "Oh Lord! Wasn't that a time?" . . . memories groping backward like roots reaching downward into the black earth of our integrity. At long last, after thirty-five years, I have met a woman that I love and we are now about to make a home together. What, then, will we do with our own lives, and how will we decide? Will we not be tempted also to obtain a fine home with a stretch of meadow and a nice, attractive, innovative school nearby for our own children — interrupted sometimes, year from year, by one less, less and less intensely necessary visit back to Blue Hill Ave or Orchard Park or the South End, where we are living now, to see if Peter is still there, or if Elizabeth is still alive?

I look at my two friends as we sit down for dinner. They are kind and gentle people. No one would say that they are doing something *wicked, sinister* or *wrong*, by buying a home, and slipping away, and settling down, and getting adjusted to a "realistic" compromise with memory and time. Yet ironies are here, and sadness too: a sense of the loss of something good and true in two fine, strong and idealistic people. My friend has made a vast success in doing research work that grew out of his four years in the Freedom Movement. In this success, he has been able to obtain a home out here, twelve miles west of Boston, costing eighty thousand dollars. It is beautiful here, and even though it is just a dozen miles away, it might as well be in Vermont or in New Hampshire. We have our dinner, then big mugs of good strong coffee. "You want to hear that old Pete Seeger record?" Scratchy and worn, he gets it out. We hear the songs we used to sing and live by: "Just like a tree standing by the water, I know that we shall not be moved . . . We shall not . . . We shall not be moved . . ."

We are sitting here: four people, former allies, fond of one another, with good memories of things that we have done together. In the midst of it all, I find that I am looking out the window into the trees and darkness and the shadows of the streams that run down by the lower meadow in the back part of this house, beyond the pattern of lights thrown outward by the kitchen windows. We go home early. Late at night, I walk in the neighborhood for hours.

VI. SUNDAY AFTERNOON NEUROSIS

". . . It is not so easy to grasp fear and terror by reading books, but surely through an act of human imagination one may, in some sense, grasp the terrible suffering, the sadism, the torture of the concentration camp . . . If such a response were impossible, man's moral responsibilities would atrophy."

— Richard Means

MOST GREAT FICTION, almost all important verse, are written on one of three essential truths: love, death or pain. None of the three is ever consciously conveyed within the public schools.

Death, in the school, is seldom sad and never devastating. It is, indeed, all but impossible to understand that *people die* in school materials. The standard, dull and anti-ethical textbook-automaton called George Washington represents an ideal instance of the sense of plastic simulation. Washington does not "die," just as he never seems to "live." In place of death, he comes to the end of his section, or sub-section, and then receives the schoolbook version of a presidential epitaph in a set of unit-questions: "What are the major points that we have learned about the Father of Our Nation?"

Discussions of issues such as these — the lives of presidents or the death of children — convey in almost every case the same experience of simulation: of seeming to be like some other thing that we would call a *real* discussion. "The school's imitations, like fake fireplace logs, are not combustible," John Mann has written. "The illusion can be created by holding a gas-flame under them . . ." It is pursuit of this effect, he says, that gives rise to those glowing and impressive learning packets, as well as to all the light and optimistic talk concerning childhood motivation: "It's still a fake if it doesn't go outward to where the real fuel is."

Questions teachers ask of children echo, from the first, the same glass-coated character: "What does the aging salmon do in shallow water as he comes ever closer and closer to the place of death?" If we ask ourselves what is bizarre, unreal, impalpable about this question, I think we find the answer is as follows: It is only in the classroom that one person poses questions, as a matter of routine, to which he does not need, or wait in expectation for, an answer. Children sometimes grow impatient and ask teachers why we ask them questions if, in fact, we know the answers. The teacher frequently replies: "It is because I want to see if *you* know." I have heard a strong, irreverent child answer at this stage: "I think that's idiotic. Why don't you come out and *tell* me something if you know it?"

Even when children leave the school behind, or ask a "non-school person" to come in to visit, still there is that sense of simulation. The visitor most often finds himself exposed to a peculiar sense of "narrative imitation" as he walks into the corridors and classrooms of the school. It is the school-disease: unreal dispute, as-if response and imitative truth. Unless he is, himself, a trained performer, the session with the children is inevitably dull. The teacher, no matter with how little overt intervention, tends to mediate between the visitor and children. He translates genuine questions into school-like questions. He shepherds the children's answers into school-like items of response.

The same feeling of the NOT-FOR-REAL comes into effect when children leave the school to go off on a "research visit." The teacher often says to visitors, with some bravado: "The children in this class are able to leave school behind and go out into the real world." In truth, however, they bring most of the glass-coated mood of public education *with* them. Look at a group of children closely when they travel with their teacher to the local war memorial or City Hall. Their legs are moving and their voices are excited; but their eyes will tell us they are still in school.

There is, at last, a point of no return. It is the point at which the plastic quarantine of public school ceases to be a space-specific matter but starts to spread out like an abstract protoplasm of denied intensities. The jargon speaks of "bringing the real world back into the school." In truth, it is the opposite which now takes place. The twelve-year simulation of THE REAL THING comes, at last, to be the lifelong sense of not-quite-real revolt, as-if rebellion, seeming-to-be guilt, looking-on-at-something-very-much-like pain. It is only at this point that men and women are effectively prepared to be controllable automatons for the voting booth, efficient business leaders and untroubled bombardiers.

The U.S. soldier, trained not to believe in the specific, real and tragic character of death and pain is, from point of view of an efficient murder-apparatus, the ideal man to press the button that releases bombs and napalm on a village of unseen and (to his own mind) unreal children and old people. War itself, within the mechanistic consciousness of such a man, comes, before long, to be perceived as something like a "game-plan." It possesses, at its most intense, the vividness of a wide-screen movie with a realistic speaker-system. Indeed, it may well be that there is no real difference for most people, anymore, between the sense of observation of a vivid and expensive film and that of their participation in a vivid and expensive war. The difference may well be no more than this: The sound is often better in the film than in the real world.

In "Politics and the English Language," Orwell speaks of this. Public speech, he says, is skillfully contrived to forge defenses for the indefensible. Planes bombard a helpless village from the air. Soldiers drive inhabitants out of their homes. Machine guns kill the cattle. Incendiary bullets set the huts on fire. "This is called *pacification*." Soldiers rob the peasants of their farms and drive them out onto the roads with no more than the goods that they can carry. "This is called . . . *rectification of frontiers*." Governments lock up prisoners for years without a trial, execute them or else send them off to die in lumber camps. "This is called *elimination of unreliable elements*." Language of this kind is necessary, Orwell writes, if people need to *name* atrocities but do not dare to summon up the pictures that go with them.

The same device is in effect today. Pentagon experts, going back to 1945, in reference to the impact of an air attack on non-strategic targets, employ the phrase: "profound psychological impression." If we examine this grotesque expression, it emerges in a simple, clean and uncomplex translation: "maximum possible civilian slaughter." The words our soldiers use in speaking about death are only slightly less grotesque. A witness in the trial of the My Lai murderer, William Calley, explains to the court that the military uses the word "waste" (for "kill") because it involves the soldier in no sense of guilt. It avoids the word "kill" because the use of this word ("kill") would create a psychological dilemma for a man who has been taught to feel that murder is unjust. The word "kill," in the Army's point of view, creates "a very negative emotional reaction." The translation for "negative emotional reaction" is A BURNING AND AN UNAVOIDABLE SENSE OF HORROR AT THE TRUTH OF WHO I AM, OF WHO MY VICTIM IS, OF WHAT I DO TO HIM. Loss of purchase on real recognitions of events of our own instigation is extremely close to standardized psychosis. It is, however, different from all other mental illness in one horrible respect: It is psychosis reinstated as one facet of efficient nationhood.

The soldier at My Lai reports his inability to feel in these words: "You feel it's not all real. It couldn't possibly be . . . They're actually shooting people for no reason . . ." This man is six months out of public school. He is six months distant from the Glee Club, Flag Pledge, textbook, grammar-exercises, Problems of Democracy. It is essential that we be precise. It is not the U.S. Army that transforms an innocent boy into non-comprehending automaton in six months. It is not the U.S. Army that permits a man to murder first the sense of ethics, human recognitions, in his own soul, then to be free to turn the power of his devastation outward to the eyes and forehead of another human being. Basic training does not begin in boot camp. It begins in kindergarten. It continues with a vengeance for the subsequent twelve years.

It is not possible to tell ourselves, in light of recent tragedies like these, that public education is not efficacious. Seymour Hersch can write a thousand books about My Lai. Robert Coles can give a million speeches on starvation. It makes no difference. It does not work. It has no power to shock: to jolt: to intervene. Death, murder, exploitation is not credible. It is "believed" as stated fact. It is not "lived through" as an actionable item of the real world. Cesar Chavez wrote: "To be a man is to suffer for others." We cannot, however, even dream to be the people he describes. We cannot suffer for others. We cannot even believe that others suffer.

Who is to blame for brutal and malignant consequences such as these? The serviceable physician who supplies us with a useful phrase such as "neurotic guilt," the teacher who informs us that it is our obligation to obey our orders and to channel our dissent into innocuous patterns of polite "discussion and investigation," the school that teaches us to modify and to dilute intense reactions to inordinate despair: these are the agencies of death and murder and of icelike alienation from the things we do, the sights we see, the agonies which we empower, watch but do not ever quite believe. The massacre of four hundred innocent people, maiming of infants, shooting of old men, women, babies, pregnant girls and young boys in the wholesale bloodbath of a village ditch, is an atrocity on the same level as the worst that Hitler's soldiers ever did; yet there is atrocity of equal order in the nation that produced these murderous soldiers and, even worse, forgave them. There is atrocity in the Army general who tries his best to cover up the things that he already knows; but there is atrocity, above all else, in this: a nation that, even today, when all is proven, said and done, still cannot say, because it is not possible to perceive, that what our soldiers did, and what we do, and how we live and dream and effortlessly kill or innocently leave to die, is *evil, real* and *irreversible.*

There is, of course, another — and entirely separate — reason for the loss of purchase I describe. Physical pain for most young people in the U.S. is not easy to "believe," for the excellent reason that it is no longer present in their lives. Technological anaesthesia fends off almost all explicit physical ordeal. Ether balms a visit to the surgeon's office. Music and carpets quiet and absorb the panic of the pediatric office. The built-in auto air-conditioner refrigerates our minds and cools our bodies as we speed across the desert of New Mexico at sixty-five polite degrees. Terror and longing, in the aftermath of devastation at the loss of someone that we love, are calmed and quieted by a ten-grain capsule (Librium): half-black, half-green. The sharpest pain that many millions of young people in this nation ever undergo is the brief incision of the Novocain needle that arrests all further pain. It is an ideal metaphor.

No one wishes to see children placed within a field of needless pain: manufactured sickness, fever, panic, devastation. Yet it is true that lifelong technological insulation — unbroken barriers of self-protection from the taste of terror — do benumb our power to fathom, and our capability to feel. The man or woman who never has known pain is oftentimes incapable of pity. This is the case, above all, when there is an excellent reason to be grateful for the barrier of self-protection. "If I feel nothing," Robert Lifton has observed, "then death is not taking place . . . If I feel nothing, I cannot be threatened by the death all around me . . . If I feel nothing, then I am not responsible for you or for your death."

Lifton's observations on this subject seem, as always, to be brilliant. It is Paul Goodman, however, who makes clear the root and cause. Children in the U.S. schools, Goodman has said, grow up within "a closed room of the imagination." The point is not just that they have been forced to live for twenty years in a closed room, but that they have been informed this room is the whole world. Nor have they the weapons near at hand by which to demythologize this false experience, once locked within it. Non-spectacular satisfaction, inept moderation, low-key delectation seem to fill the whole horizon. Goodman calls it "Sunday afternoon neurosis." Their hearts, he says, "are elsewhere" — but "they don't remember where." It is our tragedy that it could not, as Goodman wrote, be relegated to a single afternoon. Sunday Afternoon Neurosis is, by now, our national disease. The more our children and our teachers speak of pain and need, starvation and despair, the less they seem prepared to know that such realities exist.

This issue — "loss of purchase" — is compounded by a special school-obsession with lists, numbers, slots and boxes. Everything, no matter what its urgency or implication, is tagged and slotted and put into isolable spaces: "The Ten Important Points About East Harlem," "The Sixteen Major Facts About Starvation . . ." The horror in this is that it does not matter what we organize, what we examine, what we subdivide. The subject matter can be hunger in Bolivia, tooth care in Schenectady, kill-rate in Hanoi. It is the outline, sequence and assigned position in one of ten, or twelve, or fourteen numbered slots on which we concentrate, on which our toil is centered, and for which we win (or do not win) rewards.

The ritual — "list, label and container" — comes to be so automatic, by this time, that most teachers still go through with it even in the presence of essentially benign and mild subject-matter. I recall a teacher watching a young child in my class who had grown immersed in an exciting novel that was not a part of the expected reading program. The teacher seemed unsettled, threatened even, hesitated for a moment, then concluded: "That's all right . . . She's doing Reading for Enrichment." As soon as she could lock the ambiguity of a peculiar moment into a familiar slot, she no longer found it troubling.

This is an innocent example. It did not do real damage to translate the child's quiet eyes into an old curricular expression. It is a different matter when the ritual becomes a way of immunizing people to the consequences of their own behavior. What begins as one-inch margins, topic sentences and unit-summaries ends up as an automatic skill at anaesthetic insulation of the individual adult from devastation we perceive, or mandate that we marginally imagine. We learn to speak of painful issues as if they had come to be, no longer painful, but just "issues." Pain, by this device, is exiled from the public conscience, death denied, and tears in every case excluded.

The mania of numbers, and the power of such numbers to desensitize our lives, extends even to men and women who are experts in the very problem of desensitization. The most striking of such ironies, I think, is that reflected in the work of Lawrence Kohlberg: an intelligent and influential man who has given years of research to the question of the evolution of a sense of "moral reason" in an adult or a child. Even with all seeming dedication, Kohlberg cannot hold back from the use of the protective filter offered him by slots and numbers. People exist, as he reports with absolute certitude within his work, in one of six specific moral boxes: People are "LEVEL SIX" or "LEVEL ONE" or "LEVEL THREE." The labor is serious. The research is persuasive. The details are painstaking. Yet the impact of the work is not profound. It does not shake. It does not threaten. It does not bestir. Numbers cancel out the blood, the passion, the true concrete character of that which Kohlberg struggles to describe. Numbers can organize. Numbers can explicate — but numbers cannot make us cry.

Sterilization by this process is, by now, an intellectual obsession. A college recently invited me to give a lecture to inaugurate a five-day span known as "The Week of Conscience." It seems at last that almost anything can be wrapped up, refrigerated and containerized like this. We do it by units of time ("The Week of Conscience"), of subject-matter (two credit-hours on "The Literature of Disadvantage and Despair"), of specific lessons (research and term-paper on "Health Care Inequities . . .").

Grade schools, in particular, appear to be obsessed with lists and outlines: "Seven Big Headings," "Fourteen Main Ideas," "Six Interesting Questions for Consideration." Exercises of this kind do well the job that they are meant for. Pain is blood-filled, rough around the edges, messy on the insides. So too is guilt. So, above all, are rage and revolution. In a time when tears of rage are frequently the only human answer to the pain we see before us, thousands and thousands of the hours of our education are devoted to design and manufacture of containing-instruments that will protect us from the need to stand against the sky and cry out in dismay and in rebellion.

Teachers defend the process as a necessary means of bringing order to large numbers of assorted facts; yet this is not, in fact, its honest function. Too often, instead, we see the transmutation of real blood, authentic bone, legitimate grief into devitalized and non-provocative abstractions. Twenty square blocks of tears and rage, of Afro combs, Black Panther posters, crumbling schools and plywood-boarded windows on the ruined stores become a part of something known as "Problems of Youth in Racially Impacted Areas . . ." Children starving, skeletal knee-bones as in dim-light photographs of Auschwitz, rib-cage hollow and apocalyptic like the bones of cattle dying in a land of drought, red blood-cells deficient for a million children of Chicago, Mississipppi, Newark, Alabama, Boston, Tennessee, irremediable harm to learning capability and normal body-growth, become transmuted into "Problems of Nutrition for Poor People: Second Semester in the Devastation and Destruction of the Disadvantaged Child."

. The importation into public school of painful, and sometimes incendiary, data — prior to the sterilization of that data by the methods here described — is, at the least, an act of frank subversion. The younger the child, the more subversive is the act. It is only after a certain course of preparation that children can be trained to hide their tears and to subdue their sense of moral indignation. It is for just this reason that we must be certain to incorporate materials like these within the education of the children of the rich, to do so moreover at the earliest possible age, and with the strongest will to undermine the straight-line patterns of self-serving expectation for which public education is designed to train them.

Teachers, faced with statements of this kind, often respond to me with words like these: "Isn't it too much of an interruption to bring in these agonizing, and enormously disturbing, matters to the lives of children?" I hear their words. I look into their eyes. It is as if they were to speak about another planet, or a world they dream of, or a world that they recall within a passage of Vivaldi or a painting of Renoir. They tell us that we must not "bring in" rage and pain. I ask them then: What shall we do when rage walks in the door?

BOSTON, BLUE HILL AVENUE, TEN DAYS BEFORE CHRISTMAS: A child falls down in the middle of Grove Hall. She is epileptic, but her sickness either has not yet been diagnosed or else (more probable) it has been diagnosed, but never treated. Tall and thin, fourteen years old, she is intense and sober, devastated but unhating. Her life is a staccato sequence of *grand mal* convulsions: no money, no assistance, no advice on how to get a refill of expensive script for more Dilantin and more phenobarbital.

This night, she comes downstairs into the office where I work within the coat-room underneath the church-stairs of a Free School: standing there and asking me please if I would close the door and hold her head within my arms because she knows that she is going to have an epileptic seizure; and closing the door and sitting down upon the cold cement while she lies down and places her head within my arms and starts to shudder violently and moves about so that I scarcely can protect her wracked and thin young body from the cement wall and from the concrete floor; and seeing her mouth writhe up with pain and spittle, and feeling her thrash about a second time and now a third; and, in between, the terror closing in upon her as in a child's bad dream that you can't get out of, and watching her then, and wondering what she undergoes; and later seeing her, exhausted, sleeping there, right in my arms, as at the end of long ordeal, all passion in her spent; then taking her out into my car and

driving with her to the City Hospital while she, as epileptics very
often feel, keeps saying that she is going to have another seizure;
and slamming on the brakes and walking with her in the back door
where they receive out-patient cases, and being confronted on this
winter night at nine P. M. in Boston in the year of 1965 with a scene
that comes from Dante's Purgatory: dozens and dozens of poor
white, black and Puerto Rican people, infants and mothers, old men,
alcoholics, men with hands wrapped up in gauze, and aged people
trembling, infants trembling with fever; one hostile woman in white
uniform behind the table telling us, out of a face made, as it seems,
of clay, that we should fill an application out, some sort of form, a
small white sheet, then sit out in the hallway since the waiting room
is full; and then to try to say this child has just had several seizures
in a row and needs treatment, and do we need to do the form; and
yes, of course you need to do the form and wait your turn and not
think you have any special right to come ahead of someone else who
has been sitting here before you. Two hours and four seizures later,
you get up and go in and shout in her cold eyes and walk right by and
grab an intern by the arm and tell him to come out and be a doctor to
an epileptic child sitting like a damp rag in the hallway; and he
comes out, and in two minutes gives this child an injection that
arrests the seizures and sedates her, then writes the script for more
Dilantin and for phenobarbital and shakes his head and says to you
that it's a damn shame: "Nobody needs to have an epileptic seizure
in this day and age . . . Nobody but a poor black nigger," says the
intern in a sudden instant of that rage that truth and decency create.
He nearly cries, and in his eyes you see a kind of burning pain that
tells you that he is a good man somehow, deep-down, some place
where it isn't all cold stone, clean surgery and antiseptic reason:
"Nobody but a poor black nigger needs to have an epileptic seizure
anymore." So you take her home and you go back to the church,
down to your office underneath the stairs, and look at the floor, and
listen to the silence, and you are twenty-eight years old, and you
begin to cry; you cry for horror of what that young girl has just been
through; and you long not to believe that this can be the city that you
really live in. You fight very hard to lock up that idea because it
threatens all the things that you have wanted to believe for so long;
so you sit alone a while and you try to lock these bitter passions into

secret spaces of your self-control. You try to decontaminate your anger and to organize your rage; but you can't do it this time; you just can't build that barrier of logical control a second time. It's eleven o'clock now, and soon it's quarter of twelve; and it's cold as stone down here beneath the wooden underside of the church-stairs, and still you can't stop trembling. *Grand mal,* you think to yourself, means a great evil; it's twelve-fifteen and now you are no longer crying so you get up and you lock the door of the coat-closet which is the office of a Free School underneath the church-stairs; and you go up the stairs and turn out the light and then you close the door.

"Freedom," Paulo Freire has said, "is acquired by conquest, not by gift."

In visiting with teachers, I speak sometimes about forms of exploitation such as that which is described above. There are some teachers who, of course, react with instantaneous withdrawal from the first suggestion of the introduction of such narratives into the public schools. Even those, however, who do not refuse, in principle, inevitably find reason to demur in any concrete situation. "In general," they say, "kids ought to know of hunger, slums, starvation and the like . . . Do you really think, however, that this is the proper age?"

Whatever the age, the level or the grade, it is in every case *one level short* of the "appropriate" age at which one ought to deal with matters that pertain to ethics and fair play. When children are small, their teachers say they are too tender and too vulnerable. When they are older, getting into teen-age years, we say they are too volatile and too intolerant. When they are in college, we say they are impatient. We do not grant them, in any sense, the right to view the bars until they have been locked into the prison. Once they are well locked-in — to life, husband and wife, child and mortgage-payment — then cynically do we allow that it is time for them to know the world of grief and pain from which they will henceforward be most mercifully excluded. I think we know that this is not the way to educate free citizens or decent children.

It is impossible to write these words without a realistic recognition of the distance that exists between my own position and the pedagogic fashion of the Nineteen Seventies. The level of "joy" or "joylessness" in public school is held today to be of greater interest than its ethical direction. It must be clear, by now, that I do not accept this point of view. Innocence, pleasure, peace, delight and whim are obvious blessings in a mediocre, grim and unecstatic social order. They are, however, less important than the need for fevered confrontation with the evil actions that our parents finance, tolerate, connive in. When children are old enough to eat the food their folks have stolen from the tables of the poor, then they are old enough as well to learn the definition of the noun-form *exploitation,* and to figure out as well which side their folks are on.

The general's daughter ought to be *compelled* to know her father's hands are dripping in the blood of innocent civilians. The slumlord's daughter ought to be *obliged* to know the misery and squalor, rats and stench her life is built upon. The bank director's child, the foreign investment analyst's son, ought to know well, beyond all respite and all hesitation, the barbarism that their food, tuition, clothes and charge accounts are built upon. The privileged children of an unjust social order *need* to be disturbed, amazed and shaken by the consequences of the unjust privilege by which they live: and certainly many years before the vested interest which they otherwise will gain in self-deception long-sustained has first created, and then solidly nailed shut, an ice-cold quarantine they cannot break.

If children cannot learn to look into the heart and center of death, love and pain, then there will be little of sufficient awe to counteract the cynical power of sheer acquisition. Without the close and tragic truth of death and pain, there is little likelihood of years devoted to deep dreams of justice, struggle and fair play. The method of presentation of such concrete issues as class-exploitation, as now taught within the U.S. public schools, both by selection of an antiseptic set of words and by the use of sterile boxes, outlines, lists and names, guarantees the child's non-responsive state of mind; defuses war; dehumanizes love; bleeds dry the dead and dying. In a time of torment, in a decade of ordeal, few crimes seem quite so difficult to forgive.

VII. GREAT MEN AND WOMEN

"I don't give a damn about semi-radicals."
— Helen Keller, 1916

TEACHERS in the Nineteen Seventies face a difficult job when they sit down to work out lesson-plans on U.S. history. How do the ideological hand-servants of the leading counter-revolutionary nation on the face of earth cope with a history that has been studded with so many bold, and revolutionary, and subversive, and exhilarating men and women?

Schools know well the dangers that can be provoked by ethical upheaval in the consciousness of those within a social order that depends on managed views, on manufactured tastes and falsified perceptions of our own experience. Private ethics and public management are not compatible. Schools cannot leave it to the idle chance of later years to see how open minds respond to burning mandates. Instead, the mandates are themselves examined, outlined, categorized, congealed, within the basic framework of our school experience. Each radical name, each dangerous idea, is given its ordered place within the course of study. Each name, each statement, each quotation, snaps and fits into its own pre-designated slot. If each item can be locked into its proper place, there is no risk of confrontation or surprise in later years when we are on our own and do not have, between ourselves and justice, a curricular protection.

There is, by now, a sequence by which historic figures of strong radical intent are handled in the context of the public school. First, we drain the person of nine tenths of his real passion, guts and fervor. Then we glaze him over with implausible laudations. Next we place him on a lofty pedestal that fends off any notion of direct communion. Finally, we tell incredibly dull stories to portray his school-delineated but, by this point, utterly unpersuasive greatness.

Dr. King, by classic process of detoxification, comes to be a kindly, boring and respectful "Negro preacher" with very light skin and rather banal views, who went to college to "improve himself," believed in God, believed in "fellow man" and won, as a reward for his respectable beliefs and his non-violent views, the reverence of most U.S. citizens, "both white and black" — and, then, the Nobel Prize for Peace. Left out of focus is the whole intensity, the tactical genius and the ardent fervor that awoke within his soul for just one hour, yet which inspires and establishes his greatness. Teachers do not tell their pupils, if they are not forced, that Dr. King urged his disciples to defy the law, to interrupt its normal processes and openly obstruct its execution, so long as both appear to stand in conflict with good conscience.

Thoreau comes to mind in much the same regard: a man to whom, today, the nation pays considerable — but nervous — tribute. For fifty years after his death he was ignored. In his own day he was no more well-received than younger rebels of his stamp and character are loved today. He spoke of freedom, conscience and dissent and offended nearly everyone then living in the State of Massachusetts. Moreover, he did not restrict himself to words alone, but took explicit action on his views: "How does it become a man to behave toward this American government today? I answer, that he cannot without disgrace be associated with it."

In evidence of this conviction, and in clear enactment of the sense of disaffiliation, Thoreau refused to pay his tax and was, for one brief night, put into Concord jail. His willingness to stand out from his neighbors and to differentiate his own views from those of his time was seldom blurred in the accepted manner that is taken for agreeable dissent in our own decade. Thoreau sought none of the palliations that are used by those who cloud their statements with the satisfying ambiguities that pass for truth within the press and public schools today. "The greater part of what my neighbors call good I believe in my soul to be bad, and if I repent of any thing, it is very likely to be my good behavior. What demon possessed me that I behaved so well?" He also wrote: "You may say the wisest thing you can, old man, — you who have lived seventy years, not without honor of a kind, — I hear an irresistible voice which invites me away from all that. One generation abandons the enterprises of another like stranded vessels."

In 1844, Thoreau made up his mind to leave behind his neighbors altogether and went to live alone outside of Concord. There was, throughout this time, a sense of living absolutely at the center of his soul, at that decisive place within himself at which he knew that it was he alone who lived his life and that it could not be lived for him by any other: "When a sixth of the population of a nation which has undertaken to be the refuge of liberty are slaves, and a whole country is unjustly overrun and conquered by a foreign army, and subjected to military law, I think that it is not too soon for honest men to rebel and revolutionize . . . As for adopting the ways which the state has provided for remedying the evil, I know not of such ways. They take too much time, and a man's life will be gone."

Thoreau had words of scathing hatred for the cautious philanthropic people of his day. He also made clear what it was within their brand of philanthropic action he despised. They knew very well that what they did could not transform the social order, nor undermine their own unshakable position at the top. Thoreau, himself, did not abstain, of course, from straightforward ethics — nor from compassion of a strong and active form. Nor did he hesitate to claim a moral basis for his work or to take recourse, in a time of indecision, to the voice of his own conscience. It was the *guarded* character of philanthropic action and the pompous tone of philanthropic self-promotion, which he hated and attacked. They boast, he said, of spending "a tenth part" of their income in charity; perhaps they ought to spend "the nine-tenths so" and then be done with it. His own rebellion, at once more bold and less confined, took him in a more exhilarating and more dangerous direction: "We should be men first and subjects afterward . . ."

Today Thoreau is well-entombed in high school literature courses, wherein he is given limitless admiration as a nature writer. Those who wish to probe a little deeper into the political and moral implications of his views are urged by their intimidated and uneasy teachers to wait, if they can, until they are "a little older."

None of this should come to us as an immense surprise. The government is not in business to give voice to its disloyal opposition.

Thoreau is dangerous. He disobeyed the law, in keeping with the dictates of his own intense and uninhibited conscience and, from this action of good faith, derived that intellectual and personal integrity that lends so much of leverage, strength and of sustained veracity to his best work. Public school is not in business to produce Thoreau and, even less, young citizens who may aspire to lead their lives within the pattern of his courage and conviction. School is in business to produce reliable people, manageable people, unprovocative people: people who can be relied upon to make correct decisions, or else to nominate and to elect those who will make correct decisions *for* them.

It should no longer be perceived by us as either unreflective, unintended or "erroneous" that public schools will view with reservation and contain with care the words and voices of those men and women who call forth in us the best things we are made of. To pretend that public schools cannot perceive, and will not logically suppress, the danger constituted by the burning eyes of Malcolm X or the irreverent brilliance of Thoreau is to assign to those schools a generous ineptitude which they do not in fact possess. To undermine a man like Martin Luther King, or to speak of Thoreau as a naïve, brilliant but eccentric country-farmer, is not, as liberal critics like to say, a mindless error of the U.S. public schools. It is an ideal instance of their true intent.

The manner in which the schools contrive to decontaminate exhilarating women is, in part, a separate issue. In this situation, it is not so much a problem of the ethical debilitation of specific women. It is, instead, a matter of their virtual exclusion. In practical terms, great women don't exist in public school. Those who do are, with few notable exceptions, sterile relics of devitalized respectability: Martha Washington, Betsy Ross, Mary Todd Lincoln and the like. Harriet Tubman comes out of the wash with more than the average portion of her spirit still intact; yet even she ends up with much of the same bloodless character as Dr. King. Dorothy Day is not yet canonized by public school. Once she is dead, we cannot help but fear what will become of her. She will, no doubt, be treated generously, but with skilled patterns of domestication. Emma Goldman, Elizabeth Flynn and Rosa Luxembourg, having spoken in specific revolutionary terms, will not likely win a place in public schools for decades yet to come. If, and when, in fifty years, one or another of these women wins her paragraph, or her "sub-section" in a text, it is not easy to believe she will escape that special exercise of decontamination that is reserved for those who voice not only earnestness, but pain: not only righteous protestation, but authentic rage.

Helen Keller's decontamination in the public school offers by far the clearest parallel to that of Thoreau. Most of us know well by now the standard version of the deaf-blind-mute, glazed, dead and boring Helen Keller of the Fourth Grade bookshelf. In classic version, she emerges earnest, brave, heroic and undangerous: Harriet Tubman with white pigmentation, Eleanor Roosevelt with a few less faculties, but with the same high-pitched, pathetic voice.

"Helen Keller is a famous deaf-blind lady who can read, write and speak. She fought against great, even formidable odds, a battle that many people felt could not be won — and never would, perhaps, if it had not been for her trusted friend and teacher. Together, the two achieved things that seem all but past belief. Among the many important people whom they knew were Andrew Carnegie, King George, Queen Mary, Samuel Clemens, Lady Astor, Alexander Bell. In every respect, Helen Keller represented courage, perseverance and the highest moral values of her day . . ."

This is the standard Helen Keller whom two million children read about each year in public school, about whom they write tedious book reports, almost unreadable because, in forty years, they have remained identical, unchanging, banal and, in factual terms, dead wrong. Here, for one moment, is the voice of Helen Keller as in fact she lived and spoke, fighting with passion to expose the unfair labor practices of the first decades of the Nineteen Hundreds and to do battle with the U.S. social order as it still exists today:

"Why is it that so many workers live in unspeakable misery? With their hands they have built great cities, and they cannot be sure of a roof over their heads. With their hands they have opened mines and dragged forth with the strength of their bodies the buried sunshine of dead forests, and they are cold. They have gone down into the bowels of the earth for diamonds and gold, and they haggle for a loaf of bread. With their hands they erect temple and palace, and their habitation is a crowded room . . . They plow and sow and fill our hands with flowers . . . Their own hands are full of husks . . ."

In another passage, Helen Keller speaks of factory visits she has made: "I have visited sweatshops, factories [and] crowded slums. If I could not see it, I could smell it . . . With my own hands I could feel . . . dwarfed children tending their younger brothers and sisters, while their mothers tended machines in nearby factories." She then says this: "People do not like to think. If one thinks," she writes, in one of those remarks which, taken at face value, would transform from top to bottom every school in the United States: "If one thinks, one must reach conclusions . . . Conclusions are not always pleasant." She then makes clear her own conclusion after visits in the factories and slums: "The foundation of society is laid upon a basis of . . . conquest and exploitation." A social order "built upon such wrong [and] basic principles is bound to retard the development of all . . ."

The result, she says, in words prophetic of Marcuse, "is . . . false standard." Trade and material reward are viewed as the chief purposes of human life: "The lowest instincts in human nature — love of gain, cunning and selfishness — are fostered . . . The output of a cotton mill or a coal mine is considered of greater importance than the production of healthy, happy-hearted [and] free human beings. . ."

Of war, she says this: "The few who profit from the labor of the masses want to organize the workers into an army which will protect [their] interests . . ."

Of voting, she says this: "We the people are not free. Our democracy is but a name. We vote? What does that mean? We choose between Tweedledum and Tweedledee."

Of education, she has these choice words to speak: "We can't have education without revolution. We have tried peace education for one thousand and nine hundred years . . . Let us try revolution and see what it will do now."

Of revolution, she says this: "The time of blind struggle is drawing to a close . . . This is not a time of gentleness." It is not a time either of lukewarm beginnings: "It is a time for . . . open speech and fearless thinking . . . a time of all that is robust and vehement and bold."

Is she afraid? Is she intimidated by her chosen stand? Far from intimidation, she is inflamed with passion: "I love it . . . It thrills me . . . I shall face great and terrible things. I am a child of my generation. I rejoice that I live in such a splendidly disturbing time."

There is the temptation to go on: to quote page after page of this undaunted and subversive prose. Less "clever" than Thoreau, less skilled as craftsman in the use of words, she is more capable of soaring indignation.

The point at stake can be subsumed in these words: The special humiliation women undergo within the twelve-year interlock of public school (and, to a degree, still worse, within the Schools of Education) is evil enough to call for anger on its own. In the particular case of Helen Keller, I believe, she is not decontaminated in the public school by special reason of her being "woman," but rather in the same way as Thoreau — and for much the same cause. She comes out: laundered, low key, "admirable," heroic and yet, somehow, "non-infectious." Schools speak often of the dangers of infection among children. They offer tetanus shots to ward off tetanus, Salk vaccine to ward off paralytic illness. The way they fend off ethical epidemic has a genius all its own. It is difficult to think that Soviet teachers, for all supervision and political control, ever could fashion a more gross, more ruthless or more wholesale labor of historical revision.

There are, however, certain men and women who break all the rules and cannot be defused with quite the same deceit and glib abandon as Thoreau or Keller. These are, for the most part, rebels of a saintly, somewhat self-abasing character, often with religious ties or implications: people, for example, like Saint Francis, Gandhi or Saint Joan. The radical provocations of these kinds of "heroes" are such that the schools cannot with safety satirize or with immunity deny. For a number of reasons, having to do with many contradictions and pretensions that exist within our body of traditional ideas, school does not dare to label men and women of this sort as evil or insane. Whatever public schools may wish, therefore, a certain number of prophetic figures of this kind must, in some fashion, be respected or revered.

There is, however, a vast gulf between respect and imitation. It is at this point that the schools have carried out a solemn act of disaffiliation. The knife-blade falls between respect and imitation: between a "conscientious interest in a decent, and, indeed, an interesting and important person" and unclothed dialogue with the mandate which, in his utterance, resounds and resonates.

There is a quick and bitter instant of semantic surgery. Some people, we say, command our love and adoration. These, we say, are fine and admirable people. In certain ways, we say, they are the best and bravest, most remarkable, most admirable of human beings — but therefore (as we seem to say) just for this reason, not in any sense, by no miscalculation, no bad luck or evil fortune, are they anything like ordinary folk: i.e., like you or me. To be a brave, heroic and risk-taking man or woman, to be a person who is not afraid to be entirely different, whether saint or soldier, martyr or eccentric or incorrigible rebel: *to be someone like this is not to be someone like you or me.*

It is affirmed to start with, it is comprehended, it is unconditionally agreed, that we can afford to pay lip service to these dangerous and intoxicating human beings only because we do not have the obligation to be *like* them. Some people we honor; others we emulate, reward and ask for cocktails. This is an ugly but, I think, realistic designation of the range of proper options open to a person who intends to grow into serene and uncomplex adulthood.

"The social purpose of education," Friedenberg has said, "is not to create a nation of actively insatiable truth-seekers . . . It is to create a nation which can see clearly, and agree on what it sees, when it looks in certain directions." What it is expected to see, when it looks in the direction of Saint Francis, Thoreau, Helen Keller, Dr. King, is a possible object for arm's-length admiration and respect, but in no case an appropriate model for acceptable or even sane behavior.

There is, of course, a cold and brutal desecration in this process of dichotomy and insulation. It is, however, more at our expense than at that of those men and women whom we so insultingly, and so inadequately, revere. In the long run, as we seem to say, we are not sufficiently important — not enough "central to our own lives" — to believe ourselves good people but just "ordinary" folks. We live out some place on the flatlands where the stakes are low and

where the issues do not count. Unlike Dr. King, we have not been
to the mountain and we do not plan to go there. If we did, we might
come back to our old friends and "fellow man" with a sense at very
least of disconcerting irony. What then would we experience?
How then would we be able to respond? What would we say?

The man who has been to the mountain does not come back to
pick up in the conversation where he left off. If he comes back at
all, it is to interrupt the conversation. It is to say he is no longer
what he was before and that he cannot answer to the same ideas
with the same mixture of delight and acquiescence. It is, most certainly, not the business of a school that serves the interests of a
social order such as ours to send its pupils out on pilgrimage, or even
on a two-day round-trip expedition of this kind. I believe it is at
least in part for just this reason that we have been trained to feel
respect for people of this sort only in their distant power or past
excellence. We honor decent people *after* they are dead: cowards,
cynics and amusing people while they are still living. There is no
danger that a dead man will arise to tell us that we are degrading his
best work, or that we have been invalidating all its deepest worth.

It is still more than this. A man, once dead, cannot come back to
say to us that we might someday be strong and courageous too. He
cannot look to us with trust, or with a sense of love or invocation.
He cannot tell us to leave what we have been, and who we are, and
go with him. This point goes beyond the realm of politics alone. It is
not a mere decision as to which of certain men or women we may
find most suitable to our ideas. Rather, it is a matter of belief that
any person who, in any sense, has lived deeply, and felt strongly,
and struggled bravely and spoken boldly, with a voice of real conviction, is a person with whom we might converse as child and teacher,
follower and leader, friend and friend. Everything in our education,
and much in our social order, takes away from us the sense of power
to look to the people that we most revere as fitting correspondents
for our inept dialogue. They are too lofty: We are too banal. The
distance from the flatlands to the mountains is too far.

"In this life," Robert Coles has written, "we prepare for things,
for moments and events and situations . . . We worry about wrongs,
think about injustices, read what Tolstoi or Ruskin . . . has to say . . .
Then, all of a sudden, the issue is not whether we agree with what

we have heard and read and studied . . . The issue is *us,* and what we have become.''

It is clear, by now, that ''what we have become'' is, to a considerable degree, what we have first been told it is within our right or ''logical range of yearning'' to imagine that it is appropriate to wish to be. The writer who tells us: the teacher who instructs us: the schooling-apparatus that persuades us that our logical, sane and proper place is on the flatlands of relaxed intent and genial undertaking, has exercised thereby a fearful power. It is the power either to endow our dreams with richness and vocation or to reduce our aspirations to the size of an inept concern and the dimensions of an uninspired concept of inert compassion.

Low expectation, as we learn in the teaching of reading in the Third Grade, is a self-fulfilling prophecy. Children become, to a considerable degree, what they are told it is ''appropriate'' to *wish* to be. In this respect, I think it can be said that most of us need a sense of ''sanction'' or ''authentication'' — an ''empowering voice'' — in order to believe it is our right or our vocation to become just, passionate and risk-taking human beings. Conversely, there is limitless power of expropriation, for most children, in the voice that tells them it does not belong to them to yearn to be such men or women. We build perimeters around the ethical aspirations of our students by the very terms we teach them how to bring to their own act of self-description.

The schools instruct our children to believe in their own marginal position in relation to the kinds of people they are trained to look upon with reverence, adulation, love. The schools instruct our children to regard these women and these men as dwelling apart, within another realm, beyond our small, peripheral existence. These people, as school seems to say, command our love but live beyond our dreams. Dr. King goes to the mountain, Thoreau to Walden, Christ to Gethsemane, and Gandhi to the sea. As for us, we stay in class and write term-papers on the ''question'' of vocation or about the ''symbolism'' in a young man's or young woman's quest for truth and justice. Moreover, school goes further and makes certain that we get full credit for the time that we put in, whether in terms of grades, degrees and recommendations, prizes, publication or material reward. In such a way, school does not only stand between the child and the person he reveres, but also cheapens the relationship between them by showing the child how to turn his sense of admiration into coin that can be bartered on the common market. In a nation in which all forms of produce, intellection and vocation can be sold, consumed, exploited or traded-in, the ultimate triumph of the values of the state and social order in the face of those *real* dangers which subversive people such as King, Thoreau or Keller represent is to be able to turn them into a term-paper.

Nothing is sacred: least of all a man or woman whose whole being constitutes an invocation to the sense of risk, of ethics, of rebellion. It is bizarre that we should look for something different. What do we really think these schools are for?

VIII. FIRST PERSON

"Life and strength seem to exist only where one is not . . ."
— Erik Erikson

THOREAU, on the first page and in the second paragraph of *Walden,* set down these words: "In most books, the 'I', or first person, is omitted; in this it will be retained; that, in respect to egotism, is the main difference." Twelve years in public school render such words, such insolence, such recognition of the role of self, almost beyond the limits of conceivable expression. We all but die inside before we find bravado to make statements of this kind.

Only those, ironically, who — whether by exile or by prison — have been held outside the normal channels of self-diminution and reward, people like Eldridge Cleaver, for example, or like Malcolm X, still seem to sense the "sanction," or the "license," at particular times, to speak as if they knew, like Thoreau, that they might exist within their own lives as the only agents of control or transformation. "I should not talk so much about myself," said Thoreau, "if there were any body else . . . I knew as well." A person today must very nearly be the beaten prey, imprisoned victim, bound and manacled prisoner of the nation that first gave him birth, to speak, and dream, and yearn, and cry out in first-person pronoun undisguised, declarative mood, determination of the present soaring upward into future aspiration, cleverness, indirection and sophistication burned away like slag in fire.

To me, this failure seems a kind of crack within the wall of our self-etherized condition, a sudden, unexpected look into the mechanism of the abdication of our own beliefs. Frequently, I feel, when we are most intent upon articulation of a viewpoint which we most devoutly hold, then above all do we appear to wish (or need) to step away, outside ourselves, and speak our words in the third person. It is as if a man were to subtract himself from his own statement of belief and, by a reflex action, give his passions and conceptions to third persons: "alien quarters," "certain scholars," "a respectable body of opinion . . ."

Students, from the earliest years, are trained to step away before the open and unfrightened use of the first-person subject-pronoun. Grade-school teachers, in a formula of speech which by this time is almost classic in its ring, refer to themselves as if they were third persons: "Is that any way to speak to Miss O'Brien?" It is as if the teacher were not *there*, as if she were not present and pulsating in the room, but locked up somehow in the closet with the chalk and chalk-erasers. It is as if some other person spoke these words and she were only hiding and observing from a well-protected vantage-place.

In the university we hear much the same thing, though in a different set of words: "One might well ask if this could be described . . . It seems at least within the bounds of reason to propose . . . One might suggest . . . It could, I think, be argued by some people . . ."

I hear this kind of conversation frequently among my friends and former teachers, above all in sophisticated circles around Harvard. It is as if these elegant and prestigious men are scared that they may have engaged unwittingly in an illicit sexual offense by having arrived at the unlooked-for consummation of *a real idea*. It is as if they fear their progeny will not be licensed, or legitimized, unless they can assign it to a neutral party, anonymous imagination, alien parenthood, "another intellect more admirable, but less accessible, than mine . . ."

Businesses incorporate themselves with somewhat the same goal: in order to achieve immunity from consequences of their own behavior. The French expression for a business-corporation, like the phrase in Spanish and Italian, is "Anonymous Society." Ethical anonymity, I think, lies at the heart of all semantic methods of self-abdication. In a sense, the academic mind "incorporates" itself, achieving the condition of Anonymous Imagination, by just this method of third-person alienation of its own beliefs. It is more than a sophisticated trick of educated intellection. It is a hint of just how much we have already lost and forfeited. It is a way of saying that we are not really here; or, if we are, we do not feel it would be safe to say so in a voice too loud and clear.

Assignment for term-papers: "You will consult at least fifteen separate sources, half of which are books and half periodicals. Take notes on four-by-six cards, not three-by-five, and be prepared to present them upon demand. Bibliography and footnotes will follow the M.L.A. Style Sheet. At least one thousand words, with a cover sheet that includes a statement of purpose. The paper should have a clearly indicated introduction, body and conclusion. Do not use the word 'I' except in the conclusion of the paper."

Much of our education and a large part of our adult interchange reveal the same invalidation of our own experience: not only the third-person pronoun used so often by the horrified and self-intimi-dated commentator but also the conditional verb and the subjunctive supposition, both of which subvert so much of academic dis-putation. Subjunctive is the verb-form of hypothesis ("as if"); con-ditional is the syntax of tangential likelihood; third person is the pronoun of self-abdication. Together, they constitute the ideal rhet-oric of citizen or child whose hands are skilled but heart is dead and conscience is in exile.

"If one were to look without remorse into a matter like the prob-lems of the urban poor . . . if one were to consider, in all its solemn implications, the viewpoint often expressed by any number of intelli-gent and interesting men in course of recent years . . . the view that democratic process may perhaps have little meaning, and Civil Lib-erties may be of little worth, in a situation of immense despair and of intolerable dismay . . . if one were to so hypothesize . . . if one were in fact to come right out and *say* . . . that these were grounds for serious upheaval, and for major allocations and reallocations of the policies of recent days . . . then it might be time to look with favor on the search for new approaches and for parallel avenues of exploration . . . It might, indeed, be time to speak of ways in which to intervene and interrupt the tranquil course of academic specu-lation."

The man might speak of heroin overdose in Boston or Los An-geles, of "price-wage spiral" in the highest councils of the Chase Manhattan Bank or tactics of police protection in Chicago. His words achieve a level of such perfect and complete self-abdication that he might just as well be speaking of vanilla ice cream.

Even the Rebel Left, in its rebellion, indicates too well the long-abiding power of those processes which it rebels *against*. The dialogue of social revolution is pervaded with the grammar of debilitation: the interposition, for example, of the preposition or conjunction of arm's-length invalidation ("like") before all statements of intense conviction or denunciation. It's "like" we weren't alive. It's "like" we lived our lives through metaphor. It's "like" we lived in a land of sad deception. It's "like" the poor were starving and the dead were real. It is a terrible struggle often, for myself, as for large numbers of the people that I know, to overcome the hesitation to speak out directly in the strong and undisguised first person. Like many others, I prefer to generalize my own ideas as "feasible" or "interesting" suppositions. I would prefer to say that "some might choose" or "one might wish" to "entertain a certain body of respectable ideas . . ." I know that it is not unusual to feel this inclination; yet it is something that is not less sinister for being shared with others.

I hear kids speaking often of the most important processes of human struggle and of social change as if the passages of human transformation that they had in mind were relegated, from the first, to film or chronicle, past ages, "distant possibilities" or "alien suppositions." There is the sense that serious matters take place, by inherent choice, either in other lands or else in former centuries: *never where we may be and while we live.* "Important events do not take place within the same space as the lives we lead and passages of action that we undertake. These processes are not of us, not of our time and place. These things are: of great interest, worthy of examination, proper objects for astute concern. They do not, however, bring us with them into history. If *they* are of history, then *we* are not."

Students in suburban schools speak, day after day, of "urban crisis," "minority unrest," "difficult challenges of racism" in "impacted regions . . ." If they are in Evanston, they speak of racism in New York and Boston. If they are in Lexington, they speak of racism in Chicago. If they are in Scarsdale, they speak about racism in the Deep South. This is the feeling that I often have about the way they speak: It is not so much as if they are defending their own school or neighborhood or temporarily endangered conscience. It is more as if they are defending their own sense of marginal existence — as if they have become accustomed to the sense of "looking on from outside" at all serious events such as those which take place nightly on T.V. or such as those which take place in the pages of a book. It is as if their vantage-point has been in every case, up to this time, that of compassionate but disentangled viewer or, at most, narrator. This is, I am convinced, one of the strongest reasons for the fact that "class discussion" in these schools is carried through, forever and again, at such a low caloric level. It does not really matter who will win the game if none of the children is obliged to think that he is on the field.

The way in which we learn the use of words prepares us for renunciation of our own beliefs. The way in which we learn of history and social change prepares us for renunciation of our will to action as the consequence of our perception. Events in the external world are first presented, then accepted and at last perceived, as if they were non-human processes, initiated always by an outside force, related to each adult or each child only in the same way that the verb may be related to the direct object. Education, books, the university, the public school seem to be things, not that we *do* but that are *done to us*. History comes to seem an automated process that "transpires" nightly in a blue-green space of moving lines on T.V., narrated by a competent man with solemn voice and horn-rim glasses. After ten years, it is transformed into a process that exists in parallel columns of gray ink with boldface headings and "ten major questions" every fifteen pages. In a terrifying way, the existential hero of the time in which we live is the man who narrates war, not he who wages it or dies its victim: the man who sits within the glassed-in booth and narrates the political convention, not he who has been nominated or elected. There are, it seems, a certain number of intelligent and reasonable men who tell us the tales of great events and interesting deeds: but *no real deeds initiated by real people with real recognitions of the actions and events that they provoke.*

Children, by direct result, soon learn to look upon historic transformation not as the product of their own intentions, aspirations, dreams, but rather as the hard end-consequences of large and sequential processes initiated long before and far away, or — if more close and recent — then by people of more power, grandeur and imagination: "History takes place within the lives of other people, other places. Agony is for the theater, passion of the grand order for the stage. Important events take place, by their own preference, in the lives of those who matter more than I."

It is tragic enough that millions of young people have no sense of Active Ethics; yet this is not the worst. They have no sense of leverage either. Power is beyond them. Transformation is above them. Indignation, in itself, appears too grandiose a word to use in reference to the level of emotion they can undergo. Even "desperation" seems, most mornings, too impressive for such well-domesticated people: "Important people know the sense of desperation . . . people like Thoreau or Kierkegaard . . . As for me, I am just a little bit downhearted and depressed . . . It is a low-key business . . . not a serious matter after all . . ."

The most alarming evidence of real success in training children to remove themselves from processes of human transformation is to be seen if we look back upon the sequence of political upheavals which have dominated black and New Left struggles for the past ten years. Hundreds of times, we see the sudden abdication of real power in the face of the completion of a looked-for goal. Just at the edge of action, right on the threshold of real generative force, there is an instant of amazing failure: fractional passage of imaginative loss and of emotional collapse, which sometimes seems, remarkably, to yearn to forfeit everything. Like kids who work for days to build a treehouse in the sky, then break their leg as they attempt to climb it, people will toil for years to build a structure of articulate conviction, then fear to take the little extra step of *living* in it.

Truman Nelson writes about this sense of "threshold-terror." He speaks of the enormous fear that paralyzes many writers and respected scholars — the fear that listeners, or readers, may be stirred by what he has to say and then may ask him to be equal to the power of his exhortation. There is a kind of man, he says, who trembles with alarm when friends or students, moved to action by his words, come forth with clear-cut plans and workable intentions. The very strength and energy of such a man consists too often in the comfortable sense of unreal aspiration: that is to say, the quiet reassurance, or belief, that no one plans to act on his ideas. If, after hours of persuasive exhortation, he should receive a message from somebody ("Yes! Let's do it!") he collapses utterly, or else retreats to sudden circumspection and last-minute reconsiderations.

FEAR IS THE ISSUE. We have stood for so long on the outward cordon of our own experience, tangential in all serious respects to our own recognition of our own beliefs, asking for permission to reoccupy the center, pleading for the right to repossess our own ideals . . . It is a horrifying moment, after this, when we perceive ourselves to stand at last upon the margin of our own effectiveness. I know that it intimidates me most of all to be accepted by young people who believe in me. There is real terror, for an alienated man, at being taken at his own word and, in this way, winning followers. It is an unfamiliar feeling to be trusted to lead emigrations from old rooms and ancient places into new structures and into purposes unknown. It is to sense the right to grant ourselves the sanction to do what we do and to carry it off in face of all defiance, failure of nerve and skepticism. The New Left will to have "no leaders" is often, in my judgment, less an evidence of faith in democratic process than a fear of the first person. The will to *have* no leaders is a disguised form of the fear to *be* one. It is, in the long run, an overwhelming anguish at the likelihood of a fulfilled and actuated passion.

It seems almost impossible, after twelve years of public school and four of college, to stand and speak in the first-person present, undisguised: "I AM ALIVE RIGHT NOW. I SEE THE WORLD AROUND ME. I SEE MUCH IN IT THAT IS UNJUST AND EVIL. I HAVE POWER TO CHANGE IT."

The issue is, of course, complex within the Left today. For those who have been working in the social struggles of the past ten years, it has often been a devastating form of inhibition. Many people on the Left fear leaders who can speak in the first person more deeply than they fear defeat of dreams and loss in confrontation. Too many times, the words we choose when we are most intent upon articulation of our own beliefs reveal too well the bitter truth that there is no one left to make the statement. It is as if the theater had been filled, the play composed, the set completed and constructed at great cost, but all at once the stage were empty of performers.

Frequently, among the people I know best, there is almost an artistry and sculpting care with which we go about the process of enacting impotence. It seems as if some of us really do prefer this state of mind, as if it were more bearable to us (and surely more familiar) than the anguish which might otherwise be felt if we were to succeed. There is at times almost a sigh, as in the fresh-washed air after a rain: "We did not win and are not burdened with the future." Instead, we can externalize our failure, blame the Congress, blame the Ford Foundation and reflect, perhaps with eloquence and with a lot of sensitive insight, on the comfortable vista of a lost campaign. Eloquent failure comes to be our version of success; and there is a kind of heroism in it after all, the heroism of "defeat but of good struggle" and abiding faith in decent values and many relaxed and knowledgeable interpretations of our own narration of surrender. An eloquent loser can record his failure in a moving and reflective piece of prose and can adorn the present with narrations of his failed rebellion. A man that wins must stand within the center of the stage and undertake the burden of the future.

There is a too-familiar memory by now: the failed radical lying on the lawn of someone's radical estate, disciples of a sort about him in a scattered and uncertain disarray of pleasant retrospect on unsuccessful ventures. Little birds chirp after the rain. Friends and students, innocent in bare feet, sit nearby and tell us that it is okay. We did good, we tried hard, and came out unscathed, undirtied by our work, and there was "one hour anyway" in which we did something "quite beautiful" — something that we can remember with good pride and satisfaction.

It may be pride. It is not consummation. It is the elbow-resting posture of the well-indoctrinated man who narrates the most important moments in his life because he does not dare to *live* them. He contemplates in the conditional, aspires in the subjunctive and regrets in the pluperfect. There are few moments when he dares to speak and live in the first-person present. Listening sometimes to the student-organizers speaking of those processes in which they are, themselves, as I would think, enormously involved, I get the sudden terror that they too are somehow curiously looking on and watching from outside. They speak of those "objective conditions" necessary for a certain type of confrontation. It is as if it were a matter of the long-range weather possibilities: a super-lunar complex of external truth and automated fact, congealed in Heaven and verified on T.V.

There is a method in the seeming madness of our public schools. Revolutions are not made by those who live and speak in the third person. Exhortations are not verbalized in the subjunctive. Statements of conscience are not posed conditionally — nor indirectly given voice. It may well be that any nation that can do this to its children has little need, in future years, to call out armies.

Nineteen Seventy-two: I ask this question to a class of Twelfth Grade pupils in a school in upper New York State: "What is the purpose of your work in history? What *is* history in your point of view? Why do you study it? What is it for?"

"History is everything that happened in the past and now is over."

"History is cycles . . . processes . . . inevitable patterns . . ."

"History is what is done by serious and important people."

I ask this question: "Is it in your power to *change* history? Is it in the power of someone within this class?"

The answer: "No . . . not us . . . Not ordinary people."

I ask them, then: "Who *does* bring change into the world?"

One student says: "I guess . . . the leaders do."

I ask: "Could *you* be leaders, if you wanted to be leaders?"

He answers: "No . . . None of us comes from the important families."

Then I ask this: "Is there another time within your life, maybe in twenty years, when you might have a different sense of your potential impact on the world, or on this nation?"

One student laughs: "Give us two hundred years."

I ask: "How do you get that cold, sarcastic sound within your voice?"

He doesn't grow defensive. He just answers in a calm and lifeless tone: "I know very well that I'm not going to be part of anything that matters . . . not anything that matters here and now . . ."

Then I say this: "How is it that some people, somehow — Lyndon Johnson, for example — can be part of history, but others, you, for instance, have to stay on the outside?"

The student who has spoken to me most, listens a minute, holds himself in check a minute longer and then answers in a set of slow and measured words. He is a lanky boy, well over six feet tall, with cold blue eyes and with a sharp-edged look along his jaw. "History," he says — "it's like those movies that they have on Forty-second Street in New York City. For kids at least . . . THIS SHOW IS RATED X: KEEP OUT."

On one corridor in the social studies section of this modern, antiseptic, nearly all white school, there is a poster: "Occupations To Which Interest in History May Lead." The list is devastating, perfect and consistent with the words and comprehensions of the children that the school turns out. If the children work hard, and can demonstrate an interest in the field of history, then they can expect one day to be one of these kinds of specialist or expert: (1) archaeologist, (2) historian, (3) curator, (4) writer, (5) critic, (6) anthropologist, (7) research assistant, (8) librarian, (9) teacher of history.

Nowhere in the list do I find two words to suggest the possible goal of being one who *enters* history. Every job or dream or aspiration listed here is one of narrative description: critic, commentator, teacher, curator, librarian . . . not union-leader, student-organizer, rebel, revolutionary, saint or senator. "Why study history?" asks the wall-sized poster. The answer that we get is plain and uncomplex: in order to *teach* it, *total* it, *tell* it in writing, *cash* it in for profit, or *list* it alphabetically on index cards.

School teaches history the same way that it teaches syntax, grammar and word-preference: in terms that guarantee our prior exile from its passion and its transformation. It lifts up children from the present, denies them powerful access to the future and robs them of all ethical repossession of the past. History *is*, as the sarcastic student says, an X-rated film. The trouble is that everyone we know, love, touch, hold, dream to be, or ever might become, has first been told: I CANNOT ENTER.

IX. IMPOTENCE

"To criticize one's society openly requires a strong heart, especially when criticism is interpreted as pathology . . . No matter how eagerly the audience awaits or how well prepared the set, only courage can take a performer to the stage. There are many kinds of courage . . . the courage to risk being wrong, to risk doing unintentional harm . . . above all, the courage to overcome one's own humility . . ."

— Kenneth Keniston

I TALK WITH STUDENTS in the high schools of the all-white suburbs west of Boston. The students here are, by and large, incredibly well-trained, skillful in math, adept with words, successful in exams, confident of their prospects and well-padded by the social situation of their folks. It is apparent, nonetheless, that most of these students feel inhibited, constrained and impotent in every way that really matters to their sense of fair play. It is not a part of their inheritance, it seems, to think they have the right to be at once both ethical and efficacious human beings. How does this come to be?

One of the ways in which schools tutor children to the idea of their own futility is by a standard exercise of pre-planned effort-and-denial. We learn in school to ask for things we secretly know we won't receive in order to be pardoned, by refusal, from responsible pursual of the thing we ask for: "We did our best, put out the most we had, and failed despite this." The exercise proceeds in such a way as, first to challenge, then exhaust by disappointment.

There is a form of this familiar to most children. It is an exercise that might go under the description of "The Letter of the Earnest Citizen," a letter, for instance, to our representative in Washington, the purpose of which is to request a certain action, or correction of a certain evil, something perhaps that we have researched in our

Social Studies class and to which we now wish to direct our Congressman's attention.

The teacher passes out the white, lined paper and writes across the board the name and proper spelling and correct address of Congressman O'Neill. It is, I always feel, not just a lesson but a ritual — and one, therefore, which has a certain number of complex details. The teacher goes about it seriously; so do the children. The letters are composed: some strong, some weak, some gentle, some impatient. One day they go into the mailbox at the nearby corner. If the kids are lucky, they may each get back a separate letter. Probably, however, they get back only a single letter for the whole class. The letter, either way, will be receptive, warm and serious. In tone, as in whatever substance it contains, it will pay due recognition to the very special ritual we have performed.

We will, to start, receive the firm assurance that our Congressman was glad to hear from us just at this time because he needs to know what we believe in order to arrive at his decisions. In this way, he will conspire with us to let us believe that we were "really doing something" when we wrote *our* letter. The truth is, he receives a hundred letters every day and knows quite well from independent polls how people in his district feel about this point. Imagine, for example, that it is the old dispute about School Integration. Two years ago, after the last of ten reports relating to the matter had been published, and the last of fifteen delegations, representing fifteen separate power blocs, had come to talk with him, he had come to his decision: *against* racial integration. It was clear that it would lose him votes with those he counted on for serious support and would not help to get him re-elected. He has been silent on the subject ever since.

Thus, in his letter (which, in fact, is a "non-letter," to correspond to what, transparently, was our "non-request") he tells us that he feels it is "unquestionably a most important matter," one which warrants "most painstaking care." Many people are now busily engaged "in various research-projects" which relate to this. A pilot-program ("House Bill 62314") was introduced by Congressman Stevens. Senator Smith has made a recommendation to the subcommittee dealing with the problems of "The Disadvantaged Child." We all, says the Congressman's aide — in this letter which the Congressman will probably not even see but to which his signature will have been stamped — we all are working to bring change "in this most serious and solemn area," and students "conscientious enough to write their Congressman" are, "in a certain sense, doing the most important work of all."

The letter winds up with felicitations and the printed signature. The children did their research, followed through and had their class discussion. After something like a week of preparation, they composed a letter to tell someone of their views. A Congressman's assistant wrote back and told them of *his* views. Nothing has changed. Nothing *will* change. Skies will not fall and little black kids will not appear in frosty doorways Monday morning. Indeed, deep in their hearts, there are a few who knew it would be this way. "At least," it will be said, "the letters have been written. And at least we have in the (predicted) answer (that the Congressman's aide sent us) a handy and straightforward summary of all the things he is (not) doing. Perhaps this will help. At least we can only hope and pray so." It is a desperate consolation, but it is the only one we know.

All letters written to a person in high office are not futile, and all teachers who suggest that we might write such letters are not necessarily corrupt. The ritual at stake in this, however, is alarmingly familiar in the public school: above all, in the kind of futile plea we learn to bring to those who, as we somehow know, before we start, cannot respond as we would like, but whom we ask in any case — and oftentimes, in simple truth, *just for this reason.* "Ask, and ye shall receive" is the invocation to effective action given to us in the Gospel of Saint John. In schools across the nation, as in the working-patterns and imaginative viewpoints of large numbers of our adult citizens, it ought to be revised to read as follows: "Ask, and you may rest assured that you will be refused, but you will have done as much as you should, or as much as anybody has the right to ask, by the very fact of making the request."

It is not the effort, not the wistful try and not the good idealism I condemn. It is the will to lead ourselves to think that we are "doing something" *if we are not doing anything at all* except to carry out a ritual of effort-and-denial. "With earnestness we will petition if with compassion you will promise to refuse." This is, by now, a bedrock item in the course of classroom preparation: Ask, try, fail and be refused. Speculate somewhat (write a little essay) on the reasons for that failure. Now go on to a new subject.

The quite remarkable success that schools have had in getting across the message of inherent impotence to earnest children is seen in both the poorest and the richest schools in the United States. To me, it seems that it is viewed perhaps in its most bitter outlines in the richer schools and more expensive neighborhoods; for it is in these neighborhoods and it is in these children, above all, that the Myth of Impotence contrasts most vividly with the presence of real competence and with the acquisition of real technological and mathematical and scientific skills. The sense of ethical asphyxiation which these kids experience, and attest to, contrasts as well — and perhaps even more vividly — with the truly unprecedented range of physical freedom, economic license and topographic leeway, which these children in large numbers recognize, inherit and enjoy.

It is two o'clock on a Tuesday afternoon. We are sitting in a small, well-furnished room: soft lamps, warm carpets, Paris posters on the walls. It is two o'clock at one of the most modern, well-supported and prestigious senior high schools in the Boston area. We are sitting in a little room designed for "casual conversations." In front of me are twenty students who have been here for four years and will, three months from now, be going on to college. Their fathers are bankers, architects, attorneys and physicians. They travel with their families to Madrid and Paris, San Juan, São Paulo, Rio de Janeiro. They fly alone to Switzerland for Christmas, spend summers working in Nebraska or Vancouver, hitch-hike to Colorado, read Spinoza, Hegel, Tolkien, Robert Lowell, build their own cyclotron, get Math 800 on their College Boards, turn down admission to Harvard, Yale and Vassar and prefer to go to Oberlin or Berkeley, Reed or Bennington.

I look at them: *Who are they?*

They are the skilled and brilliant, sleek and slender, well-fed, strong and understated children of the men who govern, possess, design, appropriate, invest in and develop, knock down, build up, export from, import into, fly out of, buy up, into and around, between one half and two thirds of the earth we live on. They can program computers, hitch to Palo Alto, drive to Putney, phone long-distance to Geneva, visit their friend in Venezuela, thumb their nose at Yale and Harvard, build perfect scale-model versions of the Eniwetok H-bomb, mold steel medallions, sew flags on the rear of their blue jeans, make love with each other in the meadows and arrange their own abortions, if they need to, in Manhattan or in Copenhagen; but there's nothing that they can do about poor people.

They inherit the earth but, somehow, not their soul. What is it that is going on here? What is the quite extraordinary ritual of self-delineated impotence that is enacted by these bright and earnest kids?

She sits there, gentle, serious and well-intending, a reflective student, hands wrought up in a metaphor of anguish to express her sense of curious frustration: "I mean, like we know there's a lot of stuff that's just not fair and democratic and . . . like race . . . and like the system's just not right . . . We know that stuff . . . We know it isn't fair, but we can't hassle with it now . . . It's just too hard . . . There's too much there to understand . . ."

Her words, so gentle, earnest and aspiring, drift in the quiet space of air and lamplight, rugs and Paris posters. There is real sadness here, the bleeding-away of something good and brave within her eyes, and in those of her friends about her, as she speaks these arduous and jargon-interrupted words. Her hands, still twisted, rest there on the floor before her now, symbolic of her twisted and defeated aspirations. Then somebody else who's nearby on the floor, a plump girl, younger, with a face somehow benign, and bovine, and straightforward, adds on, in a nice voice too, and earnest also, like some soft sound out of the kindergarten hours, or out of the hours of the First Grade teacher with the polished nails and blue-dyed hair, a voice that rocked you back and forth with reassurance: "Well . . . I think that the very least that we can do is care."

The two ideas are like the plainsong of our self-defeat: First we recognize our sense of ethical ineptitude, then we seek to still our sense of unrest with the pacification of a well-remembered phrase. It is some triumph, and some testimony to the deep-down surgical effectiveness of public school that kids like this, with all the hard unquestioned competence, inherited wealth and physical freedom which they do possess, can be so well persuaded of their impotence.

That this should be is not an accidental outcome of the schooling process in this nation. It is the real proof of success.

What is the truth? Are these students powerless — or are they not?

This is the truth: Five hundred kids like these, refusing to take food or making up their minds that they would not obey the school-attendance rules, could shatter the patterns and shake up the mold of life in Salt Lake City, San Diego or Seattle for one hundred years. Five hundred kids in Westport or in Darien who stood up one day and announced that they would not go on from a rich person's high school to expensive colleges in certainty that they were treading on the broken hopes and cheated dreams of poor kids every bit their human equals, could overturn the college-admissions patterns in one season. One hundred kids, refusing to take private medical care while poor kids in the nearby ghetto went untreated — one hundred kids who put their bodies on the line in this most literal respect — could force the demolition and the wholesale reconstruction of the health-care distribution apparatus in an area like Hartford or New Haven, Syracuse or St. Paul.

Events like these are messages and testimonies which cannot be neutralized into a meaningless consensus. It is for this reason that our schools try to make certain that ideas like these do not occur to us. Instead, we are instructed in the best of ways for acting out our impotence by writing letters to the local press, enacting processes of futile plea and impotent petition in the selfsame terms and by the selfsame channels that have failed already twenty times before: "We will petition. You will turn us down. Each of us will have the kindness to pretend that we are doing something well-intended and sincere. In this manner, neither of us will run the risk of making painful transformations in our lives, but each will have the simulated sense of earnest enterprise to still incipient unrest." It is a low-cost way to tell ourselves we are good human beings.

The sequence of an earnest plea in search of a compassionate and credible refusal, of towering ardor flawed in every case to obviate a realistic consummation, is more familiar and more glaring at this time among large numbers of the college students in this nation than among any other single group or social class. A student leader raced into a crowded English lecture at a major university in New York

State during the student protests which took place in spring of 1970, approached the rostrum, pushed away the teacher and placed hands upon the mike. Dark eyes burning, red band of revolution on his rolled sleeve, he turned to the English scholar he had just supplanted:

"Excuse me, sir . . . We're trying to take over the university. I'd like to interrupt your lecture if you don't mind."

The professor turned about with rage upon the would-be rebel. "Get out of here, you little jerk," he roared. "You'll never pull it off if you have to ask your goddamn teacher for permission!"

It ought not to surprise us any longer that we learn this kind of lesson in the public schools. It is an age-old ritual by now, among well-educated U.S. kids, to "ask permission for the revolution" from the very agencies that we revolt *against*. For twelve years we lift up our hand and ask permission to get up and leave the room and "go downstairs" — or else "go down the hall" — i.e., to pee or to throw up. After twelve years, it is not surprising that we also learn to raise our hand and ask if it would be okay to go outside and "have a revolution." Nine tenths of liberal impotence in the United States is built upon this ritual of guaranteed defeat.

The White House Conference on Children and Youth, held five years ago in 1970, seems to me a perfect case in point: Five thousand people, from all sections of the nation, arrive in Washington with portfolios of plea, petition and position-paper carefully composed and intricately amended. The scenario for the entire conference can be written long before it starts.

The conferees arrive. They hear the President deliver a benevolent address, in which he speaks of his commitment to the ethical and independent qualities of children. The conferees dishonestly applaud the President for this dishonest speech, then head off into sessions of debate, discussion and delay. Soon it appears that this is going to be another week of endless talk and skillful pacification. A caucus is formed. The liberals argue with the Left. The press gives third-page coverage to the caucus, first-page coverage to the President's address. The dissonant conferees complain that none of this has led to real results. They go home, tired and frustrated, and report to their co-workers that it did not satisfy their plans.

What they cannot explain to their co-workers, or themselves, is why they went there in the first place.

The exercise of "going again to ask once more and once again to be refused" is based upon the pretense that there are no realistic power-oppositions in this land, that a President who finds his bed-rock of political support in cash, conservatism and reaction can also call a national convention, in good conscience, to take action on the needs of those whose vote he has discounted and without whose backing he believes that he can be elected. Naïve citizenship requires just this simulation. Honest conflict is denied. A falsified and dysfunctional consensus is enacted. There will be another conference like this four months hence. It will be just as well-attended, and by some of the same people.

Nineteen Seventy: A reporter is on visit in the New York Public Schools. The school she visits is not, like the one that I described above, in a suburban neighborhood. It is in a mainly Puerto Rican section. The time is winter. The room is dreary. The building is depressing. The teacher has begun an "innovative" social studies unit with her Fifth Grade class. The unit was developed (we are told) by an important "urban research team" with Federal backing.

The teacher writes across the board: "Today we will begin our work in urban social studies . . . We are going to talk about our neighborhoods . . ." She then proceeds, according to instructions that accompany the unit, to give the children an "experience of participation" in the process of the lesson. "Where is your part of the city?" she inquires. "What kind of building do you live in? How many apartments are in your building? . . . Are we always satisfied with the place we live in?"

On cue, the children chorus: "No."

The teacher asks the children to describe the problems in their neighborhoods. Suddenly, they start to warm up to the subject and begin to tell about the various troubles that they have to live with: hunger, junkies, crooked cops and firetrap apartments, untreated illness, trash on the sidewalks, and the rest . . .

While they speak, the teacher moves around the room and hands out bright new Social Studies workbooks. The reporter tells us that they are "complete with maps and charts to be filled in." The teacher starts to speak of her home neighborhood. She says that she still lives where she was born and that she feels quite safe there since she knows so many people. Her son-in-law, she tells the children for some reason, is a fireman.

It is at this point that the class discussion turns into an area described to children as "effective action." What can we *do* about a situation that we do not like? The answer, as we find, is not too different from the one discovered by the children in the upper-class suburban school I spoke about before. The teacher tells the children that the way to deal with problems like bad housing, insufficient heating or excessive rent is by a letter to the landlord. Tell him what's wrong so he can come and fix it. The way to deal with junkies is somewhat the same: Write a letter to the precinct captain and describe the problem to him.

"We're going to have to see and report things we don't like," she says. "Each child has a different problem and each one can find a way to work it out. We can help make our neighborhood a better place to live . . ."

Then, as the reporter says, the teacher tells the children that the Social Studies lesson is complete: "It is time to get on with their regular work . . ."

What is the lesson *taught* here? What is the lesson *learned?* The lesson taught has to do with social change; but the lesson learned is the lesson of despair and impotence. The teacher's voice, the words she uses, the suggestions that she makes, all speak of implausible enterprise, unhopeful ardor, profitless endeavor. To suggest to kids that they inform a slumlord of the absence of hot water in the cold of winter is a pre-planned exercise in self-defeat. To suggest that they should tell the paid-off cops about the helpless junkies is ironical: grotesque. The next step is to write to Gerald Ford about school segregation, to write to William H. Westmoreland about U.S. military ventures in the Third World, to write to Daniel Moynihan about starvation.

These kids are ten years old. The White House Conference is held once every decade. In 1980, if they are not dead, on drugs, in prison or in exile, they will be old enough to attend the next one. School teaches us futility. It is one part of the training for adulthood which we are compelled by law to undergo. The poor learn to live with patience, and the rich with guilt. Few of us ever learn to live at peace with our own conscience.

POSTSCRIPT: There is one cruel, and saddening, end-point to which many men and women often come, if they do not recognize ahead of time a danger which is at all moments present. It is a point of calculated and of well-contrived self-deprecation: one which offers each of us a mask, or a disguise, for deep-down terror at the thought that each, at some unfathomable point, might be compelled to face his own effectiveness.

The Trustees of exclusive, all-white colleges and universities, for instance, often speak of their inherent limitations (i.e., *as* white upper-class institutions) in justification for the absence, or low numbers, of black pupils: "We aren't prepared for projects as complex as rehabilitation of the black, the poor, the Spanish-speaking . . ." Suburban schools exploit the identical idea, insisting they are still unable to accommodate black kids because they don't yet know the way to deal with "serious issues of this kind." In plain terms, these people use their own time-ratified oblivion — in regard to basic points of right and wrong — in order to avoid the obligation to do anything at all to change a situation which, at present, serves their own self-interest.

It is, I am convinced, out of this fashion of attractive, modest and yet well-contrived self-deprecation that we end up with all those bland and even-tempered men who work for institutions such as I.B.M. and E.D.C., men who do not choose to take such actions as might threaten income or position, but manage to "toy" with education at that low-key and that unimportant level that transforms no disproportion and exacts no price from anyone concerned, but justifies its own inept dimensions by the skillful pacification of contrived humility.

Too often, we are willing to perceive a kind of charm and fascination in the type of person I have now in mind: the fellow who "tinkers a bit" with classroom innovation, dabbles with "a rather good idea" for teaching number facts, urges kids to call him by his first name — and tells other teachers how to "revolutionize" their rooms with plastic cushions. Over cocktails in the Education College of the local university, he gets some social mileage out of his week's labor. "I don't want to change the world," he says. "Perhaps I do a bit of good — who knows?"

He says it all with ease and understatement; yet he knows well, and phrases it just right. "A bit" is modest, reasonable and realistic. He does not plan to change a world that grants him such a pleasant way of life: certainly not. Nor does the bright and well-credentialized young fellow in the chair beside him. Thus, in Fake Humblehood, these men discover their true shelter: "Ethics exist, but not within the world in which I dwell. The power of intervention is not mine, but that of those who live with more expansive dreams, more glorious goals . . . and less humility."

None of us, Coles writes, "is in a position to gloat . . ." He is correct; yet each *is* in position at all times, by right of our shared lot as men and women in a world of pain, to make unfrightened statements of our own beliefs. If we do not dare to fight with all our hearts to disavow the pretense of political and ethical debilitation (a pretense which has always served so well the economic interests of the rich), we end up then within a devious position: We "judge not," for the very good reason that we live in fear of being judged by *others*. By legislation of a set of unambitious expectations in the ethical behavior of our own co-workers and our friends, we guarantee the same protection for ourselves.

Amiable habits of self-deprecation are today the going fashion in this land. Those who plan to stand up in the face of processes like these must be prepared to do so early, and sometimes alone, without the terror that they might be charged with "excess moral fervor" or the like. It is inevitable that they will be so charged. Nothing comes out of nothing. Nothing that matters ever comes for free.

X. ENEMIES OF REVOLUTION: NEW WORDS FOR OLD DECEPTIONS

"A Denver school cools the spirit of rebellion with a radical new program. . ."
— from a Life magazine essay
on the Open Classroom

IN RECENT YEARS there has been a well-sustained campaign to popularize the idea of a painless revolution in the U.S. schools through something known as "open education."

The warm reception which this slogan has received, above all in the upper-class schools which wish to have an innovative image, demonstrates the panic that is felt by those who recognize incipient stirrings of an insurrectionary nature in the consciousness of children and young teachers. It is not safe to leave such stirrings uncontained. The myth of open education — and the ideology of "neutral schools" on which it totally depends — now represent an ideal method of domestication and co-option by a generation that has not yet grown up from the myths created by the anti-Communist writers of the Cold War: people who, in pain and panic, wish to rid their hands of politics forever.

Education, wishes of such people notwithstanding, is not neutral. It is political, ideological, partial and, in every situation, involves some form of adult-imposition. A public school, as Lawrence Kohlberg has observed, is no more committed to neutrality than is the government or law: "The school, like the government, is an institution with a basic function of maintaining and transmitting some, but not all, of the consensual values of society." This is the truth. Education, in a land like the U.S., can never be neutral, open or impartial. It is not now. It has not been before. It will not be after we have finished with the struggles of our times. "The real question," as George Counts observed approximately forty years ago, "is not *whether* imposition will take place, but rather from what source it will come."*

The ideology of open education is built upon a number of ingenious areas of child-manipulation. The heart of the deception rests, however, on a single, well-constructed lie: the pretense of free choice within a managed framework of "alternative" ideas. This point lies right at the heart of the effectiveness of public school. It does not do to lock up children in a diplomatic compound unless we can induce them to believe that they are living in an ordinary structure — and, still more important, that they live there by their own free will. There must be the illusion of free options. There must be, too, a certain area of seemingly free motions. The compound must not seem to be a compound. The quarantine must appear to be no quarantine at all, but only a convenient form of tactful disaffiliation from unpleasant matters in the outside world. The prison must not seem to be a prison if it is to do the prison job correctly. There are new and older versions of the same deceit.

In certain ways, methods which today are advertised as "open," "innovative," "free" are infinitely more successful in achieving the old goals than the conventional devices. There is, for instance, a familiar way, by now, of "dealing" with a controversial subject in the public school: a method that appears to children to be conscientious, honest, open-minded, and leaves us later on with the experience of "having faced the issue," and yet in which the odds are really fixed before we start and the goal is not to meet the issue but only to be able to tell ourselves we did. Teacher and child alike regale themselves, in later years, with the idea that they have just looked down into the jaws of ideological temptation and emerged victorious. In truth, however, this is a dishonest and a grandiose description for a process of straightforward self-deceit.

Unitarian churches, liberal synagogues and such, often ask a controversial speaker to come in and talk. A listener who did not intend to think, or feel or struggle anyway, is able to depart with the distinct "experience" of having undergone an hour of great power, depth and richness. In fact, the only thing he really feels is the athletic satisfaction of an hour spent in *warding off experience*. This is the way most dangerous ideas are now defused in public school.

* My emphasis.

Teachers pretend to open up the issue; in reality, they close it more emphatically than it was ever closed before. The teacher who facilitates this false sense of encounter with a serious and painful point denies more to his pupils than a teacher who avoids the issue altogether. The latter, whether he knows it or not, at least has left the chance that children, in rebellion, will search out the area in later years, and find there something to provoke or challenge them. The pupil, however, who has had the false experience of confrontation with an issue in a classroom that was stacked against it, has seen the issue sterilized forever.

The pretense starts out in the early years of school. It is the class, for instance, in which children only tentatively and flashingly perceive that something inauthentic is about to happen; the class perhaps in which the child only hesitantly and vaguely understands that he is looking at the nature of another social structure, not to find out *whether* it might work, but only why it *can't;* the class in which both child and teacher take "a good long look" at our own form of "democratic process" in order to find out how to make it "just a little bit more fair and democratic," but never to ask if there is something unjust and undemocratic in the heart of it.

John Mann, a radical educator working in New Mexico, has made this point by use of a precise distinction: The innovative teacher likes to speak in terms of "smorgasbord" instead of pre-planned meals. The smorgasbord, however, is only relatively better than the single bill of fare so long as that which has been advertised as *choice* turns out to be no more than *whim*. "Whim," he writes, "is when you select potato salad instead of french fries today . . . french fries instead of macaroni tomorrow . . ." He then says this: "By agreeing to behave as if whimsical selection among proffered alternatives were choice, one enters into complicity with a system that deals in defeat of the human spirit."

The key ingredient is the pretense of free options. The corollary point is stated often, and in numerous ways, within the writings of Paul Goodman: Children can only choose for what they see *as* choices. Children can only opt for what they see *as* options. There are no serious options to be taken by a child who does not know what his real options *are*. Children never choose to learn of something that they have not heard of. They can "choose" for TIME or

Newsweek, S.R.A. or I.B.M. or E.D.C. They cannot choose for starving kids in Harlem, slaughtered babies in Vietnam, desperate people in Bolivia or Peru, if everything within the air, and on the board, and in the music on the speaker-system, and (above all) in the anaesthetic message of the teacher's alienated eyes, convey the secret meaning that such things do not *exist* — or if they do, then only in a way that cannot touch us or make claims upon our lives and our careers.

It is remarkable to see with what consistent patterns of self-insulation liberal teachers manage to ward off the truth of matters so well-proven and so long-confirmed: Children are not free in any way that counts if they are not free to know the price in pain and exploitation that their lives are built upon. To live guilt-free and conscience-clean within a world of pain that is, in large part at the very least, of our own making, is not freedom worth respect, though it is, of course, the kind of freedom that a liberal upper class finds it worthwhile to propagate. TIME magazine can call it "Civil Liberties." The Carnegie Foundation can call it "open education." It is still servitude, and it is still deceit, if the space in which it all takes place, long days before the child ever gets there, is already filled with ether.

There is a separate point: The possibilities of non-political, or neutral, education depend upon the prior existence of a neutral "field." To dream of this (it is a very happy and consoling dream) is to dream of children who have lived their lives within a sweet and unplowed meadow. Yet we know well our children do not live in a sweet meadow. They live in a minefield: one which has been crossed and patterned by high-voltage wires, planted with high-volume speakers. To play the game of neutral "resource-person" in this context is to fill a less offensive role than that of conscious salesman for a weary catalogue of patriotic lies. It is, moreover, less humiliating, since it frees the teacher from the obligation to say things he cannot possibly believe. In this sense only does it represent a lower *level* of direct deception. It is deception nonetheless.

There is one powerful area of self-deceit which is in operation here: one which attempts, time and again, to tell us that the child's inquiries are genuinely free. The vested interest that we hold in this belief is in direct accord with the more powerful vested interest of our faith in our own freedom. It is possible that there was once a time, ages ago, in some other land or even in our own, when wishes were free and wants were largely self-created. Today, whatever we may like to say, we know it is not so. The wants of the young, like those of their elders, are relentlessly controlled. "It is the essence of planning," Galbraith has said, "that public behavior be made predictable . . . The management to which we are subject is not onerous. It works not on the body but on the mind. It first wins acquiescence or belief; action is in response to this mental conditioning and thus devoid of any sense of compulsion. It is open to anyone who can to contract out of this control. But we are no less managed because we are not physically compelled."

The language of co-optive innovation speaks forever and again of open, free, spontaneous education; yet teachers know quite well their students cannot ever choose for things, or side with people, that they have not heard of. Nobody, without explicit provocation, walks into an airport and requests a flight to go to Rio de Janeiro if he does not first know it is *there*. Nor does he walk into the fifth floor of a slum tenement in Harlem, the Emergency Ward of a poor people's hospital in Memphis, the Phoenix Court, the ghetto schools of Pittsburgh or St. Paul. Nobody "goes" to any of these places if, within the place where he and his own conscience live, he does not know, and understand, and feel, that things like these are TRUE and TANGIBLE and REAL.

Again, the issue is the question of real options. In almost all the literature that speaks of open education, terms such as "materials," "stuff," "gadgets," "batteries" and "bulbs" are far more common than those words that speak of principles, of passions, or real people. Options offered are between hard objects: never between human needs or moral obligations. Honest choice is not the choice of lifeless objects to delight or serve the self, but human loyalties to serve and liberate the victims of a system which rewards some at the direct cost of others. Freedom based on choices less than these is not real freedom.

The children in the innovative public school "choose" between the little booklets sent into their room by Time Inc., packaged systems sent by Westinghouse and I.B.M., "urban-oriented," "multiethnic," "relevant," "up-dated" versions of the old Scott Foresman text — or bean seeds, balance scales and baby gerbils. This, then, becomes their sense of freedom: They have the right to choose without restraint among a thousand paths of impotence, but none of power, the right to demonstrate their sense of ethical surrender in ten different innovative "resource-areas" and at twelve separate levels of proficiency. Like first-class passengers on board a jet flight to a distant city, they have their choice of any drink or food or magazine or padded seat they may prefer; but they are all going to the same place, they are all going there at the same rate of speed, and the place that they are going is a place that neither they, nor you, nor I, but someone else they do not know has chosen for them. They have no choice about the final destination. They have no choice about the flight, the price, the pilot or the plane; but they can stretch their legs, and walk along the aisle, and select their magazine, and they can call this FREEDOM.

"The social worker . . ." Freire has written, "has a moment of decision. Either he picks the side of change . . . or else he is left in the position of favoring stagnation." The skillful myth of open education, and the fiction of unmanaged choice on which it totally depends, provide a means by which the teacher can pretend he does not need to choose. In truth, he chooses. He chooses for connivance, for collusion, for non-intervention, in an innovative form; yet he does not dare to tell himself that he has made this choice. He calls it "independent study,""open structure," "non-direction." He hopes that no one else will feel the need to call it non-conviction.

Teachers in these schools know, all too well, the character of whim, disguised as choice, which they now advertise to children. Most of these teachers can predict, with a good deal of skill, the items pupils will select when they are exercising their own "independent" right of option. They know, just as well, the ideological conclusions they will draw when they do "independent research." They write down in advance, on Sunday afternoon, in lesson books, the things their children will "discover" Wednesday morning in small-group discussion. The innovative classroom may well, as the jargon says, be "child-centered," but it is also teacher-written, I.B.M.-predicted, School-Board overseen. *Nobody ever dis-*

*covers anything within a well-run school in the United States which
someone somewhere does not give him license, sanction and permission to discover.*

Teachers often think they can present a neutral posture in the eyes
of children by a tight control over the words they speak. It is a
wistful, but naïve, position. Teachers never can be non-political or
neutral. They are political when they say: "Good morning." They
are political when they sneeze, break out in tears or roar with laughter. Gide said: "Style is character." In the classroom, life-style is
at the heart of education. The things a teacher does not dare to say
may well provide a deeper, more substantial and more lasting lesson
than the content of the textbooks or the conscious message of the
posters on the wall.

The teacher who does not speak to grief, who cannot cry for
shame, who does not laugh and will not weep, teaches many deep
and memorable lessons about tears, laughter, grief *and* shame.
When war is raging, and when millions of poor people are enduring
both a private and communal Hell, no teacher, no matter what he
does or does not do, ever fails to demonstrate a powerful bias in one
fashion or another. This is the case even if his bias is conveyed only
by the lesson of conspicuous abstention from a field already fraught
with possibilities for moral indignation.

What the teacher "teaches" is by no means chiefly in the words
he speaks. It is at least in part in what he *is*, in what he *does*, in what
he seems to *wish to be*. The secret curriculum is the teacher's own
lived values and convictions, in the lineaments of his expression and
in the biography of passion or self-exile which is written in his eyes.
The teacher who appears to children to be neutral, or sedated, in
the face of human pain, black-infant death or something so concrete
and evil as the murders at My Lai, may not teach a thing about
racism, birth mortality or My Lai; yet he will be teaching a great deal
about the capability of a well-set and a respectable U.S. adult to
abdicate the consequences of his own perception and to vacate his
own soul. By denial of conviction, he does not teach *nothing*. He
still teaches *something*. He teaches, at the very least, a precedent
for non-conviction. For these reasons, then, apart from all the rest,
it is apparent that a teacher cannot take a neutral posture in the eyes

of children. It is just not possible to disaffiliate entirely from the blood and the stench of the times in which we live.

Open education now discovers a well-financed ally in the so-called "educational technologies." In terms of teacher-fascination and convenience, the mechanistic, "systems-oriented" brand of innovation is both tantalizing and seductive. Technological manipulation, skillful use of all the right code-phrases, names of famous scholars and advisers linked with the design or manufacture of these innovative plans, the inclination of most educated adults to put confidence in technological solutions, the secret hope (perhaps the deep-down dream) that somehow, by some magic, we shall be allowed to spare ourselves from pain or candor, truth or revolution by the cleverness of an inspired machine: all of this works to set aside our skepticism and initial sense of reservation. There is, in all of this, so much of an *appearance* of real change. It is not easy to believe that something is not different.

Advertisements for these programs draw with skill upon the catch-cries of the rebel authors. The C.I.A. reads Ché Guevara, Frantz Fanon, Regis Debray. The men at I.B.M. read A. S. Neill and John Holt. They draw upon the least important but most facile adaptations of their work. Henceforth, as the fliers and promotional materials report, teachers have a whole new chance to share in "revolutionary" change and take their place within the vanguard of reform. No longer need a single teacher hold within his hands the reins of thought for thirty kids. From now on, a child may move forward, learn, inquire, check and self-check, question and progress, without adult-control.

Then too, it is said, materials will now be far more scientific, more diverse and more sophisticated. Teachers need no longer waste their evenings or their Sunday afternoons in striving to assemble workable lesson-plans in complex subject-areas: "Those who know much better have already done it *for* us." Henceforth, the teacher can sit still, observe, relax and work at his own ease with just a single child, get up and stroll about the room, give help where needed, offer encouragement where it might be required . . .

That, in any case, is the promoted expectation. This, however, is the serious question that remains unchanged: What does all this jargon really tell us of those things that *matter* to us as good, ethical men and women in a land of pain? What does it say, for instance, of the willingness to stand and speak, react with passion and respond with rage, to needs and devastations that cry out for strong, un-hesitant response? What does it say about the real priorities of school itself — about the need of a society like ours to polish unique items, special people, rebel children, to one size and to one shape? What does it say about the silent conscience of the ruling class? What does it say about idyllic meadows, uniform suburbs and sweet streams, removed from sirens, sickness and starvation?

It is self-evident that, in such terms as these, there cannot be a serious transformation. The child's mind is still, just as before, totally at the mercy of those, far outside his world, who make deci-sions for him: those, for example, who decide to mass-produce *these* packaged items as opposed to *those,* and then those other men and women far removed, who sit some place in cold and isolated rooms, and make decisions as to how, and with what data, and by what devices, and with what visible or by what unseen attitudes, ideas, beliefs, to shape our wishes and our dreams. In former times, deci-sion-making of this nature could be handled on the local level. It would be done by School Board, school administrator, principal or P.T.A. Now, with the labor of preparation once-removed, with the factor of decision once-subtracted from the classroom and, with some exceptions, from the local systems too, the total business comes to be more uniform, predictable, mechanical and, therefore, subject to more perfect patterns of control.

In earlier times, the teacher only did his best to *act* like a machine. Now he is, in fact, replaced by one. Before, he could at best provide, within one isolated room, a process of labor, a set of stan-dardized pursuits, which might approximate the labors taking place in other schools. Now he does not need to struggle to achieve this goal. The process in Seattle may now be identical with that which takes place in New Orleans. The process in Chicago may now be the same as that which takes place in St. Louis, Memphis, Phoenix and Poughkeepsie. In an individual school, each child may *appear* to be attempting something different from the child in the seat be-hind, but *all* will be doing exactly the same thing as children in ten thousand other schools, who will, at the same moment in the same hour and same morning of the same day, be moving with the same illusion of free options through the same set of mechanical proce-dures and the same set of pre-planned devices and ideas.

It is correct that the child on the right side of the class will be proceeding "at his own pace" in distinction from the child on the left side, or the child in the middle or the back. He will, however, for all superficial sense of independence, for all pretense of unique experience, be doing the same thing, at the same time, at the same pace and by the same procedure, as more people in more places than at any time before. In the guise of individualized instruction, under the cover of a "new," "unique," "experimental" concept and idea, the school will have created more identity of purpose, more conformity of direction, more predictability in reference to assumptions, more homogeneity in reference to end-products, than I should think that any system of indoctrination, with the possible exception of the Medieval Church, has ever had at its command.

Technological corporations, like the governments they serve, ma-nipulate and now increasingly resemble, may frequently be clever and will commonly seem liberal or benign; but they are not suicidal. It is not to their use, from any point of view, to do in public school that which they do not do on the outside. There are fifty million captive customers, future voters and potential soldiers sitting in these schools. It is a safe assumption that, whatever gadgets, pack-ets and bright boxes make their way into the public schools, few enough (and only enough, indeed, as necessary to provide the fiction of illusory dissent) will serve to trouble young imaginations. Images of hot and crowded urban clinics, mother and child sitting in the basement hallways and the odorous and infectious waiting-rooms of arrogant and crowded health dispensaries, plywood windows over corner-drug, watchful cops and desperate kids on neon-lighted nights, hunted eyes and horrified gaze on hopeless fourteen-year-old addict searching for the man that holds in his hand the bag of dreams at two A.M. on Blue Hill Ave in Boston: these visions, sounds, smells, torments will not look out at suburban children from the innovative learning packages from I.B.M. any more than they look out from age-old chalkboards or My Weekly Reader.

It isn't demonic. It isn't malevolent. It isn't "conspiratorial" by any standard definition of that term. It is, in contrast, normal, pleasant and convenient. It is a better instrument of mass-manipulation and control than state or school has ever previously had at its disposal. It enters the class under communal benediction of the politician, salesman, educator. It comes in guise of greater license, broader options, heightened power for the individual child. In the name of freedom and beneath the banner of experimental education, it comes to confiscate, to disenfranchise, to deny.

Machines cannot resist co-option. Teachers *can*. So too can students of a certain stripe and state of mind. They cannot do this, though, if they do not begin to function with the lever built of burning skepticism in the face of technological intentions. Businessmen are not in business to lose customers; public schools do not exist to free their clients from the agencies of mass-persuasion. A monolithic complex of industrial, political and academic wealth does not exist to build the kinds of schools which will empower children to subvert their goals.

In my belief, most books on open education, whether of the technological or British brand, are low key, boring or dishonest. I do not think that there is any way in which to write a serious book about our public schools, in 1975, that can be neatly called "another interesting book about nice innovative things to do with children." I know, at least, I cannot do it: much as I would like. Each of us writes at last the kind of book that we must write, and wins the kinds of allies that we need, deserve or yearn for.

XI. NONSTOP FORWARD MOTION

"Our consecration to motion is encouraged and supported in
order to keep us out of mischief. At least we know that so
long as we thus busy ourselves we shall not incur the serious
displeasure of our social elders."

— George Counts

IF MEN AND WOMEN, even in a well-divided land, were not vulnerable sometimes to a sudden period of unexpected anguish and bad
conscience, there would be no need for us to live protected.

It is the persistence of guilt, and the curious survival of ethical
strivings and potential self-examination, despite all, which makes so
many of these school-delineated exercises necessary. A hard, cold
nation, stripped clean to the bone, perhaps like Nazi Germany for
fifteen years, would not be in such need of complex forms of self-
protection. We *do* require self-protection of this kind because we
are not yet "stripped clean;" and all the methods, myths and exercises of self-exculpation that I have been trying to describe, are
there because we need them to protect us in the face of the indomi-
table and, somehow, indestructible remnants of our own sense of
compassion.

In these pages, I intend to speak about another form of school-
delivered self-exoneration. It is the ritual of Nonstop Forward Motion: motion like that perhaps of some swift, clean and low-cost form
of modern transport, one that requires no fuel and asks no nutriment
for pilot, passenger or engineer. The most important function of this
ritual, in my belief, is to enable children to avoid disturbing recognitions of their latest act of impotence and self-defeat. The faster

they move, the less time they will have to look back on those labors they have left undone and on those pre-doomed aspirations they have courted, sought and then deserted.

In school terms, the process can be stated best in something like a two-part formula: (1) "Ask for something so it can be refused." (2) "The bell is ringing. Go on to your next subject."

The myth is perpetrated that we have achieved A Real Thing by the action of petition and refusal; that we have fulfilled our dream, or our vocation, and can now head onward to The Next Thing. The next thing may be class play, a rock concert, "Pep Club" or summer in Vancouver. At the Hip (and college) level, it is a "new bag" to be "into." At the adult level, it is another research-project, the definition of a "new oppressed minority," a new movement, a new ideological position, a New Thing To Try And Fail At. From this exercise, there grows, little by little, the unsettling phenomenon that appears to many European observers of the U.S. Left as "Ideological Promiscuity," movin' on, as the folksong has it, from one moment of impotent advocacy to the next one. A friend of mine has offered this description of a fashionable movement in the U.S.A. in 1970 or 1975: "Ask, try, plead, fail. Write an interesting piece for The New York Review of Books on the subject of your failure. Now go on to a new movement."

The definition is not totally unfair; yet there is the chance, in stating it this way, that we can miss the point. That point is that "to ask and fail" is first described to us in school, and then experienced in our adult lives, as the ethical equivalent of Having Done A Real Thing. School says to us: "You did a Real Thing. You had your class discussion about race and ethics. Now go on to your next subject."

In the literary world, there is the same idea: "You did something good by publishing a book of protest. We did something good by reading what you wrote. We went even further by giving you a good review. Now get on to the next thing . . ."

In the same way, we hear one another say: "We had a Civil Rights Movement." There is the hallucination almost that a human need was answered by the mere idea, like a cloud up in the sky, of the "having" of a movement. In a sense, it *was*. A need *was* answered: not the human need it was supposed to be about, but our own need for a plausible activism. "We're into a New Thing," I hear the high school students say. "We're into Ecology," "into women's liberation," "into communes." The point is not that each of these things might not be a "thing" worth being "into." It is the idea these students have (a) that they are freely *choosing* for each thing that they go "into," (b) that to be "into" something only for the length of time it takes to try and fail is of any real worth to other human beings.

The ritual of Nonstop Forward Motion from one moment of surrender to the next is characterized today by an unending sequence of "concerns," each of which is tried, consumed, and traded-in like clothing fashions or new models of T.V.: civil rights, peace, pollution, women's liberation, welfare rights, the pathos of the white and unrespected middle class, the American Indian, the Mexican-Americans in the Southwest, Puerto Ricans in Manhattan, overworked pupils at exclusive prep schools in New England — each cause placing claims upon us in unceasing sequence, but always with shorter and still-shorter periods of perseverance. Each of these causes is legitimate. The question here is not the substance of each struggle. It is the character of our forward ambulation. We move forward not from completion to completion, but from one incompletion to the next.

The discovery of "new oppressed minorities" is a good example of this process. There is no question but that other categories of oppression are legitimate besides black skin and Spanish surname; yet there is at times transparent insincerity about the way we move on to discover, then define, at last equate these categories. The discovery by the intelligent wife of a Manhattan millionaire — ex-volunteer for Day Care in East Harlem during 1965 — that she too is oppressed, first because she went to an oppressive prep school that was not like Summerhill, second because she is a woman and cannot go down to Wall Street like her husband to exploit the poor, leads her to the final step of making an unqualified equation between her own oppression and that of the victim of the slum.

The point is not just that this is a cruel equation (her children are not born brain-injured; she is not starving; her children do not chew lead paint; her cancer, epilepsy, heart disease do not go unexamined and untreated) but also that, by such equation, *neither* form of exploitation will be dealt with in a conscientious way. Each produces literature, controversy, talk-shows, a New Thing to Be Into, a special issue of Atlantic Monthly or of Saturday Review. No one who is now in pain will be in less pain when it is all over.

Nonstop Forward Motion, in the form described above, leads by rapid stages to a still less admirable, and more self-serving, state of mind: one in which all human needs seem to be equal in their claim upon our conscience and their power of appeal to our capacity for intervention or response. The ideology of Equal Claims which soon evolves is one in which it seems not just offensive, in political respects, but even "in poor taste," to say that one thing counts more than another. ("Let's not talk about *poor* kids from now on. Let's just talk about *kids*.") The theme that follows logically from this, is that essential change is *less* essential than we think; that hunger is serious, but so, as well, are string quartets, folk concerts, river conservation; that children are dying, but so also are the ideals and aesthetic satisfactions of their teachers; that slum children may be starving, but so, in another manner, are the most important values of their doctors, lawyers, landlords and storekeepers.

Ecstasy, in place of ethics, soon becomes the major pedagogic goal of those who wish to work and prosper on the crest of fashion. "Joylessness" — not murder, pain, class-exploitation — comes to be the word that wins the quarter-million-dollar grant from Andrew Carnegie's inheritors and makes the front-page headline in The New York Times. Therapy, at length, becomes the final substitute for social change, and fair play for the oppressed grandson and the oppressed wife of the oppressive millionaire becomes, in itself, so vast and so complex and so remarkable and so intensely intricate a matter of consideration as to make old-fashioned, tedious and square those who, with memories too deep or loyalties too long, still wish to speak of where the money comes from.

The widespread substitution of the single concept — "joy" (or "joylessness") — in place of words like exploitation, segregation or injustice, is one of the most vivid instances of the full power of this exercise. In face of Mississippi, in face of Roxbury, in face of

Watts, in face of Kent State, My Lai, in the face of napalm, Nelson Rockefeller, Gerald Ford, in the face of lead-paint poison, in the face of thirty, forty, fifty small black children dead for every thousand born alive, in the face of Henry Kissinger, in face of General Westmoreland, it is no small matter to be able to convince the people of this nation that the deepest and most searching pedagogic problem of our time is not that we train children to be murderers — but only that we do so within classroom situations that are "joyless."

In an evil sense, as seen from the position of the man behind the window on the twenty-eighth floor of the Carnegie Foundation, "joylessness" provides the one, most perfect democratic resolution to the problems of our times. It is the consummate egalitarian response to the implicit dangers of a head-on confrontation with the unjust allocation of resources. The boys at Exeter are joyless. The girls at Farmington are joyless. The little boys and girls of Roxbury and Harlem and the South Side of Chicago are joyless as well. Some will be joyless businessmen and joyless brokers, joyless guests at joyless first-night theater parties, joyless customers of joyless discotheques and joyless small French eating places. Others will be joyless kitchen-maids and joyless janitors and joyless junkies. It is the joylessness of each side of the structure of oppression, the joyless hours undergone on both sides of the tilted and unequal seesaw, that bring us all together in a single democratic unity of insufficient fun.

"Purity of heart," wrote Kierkegaard, "is to will one thing." During high school visits, I have often heard kids saying things like this: "We used to be into that race and conscience bit . . . We're in a new bag now . . ." First it seems cold, then bitter, then despairing. There is a hollowness, an empty ring, about it all. It sounds less like achieved serenity than like disguised surrender. It happens in the same way with large numbers of adults. We go on from movement to movement, thing to thing. Each of the things we do may be a good thing in itself, but "moving on" is not a good thing if it is a way of spinning out our worth — and squandering our capability for love and struggle — on a boardwalk of inadequate completions. We go along beside the games of chance, trying and losing, and then moving on to try the next game. As at a boardwalk, there is much commotion, little industry and few rewards.

The obsessive character of nonstop locomotion of this kind is seen in every area of intellectual and moral aspiration. There is at least one memorable example every season.

Nineteen Sixty-nine: A book is published, *Poverty and Mental Retardation*. The author is named Rodger Hurley. The preface is by Edward Kennedy. The book is previewed in a long review by Robert Coles. It is the "consumption" and the "neutralization" of this book, rather than its tragic content, which are of importance here.

The book documents the startling degree to which poverty in the U.S. cripples its victim, not just in some cultural respects, but (far more important) in the physical respect of irreversible brain-damage. The author, financed in his efforts by the U.S. government, incorporates — but far transcends — the labor and concern of men like Goddard, Hollingsworth and others. He has the capability to get upset. Even if he did not, however, some of the statistics he sets down would burn upon the page. In demonstrating how culturally loaded intellectual criteria, along with genuine physiological damage, create a disproportionate incidence of measured retardation among blacks, he cites this information: "The most frightening instance of the over-representation of the Negro . . . is found in reports of the Eugenics Board of North Carolina. Over a period of thirty-seven years this Board has overseen the sterilization of 6,851 persons, some by means of castration. Not all of these individuals were sterilized for feeblemindedness; mental illness and until recently, epilepsy were also considered adequate reasons to subject individuals to this utter degradation.

"In the two-year period beginning July 1, 1964, 356 persons were sterilized: 124 were white, 228 were Negro, and four were Indian. In the previous two-year period, 507 persons were sterilized: 150 were white, 323 were Negro, and fourteen were Indian. *There are approximately three whites to every Negro in the North Carolina population.*"*

* My emphasis.

On infant death, he gives us these statistics: "In the United States in 1964, the overall rate of infant mortality was 24.8 per one thousand births. This figure in itself provides a significant comment on the quality of reproduction in this country, since fourteen other countries had lower rates than the United States in 1965 . . . " When this figure, however, is broken down by color, he goes on, we find the rate for non-white infants in the U.S. during 1964 was 41.1 per thousand, almost twice the white rate. "In 1962, the entire city of Newark had an infant mortality rate of 41.3 per one thousand live births, as opposed to a statewide rate of 23.9 and a national rate of 25.3." The lowest city rate throughout New Jersey during the same year was 13.9 per thousand. If this figure had applied in Newark, Hurley writes, it would have meant survival of almost three hundred infants.

He establishes too that black kids, due to poor pre-natal care, are far more likely to be born premature, and tells us something which some of us may not have known: "An infant born prematurely is sixteen times more likely to die during the neonatal period (first twenty-eight days of life) than one whose birthweight is normal." If the premature infant does survive, he is "ten times more likely" to be mentally retarded.

If we have questions left as to the level of treatment given to the poor, he also deals with this: "More than ten percent of all nonwhite mothers in this country in 1964 gave birth without a physician in attendance; this rate was more than twenty percent in several Southern states . . . In general service delivery clinics . . . quantity must of necessity take precedence over quality. This observation should not be misunderstood as meaning that clinic service is tantamount to no service at all, but the quality of medical service one receives is directly related to the price one pays. For general service delivery the poor pay very little or nothing and, thus, they 'definitely get second-rate medical care.' "

It is a horrifying book; more horrifying, however, than the content of the work is the way a book like this is "handled" by a population such as ours. The book is published. Its statements are well-documented. Its conclusions are attacked, discussed, at last accepted. It gets reviewed and praised, sold in the stores, talked about among intelligent people for a while, held in respect by many, discussed again in certain places and adopted finally as a standard text for certain areas of study. *It does not make a perceptible difference in the life of anybody,* not when it appears, not when it is first reviewed, not when it is first reprinted, not when it is chosen as a college text, not when it is finally dropped into a special, neat and clean compartment of contemporary culture labeled as "important comment on a major social issue."

The same thing takes place also among people with whom I have worked within the public schools. There is a way in which some of these people learn not only to "consume," "acquire" and "possess" each book, or fashion, innovation or idea, as it is published or put forward, but also to exploit the very sequence of these items and ideas in such a way as to provide them with a constant pretext for the inward action of surrender. Ideological consumption is tied thereby to the process of inevitable obsolescence.

We meet, within the Left, large numbers of young people who are able to take up, exploit, relish and reject new books, new notions, new allies, almost with the same rapidity as they would "take" or "drop" new college courses. The type of serious, but inconstant, men and women I now have in mind — Hip in appearance, radical in words, but desperately well-programmed in behavior — discover each year the work of someone new, discuss it with pleasure, digest it with delight, consume it with uninhibited appetite, but then make use of this new ideological appropriation as a reason to move on from where they are to something new.

They read Illich — or they go to Mexico to visit Illich — and come home, with neither caution, care nor honest comprehension, to report to all who are prepared to hear, that "school" as an effective concept is outdated. They read John Holt and they report to serious parents of the children in their school that you cannot "teach" skills in any case, so we should not waste time in even trying. They read Charles Silberman and they report to their co-workers that "joy" and "joylessness" are now the only words we need to think about, or use, in our discussions. No need, then, to be troubled about books or math materials or Building Code. They read Black Power writings — scrupulously selected, as I find — and they announce, in what they take to be the dialect of the slum, that "the white man" ought to go away and let "the black man" get himself "together" to do his own "thing." (They say this even in the midst of sessions taking place at strong, successful, integrated Free Schools.) In the end, they pack their books, lock up their conscience, put away their dedications and their skills, go off to the woods and build a whole new set of ideals and of loyalties.

The question, however, that we need to ask is this: *What loyalties can be constructed on a groundwork of desertion?* I have spoken of a teen-age boy who lives nearby. In the course of ten years, Peter has gone through six "generations" of white teachers, organizers, drifters, VISTAS, O.E.O.-supported revolutionaries and what he calls "The Hippie People." He can list the names of every young white man or woman he has known. They give him supper and they buy him shoes and take him out on hikes and sit down on the floor and play with balance scales and Cuisenaire rods for one summer and one winter, and sometimes for one spring and for one summer once again. Then they switch gears. They are into A New Thing. They cancel him out, or rather they don't "cancel" him — they cannot quite do that — but situate him rather in a slot of history or in a place of pain known as "the race and conscience bag." They make new friends and read new books and find a whole new set of words, and they are off to a new dedication.

Peter, however, does not live within the "race and conscience bag." He lives on Columbus Avenue in the South End of Boston. He is a real person. After they are gone, he is still here.

I know quite well that I would not be so disturbed at shifting loyalties and transient dedications of this kind if I did not perceive the strongest impulse of this nature in my own life. It is very, very tempting to keep moving on. It is extremely hard to stay in one place and to follow through on one thing.

There is, for each of us, the need to learn and grow, to voyage and explore, above all in the terms of our own consciousness of what "school" is about. There is, however, a much deeper need to find one solid core of concrete action and specific dedication, in just one neighborhood, or in one city, with one group of children and one group of allies and one set of loyalties, and with one deep, deep dream of love and transformation. This is the challenge that I know my co-workers and I will face within the years ahead. It is easier, in many ways, to drive out to the airport and fly off to

Mexico than it is to walk to Peter's house four blocks away and sit and look straight in his father's eyes. This is the struggle also of the New Left and the whole youth movement in this nation at the present time. It is the struggle of those of us who have been trained for twenty years to be nonstop consumers, and now must pause to teach ourselves how to be loyal to one thing that we believe in.

XII. EXTREMES AND OPPOSITIONS

"The term 'inequality' suggests a kind of passive accident. . .
It is a gentler word than racism or exploitation. . . It is an
easier word than oppression. . . Precisely for these reasons it
is a useless word."

— John S. Mann

WORD BIAS, in itself, can be a major factor in determination of our
ideologies and our desires. Words for certain things are near at
hand. Words for other things are hard to find. Words that seem the
most accessible, or those we have been trained to find most pleas-
ing, are powerful forms of limitation on the kinds of things we can
experience, or advocate, or even learn to long for.

Thoreau wrote in 1854: "I fear chiefly lest my expression may not
be *extra-vagant* enough . . . I desire to speak somewhere *without*
bounds." In terms of syntax, style and word-preference, the message of the public school is the exact reverse. Children come to
realize, early in their school careers, the terrible danger to their own
success in statements that give voice to strong intensities or to ex-
travagant convictions. Instead, they are instructed, in a number of
clear ways, not only not to speak but also not to think or feel or
weep or walk beyond the clearest bounds laid out by public school.
They learn whole sequences of moral obviation. They learn to
abhor and to distrust what is known as "unconstructive" criticism.
They learn to be suspicious of "extreme" opinion, most of all if
it is stated with "extreme emotion." They learn to round off honest
judgments, based upon conviction, to consensus-viewpoints, based
solely on convenience, and to call the final product "reason." Above
all, they learn how to tone down, cushion and absorb each serious
form of realistic confrontation.

Anger between two parties, conflict starting up between two

sides, is not accepted as the honest manifestation of irreconcilable interests (power and its victim; exploitation and its cause; victimization and the one who has the spoils) but solely as a consequence of poor communication, bad static on the inter-urban network, poor telephone connections between Roxbury and Evanston, or Harlem and Seattle. Nobody *really* disagrees with someone else once he explains himself with proper care. Confrontation, in the lexicon of public school, is a perceptual mistake. It is the consequence of poorly chosen words or of inadequate reception: "We have to learn not just to talk, but also how to listen, how to understand . . . " The message here is that, if we once learn to listen well, we will not hear things that we do not like. To hear things that we do not like is not to hear correctly. (The teacher tells us that we need more exercise on "listening skills.")

The level of speech which is accepted, offered and purveyed within the public schools is the level appropriate to that person who has no reason to be angry, or no mandate to be brave. The implication is conveyed to kids that almost anything they ever say, or hope to say, will, by the odds, be "somewhat stronger," "somewhat less temperate," than the limits of the truth require; that there will be, in every case, a heightened likelihood of untruth in a statement that appears to carry strong conviction, *more* truth in a statement that appears to carry *less* investment of belief. Conviction in itself, as children come to understand, is the real enemy; but it is the presentation, not the content, which is held up to attack.

"Linda," says the teacher, in the classic formula of admonition, "isn't that a bit strong?" The teacher seldom comes right out and says the sort of thing that might be true, or at least half-true: "Look, we're going to have a much less complicated day if you can learn to cut into your sense of conscience and integrity a bit."

Instead he asks the children: "Aren't we overstating?"

As the first assertion is restated to conform to satisfactory limits of conviction, the viewpoint it conveys begins to seem "more true," and finally wins the badge of mild approval: "That sounds more sensible . . . " In practice, as there comes to be less to believe, it comes to seem more readily believable. It is rare indeed, during twelve years of school and four of college, that pupils get back papers from their teachers with the comment: "Be more angry! Go further! You have stated this with too much caution!'' Emphasis is all the other way.

Equally distrusted is unique opinion which has not been rounded off to fit the class consensus: "Okay . . . David's said the Negro people have been fighting for their rights . . . and Susan says that we need law and order . . . Well, there might be truth in *both* of these positions . . . Let's see if we couldn't find a *third* position . . ." It is not argued in a candid manner by the teacher that the third position may well prove to be *convenient;* rather, there is the implication that the third position will be more "true" than either of the two extremes, that truth dwells somehow closer to the middle.

I have in mind a passage in a textbook that we used to use within the Boston schools, one that struck me later as a vivid example of the ritual of extremes denied and honest oppositions unadmitted. "No one can truly say, 'The North was right' or 'The Southern cause was better,' " said this textbook in its chapter on the Civil War. "For in Our America all of us have the right to our beliefs." There is the crazy notion here that either there is just no truth, no right or wrong at all, or else that, if there is, then truth by its own nature is to be discovered somewhere equidistant between Montgomery and Washington. The feeling we get is that neither of two sides is either right or wrong, but each "a little bit off center."

It is an easy step from this to the convenient view that all extremes of action end up in the same place, that radical change must bring inevitable repression. The phrase "EXTREMISTS AT BOTH ENDS" is, for this reason, a manipulative phrase. Its function is to tell us: (a) There is, in every case, a "greater truth" residing some place in the middle; (b) There *is,* in every case, a "middle situation" — one which is not artificial, or dishonest, or contrived.

The most unguarded statement of this bias to appear in print in recent years is one published in a teacher's guidebook issued by the N.E.A. The guidebook offers several bits of incidental, tactical and self-protective counsel to the teacher: one, for instance, which advises teachers not to turn their backs to children during blackboard-writing. "Learn to write . . . with only your right shoulder toward the board." The author warns a teacher who presents his back to children that the price will be "disorder." It is, however, only in the passages which deal with "class discussion" that we see the blatant emphasis on false consensus. "Avoid emotion-charged topics," says the guidebook. Discussion of such issues "may lead to an argument so explosive that fighting can result. Until a group has achieved enough maturity to keep itself under control, it is better to risk boredom than pandemonium." It is clear by now that schools have made their choice. The choice is not for pandemonium. The choice is for consensus, even at the price of boredom and the total sacrifice of every value that we hold and honor.

There is a separate point. The arrival at the moment of consensus in a class of children is most often executed in a way that does not only have a neutralizing power on the present but also has a backward-glancing influence on the past. It takes away the thing we thought we had believed. The act of compromise is thus experienced not only as a moment of immediate capitulation but also as a retroactive indication that our first position was erroneous or imprecise. This is, of course, occasionally the truth. The harder we work at it, in any case — and the longer we persist — the greater the likelihood that we can ferret out some item of sufficient unimportance to our heart and mind to constitute a D.M.Z. of shared belief.

There is always something of sufficient unimportance to provide a temporary reason for cease-fire. The assumption, though, that lies beneath this process of denial and of obviation is not honest and not conscionable. It is the pretense that there *are* no grounds within this social order for strong and risk-taking oppositions; that the more we listen and the more we talk, the more we will find out that there are *no real battle-lines* of power, combat, competition; that rich and poor, and black and white, oppressor and oppressed, have non-conflicting goals. The game is never "zero-sum" by this interpretation. Resources are at all times infinitely expanding and available to all on equal basis. The use of power plays no role at all within a world view of this kind. There is, at most, a genteel form of low-key competition: one in which we all stand equal chance, but no one ever loses.

Evasion of the role of power is, of course, the calculated luxury of those who wield it. It is, in the U.S., both a transparent and self-serving lie: self-serving for the power class within this land to understate the domination that it holds upon the lives of millions of poor people in our midst; self-serving for the nation as a whole to understate the power that it wields upon those nations that are in our stranglehold. It is the ideology, par excellence, of the Oppressor Nation in a state of rest or in a mood for genial conversation with its victims. The U.S. General goes to luncheon at the orphanage for victims of the war that we have brought to South Vietnam and distributes presents from the U.S. Red Cross. The university president or corporation banker invites the radical children in for tea.

Words that are used in school help to empower and to facilitate this form of false consensus. The school presents to children words that summon up exclusively non-causative connections, while placing words that have to do with direct opposition ("exploitation," for example, or "oppressor nation") past our recognition and beyond our reach. It is not easy to describe a state of mind for which we do not have a subject-noun available. It is not possible to designate a deed, an action, an event, for which a transitive verb does not exist or — if it does — is not made available to children at a moment when its use could lend lucidity and strength to an incipient belief or to an only half-perceived connection. The syntax of the school becomes thereby not just a syntax of enforced consensus, but a syntax also of benevolent ideals. The level of intensity to which we are permitted access is the level proper to a person who is not in pain — or else who has been trained not to believe that *other* people are. There are many adjectives of pity, but few verbs of rage, within the dialogue of social justice as defined by text or teacher in the U.S. public schools.

School does its best to shut out almost any word that can convey intentional exploitation of one person in this nation by another. Pain may exist, but seldom blame: a top man and a low man, but no seesaw. The noun-forms school allows are noun-forms of uncaused misfortune, autonomous poverty and guilt-free excess. The verb-forms are the verb-forms of benign intention, low-key benefaction or else of technological amelioration. "Deprivation" exists as a debilitated noun. "Deprive," however, as a transitive verb with a malignant subject-noun, does not exist within the lexicon of public school. Certain unfortunate children may exist in an "unsatisfactory" state of being known as "deprivation." Rich pediatricians in Darien, however, do not "deprive" poor children in Bridgeport of their right to grow up whole and sane, relieved from fever and from danger of inexorable damage to their growth or their cognition. Certain kids in New York or in Mississippi may grow up in an unpleasant state of being known as "malnutrition." The President, the Congressman, the Senator, however, does not "malnourish" them.

U.S. Civil Rights Commission, 1968: Dr. Alan C. Merman, Assistant Pediatrics Professor at Yale University Medical School, surveys health conditions in Lowndes County, Alabama. Dr. Merman reports that, of 709 children studied, eighty percent have anemia sufficient to require treatment. Ninety percent report that they have never seen a doctor. One in four needs to be given glasses., One out of the total number owns a pair of glasses. Dr. Merman tells the members of the U.S. Civil Rights Commission that eighty percent of the children and adults that he examines have approximately two-thirds the amount of red blood-cells as have the members of the Civil Rights Commission.

Dr. Albert C. Britton, Jr., black physician from Jackson, Mississippi, tells a subcommittee of the U.S. Senate that the death rate for black infants in his state, between one month and one year of age, is now five times the rate for whites. Dr. H. Jack Geiger, of Tufts New England Medical Center, states that the health of the poor is "an ongoing national disaster." Dr. Geiger estimates that poor people in the U.S. are four times as likely to die before age thirty-five as those of average income. The gap between the infant death rates of nonwhite and white, he says, *has widened twenty percentage points in twenty years.*

What is the definition of a "moderate," an "understated" or a "reasonable" answer to the havoc and the exploitation which these syllables imply? What does the U.S. Senator or committee counsel say in answer to the mother of a child dead for lack of proper pediatric or obstetric care, correct nutrition or pre-natal counsel? Medical devastation does not yield to moderate response. Exploitation cannot be discussed, or dealt with, by a syntax of consensus. Starvation of children does not have "two sides." It cannot be described within the words of moderation. There are not "two sides" to a dead black infant. Nor are there "two sides" to the idea of a doctor earning eighty thousand dollars in one year. There is not a "third position" about murder.

There is, I think, one most destructive and most brutal consequence of word-evasions such as these. It is not long before we learn not to accept as "credible" or "real" that which we cannot label with a fitting term of designation. The teacher asks the child, in the prototype above: "Isn't that a bit strong?" In time, this comes to be our answer, too, not just to words that people speak but also to the possible truth that stands behind them. Forty thousand dead black infants seem "a little bit excessive." Four hundred dead or wounded old men, women, suckling infants in one common ditch outside a village of Vietnam, seem "a little overstated." That line of orphan children outside our hotel in Lebanon, Brazil or Venezuela seems "a little bit extreme." The bias against extremes of *exposition* in the public school turns very soon into a bias against accreditation of extreme *realities* within the world beyond. It is a bias that serves the cause alike of qualified and modulated guilt in the oppressor, and quieted and sedated rage in the oppressed.

There is a neighborhood, about twelve blocks from where I live, which boasts one of the highest heroin-addiction rates in the U.S. Hundreds of people, most of them fourteen to twenty-two, are on The Avenue in search of heroin each night. They use from twenty-five to eighty dollars' worth a day. They sit on a bed or on a chair and tie a loop of rubber, or a belt, around the upper arm, to bring a bulge out in the vein. The vein invites the needle and the cylinder fills, along the notched notations, with a cloudy stream of backward-running blood. The moment comes. The syringe is pressed down. The heroin enters the vein and the body is returned to an ephemeral ecstasy.

The picture does not come out of a book, but from a real world seven minutes from my door. The kids go by the windows of the poolroom known to addicts on the block. The cops know too. It cannot be they are so blind or stupid not to know what any first-year VISTA volunteer can see and any child can comprehend. The man who runs the operation, white and arrogant, comes by sometimes to pick up the cash or else to settle small disputes. The kids know who he is, and what he does, and how important to the running of the current of the blood and snow through veins of black and hopeless souls, two thousand maybe of all ages in this part of town.

One of the kids I know best is fifteen. I've known him since he was eleven. He is still gentle, tentative and trusting. Half his friends are on the street; most are on the needle. We drive together along Blue Hill Ave one afternoon. He gestures left and right as we go by the plywood doors and boarded windows. He points to different kids he knows and talks about the world they live in and the way they get the money that they need. The white man in his Eldorado is a symbol of excitement for him: "You ought to see the women he brings with him in that car . . . There's a T.V. in the back seat with a built-in bar."

Daniel did not start to shoot up heroin, himself, until last year. Maybe there is someone in the Neighborhood Service Clinic that can help: "See a doctor?" He shrugs: "Sure, I don't mind." He is a thin kid and has a faint fuzz of defiant black along his upper lip . . .

CONFLICT RESOLUTION: The most successful method of evasion of direct extremes — that of police corruption, for example, on the one hand, and that of the fifteen-year-old victim of police corruption on the other — is now institutionalized beneath the label, "Conflict Resolution." The concept, once a part of therapeutic process and industrial relations, now emerges as a branch of university-supported social science. If the C.I.A. did not put up the money to conceive this term, then they should pay the ones who did. Few fashions could be better timed to serve the interests of the ruling class within an unjust and divided land.

"Conflict Resolution: A New Social Science." Thus reads one topic-heading in a handbook widely used by high school students and their teachers: "The principles of conflict resolution are [now] undergoing an intensive . . . study and evaluation . . . The task of conflict resolution has become a full-time occupation — and a major field of research . . ." Another publication, issued for the high school teacher by the Xerox Corporation, emphasizes — or, in this case, demonstrates — the same phenomenon: "People with opposing views do not have to adopt a combat posture . . . Instead they can be taught to value mutual clarification . . ." To change our mind, the booklet tells the teacher, is not necessarily a sign of weakness. "Stubborn adherence to a position . . . is irrational." We should, explains this Xerox publication, offer children real incentive and reward for willingness to give up views that they most deeply hold — in face, of course, of reasonable and overwhelming evidence.

None of this sounds as evil as, in fact, it is. It would be unforgivable, however, if we were to act as if we could not see the goals, as well as economic benefits, of fashions such as these. Esalen and similar institutions are the ideal instruments of counterrevolution in a social order which is scared stiff to perceive that classes, races, neighborhoods and nations do today have deep and often unavoidable need for confrontation. The tenants of an avaricious slumlord do not really need to "talk it out" with the slumowner. They do need, far more often, by whatever methods they can find, to *fight it out*. If, out of misguided deference to the will of those who have been trained to cool off cities and to lower passionlevels in the black and poor, a tenant now and then can be persuaded to "sit down and talk it through" and tell it "like it is" to the detested owner of the tenement quarters in which he has been compelled to dwell, if he agrees to this, to "tell it all," to spill his deepdown fury on the therapeutic floor, he is most likely to discover and to make, at length, extremely clear, that he was right to view this man, who lives and thrives at his expense, with hate and fear.

There is one question which the experts in this field do all they can to train us to ignore: What if, in fact, the more poor people listen and the more they talk, the more they should discover they were *right* to feel competitive and hostile, bitter and suspicious, all along? What if, the more they listen and the more they understand, the more belligerent they grow, and *ought* to grow? What if they find rich people really do prefer to think about their country house and holiday at Key Biscayne and Vail than to address the desperation of the children of their janitors and maids? What if the college dean and university Board Chairman honestly do prefer to have liaison with the research branches of the corporations and the various foundations, rather than with welfare mothers and the victims of the ghetto high school systems? What if this is, not merely "now and then," but even "frequently," the case? What if these disproportions are not accidental always, but well-noted, thankfully accepted and most gratefully received. No one likes to answer questions of this kind. Few even wish to ask them.

This is not intended as a plea for wider oppositions among genuinely amicable parties. It *is* a statement — out of my work, and observation of the work of others too — of just how readily we can be led to feel we should deflect a real antagonism by elliptic cancellation: to do so, moreover, out of motives which are not strategic but self-serving. The critic of the public schools, for instance, can with great ease translate his real objections to the economic function and political intention of those schools into a set of interesting, technical but basically undangerous prescriptions for those structural innovations which will make the prison cells more pleasant, but in no case raise important issues in a way that stirs explicit opposition in his listeners. By such a means, he guarantees at once his present status in the popular imagination ("a safe, yet controversial, critic") and future income as itinerant consultant. The person who states, with undiluted rage, that public schools are compromised above all by their perseverance in the loyal service of a murderous nation and an unjust social order risks instantly the loss of income, reassuring smiles and serene position in a middle ground of half-perceived and only half-articulated anger.

It is viewed as tactless, among liberal critics of the public schools, even to suggest that certain matters of immediate self-interest might be present in their motivation. Most men and women learn, when they are still quite young, but more and more as years go by and as they venture more and more into the architecture of domestication which the public schools and universities provide, how far to go, how much one ought to say, where to hold back, at what point to refrain, how much to hedge, at just what point to backtrack and to "reconsider."

The domination of the Low Key in the U.S. literary world is very near totalitarian at last. An entire body of critical terms exist which are, by definition, totally irrelevant to pain, yet govern our literature and neutralize our rage. Again and again, the concept of dispassion as an intellectual virtue is advertised most by those who feel the least. Liberal school-reformers tell us often they are arguing in favor of a philosophic point of view. This is not true. They argue, not in favor of a noble theory but in defense of their own deadened hearts and frozen souls. That which they cannot feel, they label "excess of emotion." That which they dare not risk, they call neurotic, needless or unwise.

"If a newscaster," writes Marcuse, "reports the torture and murder of civil rights workers in the same unemotional tone he uses to describe the stock market or the weather . . . such objectivity is spurious." Still worse: "[He] offends against humanity and truth by being calm where one should be enraged, by refraining from accusation where accusation is in the facts themselves."

This brings us back once more to the initial subject of this section: Whether within the old-time classroom or in the innovative "learning-center" of the most experimental and expensive school, public education strives, in every way it can, to make a virtue of dispassion in and of itself, to teach us how to smile at our own most earnest aspirations, to find in one another reason for applause if we do not seem to choose for highly dangerous positions, or else do choose, but in a voice which seems to say that we consider it of little import either way. Again and again, within the texts, the lesson-plans and class discussions, there is the sense of "aftermath" that follows tragic drama. It is as if our children had been doomed to live forever at the end of *Samson Agonistes*, "all passion spent," yet never having entered into combat, never lost and never won. Schools do their best to fend off the intensities of grief, the tangible realities of unjust power, and the necessity for taking sides. They teach us to look on the articulation of all ethical priorities as "egotistic," to stigmatize the saint as solemn and (still more ironical) as "sanctimonious." Above all else, they teach us how to trim the sails of our most deep and serious convictions, to limit the fury, to water down the passion and to understate the pain.

The guidance counselor tells the desperate child: "Emotion is not going to solve anybody's problems . . ." The Third Grade teacher recommends the same: "Lower your voices, children . . ." From Nothing Too Much, the basic level-headed formulation of the Golden Mean, we move full circle to the arid destination of the public school: Nothing Sufficient, Everything Low Key, Everything at a Bleak, Inept and Non-provocative Level of Devotion.

Prison bars do not need to be made of steel and concrete. They can be fashioned also out of words and hesitations: an "interesting seminar on hunger," "a reasonable exchange of views about despair." The language that we learn in public school is one of ethical antisepsis and of political decontamination. It is the language of an intellectual cease-fire while the victims are still dying. It is also a language which, by failing to concede *real* oppositions, denies a child or adult right or power to make strong, risk-taking choices. The student learns to step back and to steer away from moral confrontations. He learns to ascertain the quickest highway and the best approach to middle places of inert compassion and dysfunctional concern: places where choice does not reside and anger does not threaten.

If the child studies hard, if he assimilates the language well, and if he should grow up by any chance to be a writer, teacher, commentator or a critic even of such areas as social justice in this nation, he will have learned by then the proper means by which to make himself provocative, but not unsettling: fashionable and delightful, but not feared. He will have become, by grotesque sequences of North American recirculation, a perfect item in the same machine that polished him to size. At worst he will be somebody like Moynihan. At best he may be somebody like Galbraith. There is no danger he will be Thoreau.

XIII. ETHICS

"I don't think that these kids get too much hung up with guilt. They see this stuff as pretty realistic power-politics . . . They look on Kissinger, and men who operate like that, as pragmatists."

— Twelfth Grade teacher in a
high school near Los Angeles

ETHICAL PROTEST, in the face of exploitation, represents a major threat to social order in an unjust nation. Liberal educators do all that they can to work around this point.

Dozens of books are published nowadays on "moral" education. Few, however, seem prepared to face head-on two basic points: (1) Public schools in the U.S. do not exist to educate an ethical human being. The first act of an ethical child, after all, might well be to start the demolition of a manifestly anti-ethical structure like a public school. No institution goes about the conscious task of subsidizing its own demolition. (2) Schools *do* exist to educate defeated, unprovocative, well-balanced human beings: that is to say, the kinds of people who can be expected to keep schools like these in operation for at least the length of time it takes to educate the generation next in line.

These points having been consistently excluded from discussion, the entire debate on "moral education" comes to be unreal and hypothetical and has, repeatedly, that dry and unimportant sound that one associates with boring nights at Unitarian churches in New England towns. Everyone is saying reasonable things, but nobody is saying one thing that we all are thinking: Ethics, in the U.S. public schools, run directly counter to the interests of the people who hold power.

Schools abound, inevitably, with moral slogans, benevolent expressions, sometimes even lengthy categories of "one hundred virtues," "moral builders" and the like. Whatever the slogans posted on the walls, there is a deeper message sold to children in the public schools. Briefly stated, it is a bias against uncomplicated ethics and in favor of "the charm of realistic cynicism." Early in the game, we are instructed to look with reserve upon such serious girls and awkward boys as with gaunt eyes and urgent words anticipate, by their behavior, the unswerving honesty and ethical intrusions of such grown-up citizens as Garrison, Thoreau or C. Wright Mills.

Evanston, Illinois, 1972: A boy I meet, during a visit to a junior high, tells me that he lives with his two brothers, sister and his mother in a commune. His father is dead. He is thirteen years old. The teachers tell me that he is unique: open, ethical, gentle, trusting and non-violent. In his economic views, he is a socialist. He does not eat meat.

The rougher kids call him "a pinko," "Hippie," "garbage," "Communist" or "faggot." His mother is an excellent folk singer. The children tell him that she is a prostitute. Even the teachers who admire him do not respond with strong support or with defensive passion in behalf of his unique and non-vindictive ways, but rather with a cautious and familiar teacher-mix of kindliness and condescension.

"I guess we're willing to go part-way," one student (said to be his friend) remarks. "I think the trouble is: He goes too far. He's like the people that we read about in books. It's good — I mean, it's good for history, I guess — that there were people like that living on the earth. Some of the saints were like that. David is a little like that too. He talks about non-violence and love. He calls himself a socialist. He doesn't fight back when kids speak about his mother. He just sits there and looks amazed . . . or sad . . ."

The teacher tells me: "David has a problem. He comes from a broken home. His mother got mixed up in racial issues in the Nineteen Sixties. He quit school out here one year and commuted into one of those black Street Academies. It didn't work. I don't know why. I guess he felt the changes that were needed most, for him at least, were somehow going to be here. So he came back and re-enrolled. He's bright, you know; so getting back in touch with class

routine wasn't too hard. It isn't that. It isn't academic readjust-
ment that's got anyone concerned. It's his ideas, and his amazing
state of mind. He's vulnerable . . . the memories he has . . . He talks
a lot about the black kids that he knows . . . People come down on
him in lots of different ways. Even the ones who like him get
alarmed. They want to help him, but they feel concerned. They
think he's going to go crazy.''

I talk with the boy for several hours at the end of school, then give
him a ride home. He opens up as soon as we are outside the school-
drive. He has red hair, curious eyes, a lot of freckles. When I drop
him off down at the corner of his street, I ask him what he thinks is
going to happen to him during the next year. He seems resigned to
the idea that, somehow, he is going to give in. Soon, not now, but
some point before long:

"Everyone's forced to come to the same level as the others in this
school. Sooner or later, you can tell you're going to give in. The
kids and teachers get you in one way — the doctors in another. The
worst, in my mind, is the medical approach, the confident sense they
have that something's going to go wrong. They're always telling
you that you'll go crazy. If you hear that for about three years,
then you begin to think it's so.''

His eyes, vulnerable and kind, fill up with tears when we shake
hands. Closing the car door, he surprises me by saying to me what I
am just about to say to *him*: "Good luck. I hope that you don't let
them scare you — or destroy you.''

Public education, for most children, is a twelve-year exercise of
ethical emaciation. The needle is put in at kindergarten. For twelve
years, blood flows out in gradual pulsation. At last we come of
age. We graduate and go to college, find a job or join the military.
We are well-schooled by now in our own sense of personal debilitation. There is no danger, or small danger, that we will unsettle
those who came of age before us. I have seen this happen both
in elementary and in junior high and high schools straight across
the U.S. I also have a painful memory of the private anguish and
the cruel humiliation of a child who believes he cannot choose but
keep good faith with his own conscience and who therefore is not
able to adapt to the idea of the "good fellow" that has been es-

tablished as the norm within his school. It comes to be apparent
to a child of this sort that he has placed himself in danger of satiric
comment from his classmates and, still worse, of clinical observation, masked as pity, from his teacher or "adjustment counselor"
if he reveals himself to be entirely wracked and shaken by the kinds
of thoughts that troubled good men like Saint Francis or inspired
women like Saint Joan.

Indeed, in view of the abuse such children take from their own
peers, as well as from the men and women who control their lives, it
is remarkable that we end up with anyone like Daniel Berrigan or C.
Wright Mills at all. We learn to speak of someone of this sort in
terms that make it clear he is a proper object for satiric treatment,
clinical comment or else social quarantine. We say of a young
person of this kind, who loves Saint Francis, who reads and takes to
heart almost each word that has been written about Gandhi — who
searches for the voice of decency, of justice unadorned that he finds
when, late in the night, he loses himself in reading their own
words — we say of such a person: He is "too intense and solemn for
a student of his age." We do our best to get him to come down at
two-fifteen to try out for the Glee Club, join the other kids for
basketball or find a hobby.

The child who has a private vision, secret dream or personal
yearning for a life of justice is going to have to fight for sheer survival in the face of teacher, counselor, physician. We never send
children to a doctor if they start to sound too much like Nelson
Rockefeller; but if they start to sound too much like Frederick
Douglass or like Emma Goldman, we will lock them in a padded
room and bind their arms and elbows to the wall with belts and
buckles. There are rooms, houses, spaces, in which it is not possible
to speak above a whisper. In moral terms, the U.S. public school
is such a room in 1975.

A cruel misuse of psychoanalytic insight, in the form of high-
priced therapeutic exculpation for the conscience of the rich, has
tended to encourage and intensify this view by urging us to look
upon the presence of a tortured conscience as a symptom of neurosis. "Neurotic guilt" has come to be employed as if it were a
single word. Guilt is, we seem to say, inherently unhealthy. Guilt is
unsound. Guilt is, as business people say, "counter-productive."

The sinister part of all of this, of course, is that our logic leads us very quickly to believe that there are not some situations of unjust and brutal disproportion to which guilt might well be *the only sane response*.

I remember one young woman whom I knew in college years. She had inherited ten million dollars at the age of twenty-one. Now, at twenty-two, she worked in Roxbury with some of the most badly battered children in the city. It struck her often as remarkably unfair that she, her brothers and two sisters, through the accident of birth, should have, each one, ten million dollars to protect their lives and to assure the safety of *their* children, and their *children's* children too. It seemed unfair because she saw before her, every day, so many kids who were in every way the equals of her brothers and her sisters and herself; yet she knew very well these kids would, only by infrequent miracle, be able to break out of the entrapment of slum schools, parent despair, poor health, poor nutrition, crumbling plaster and the rest. The only way she might in later years know any of these kids would be if they were to become her servants, butlers, elevator boys or other kinds of menial laborers. The year in Roxbury hit her so hard that it grew into an ordeal for her to go back home to her own family "place," almost a private village really, with two hundred acres of uninterrupted forest, fields and pastures for the horses, even cottages for "help." At home, as would not be unusual in cases of that kind, the servants all were black.

Each time, then, that she went home — for instance, at Thanksgiving, Christmas or some other holiday — she found it agonizing to sit at the dinner table and digest her food. She began to vomit secretly upstairs, or spit out food into her handkerchief or napkin, hoping in this manner that her father would not see. Her father did see, of course, and spoke about it with his wife, then with his daughter too. Being concerned about the danger to her health, he made arrangements for her to begin to see a psychoanalyst in Boston. She did so, and in fact spent several years in therapy. Out of this treatment, which had been provoked directly by her devastation at the sight of so much poverty and pain, she gained at length a more relaxed and reasoned skill to reconcile the differences between her own life and the lives of those poor children whom she had begun to know. Simultaneously she learned, as well, to reconcile the differences between her own intense convictions and that style of life which, as she knew, lay waiting for her. Her hesitation and her gnawing sense of guilt at last abated somewhat: never entirely, but enough so that she could go home from time to time, accept the luxury of horses, servants and the rest, and summon up a kind of "realistic" will to smooth away the inconsistencies. At length she married an appropriate young man and traveled, little by little, out of the orbit of her ethical upheaval. She settled down at last into a normal, quiet and unturbulent routine, learned how to keep that residue of guilt within control, and did not need to vomit after supper.

It would not make sense, from any "normal" point of view, to say that she had just been cheated out of something decent and profound when she learned how to live in luxury without a sense of nausea, and to eat well and accept the services of family servants without guilt. I would not try to say that she was "better off" when she was throwing up her food. Yet I would wonder if there was not *something wrong,* in toto, looking back, in all that had just taken place. Expensive medical treatment, denied to all but very few, enabled her at last to share without a sense of guilt in use of just such wealth as made that treatment possible. Ironically, it also helped to ease her back into a style of life in which she would be less and less exposed to the conditions that inspired her original upheaval. A vulnerable conscience, having been explained and "understood" at last into a kind of quiet and serene capitulation, no longer troubled her now at twenty-eight as it had done at twenty-two. She became, in terms of the society, a "better-adjusted person," able to live at peace with the idea of an imbalance of advantage that once, in an earlier time, had seemed to her to be intolerable.

It is not the misuse of a psychoanalytic method which provokes this narrative. It is the view that has pervaded so much of our intellectual life, and now appears almost unquestioned in the public schools, that earnest conscience, straightforward guilt, bad dreams, unsophisticated and direct self-accusation, are, in some sense, unwholesome, unattractive, not to be admired — and, for just these reasons, properly to be "dealt with," neutralized, dismantled. It does not go at all too far to say that psychiatric exculpation on this scale would have been of great assistance to large numbers of those troubled and uneasy bureaucrats who were so necessary to the German leaders in the Second World War. Many people tend to bristle and step back from harsh comparisons like that. The parallel seems too shrill and too insistent. It is enough, in any case, just to observe that in our own life here, in our own situation as the power class within an unjust nation, the automatic identification of bad conscience with a syndrome of neurosis is extraordinarily convenient for those people who are privileged to live in safe, well-lighted places.

In another age, or in a different land, the inability to swallow pieces of rich lamb, rare beef, delicious sirloin, from imported porcelain upon a delicate linen cloth, with black maid and with black butler standing nearby in the door, while in the memory there stands the frieze of crumbling houses, rat-infested kitchens, kids without socks or boots or mittens in the freezing snow, a supper of potato chips with barbecue flavor from a ten-cent bag, breakfast of Coke and "Sky Bar" — an inability to swallow lamb and beef in such an hour might be seen as something more than a neurotic syndrome and something better than an "incomplete adjustment" to conventional ideas.

In such an age, a woman who could not contain such differences of deprivation and excess might be described, in the most simple terms, as "a good person." It might be thought to be, not an alarming process, but a longed-for and important period of human transformation, for a woman who inherits something like ten million dollars in a world of pain, to feel the need to vomit up a number of the values, memories and pieces of rich meat she has been forced to swallow in her twenty-one years of insular existence.

It will be pointed out that most of us do not possess ten million dollars. I would say, in answer, that, in relative terms, we do. By all comparative standards in the world today, especially in nations which are still within our economic domination — even within a nation like our own, in which fifteen to twenty million people live in hunger or starvation — we are very much in the position of the student I have just described. Our excess is not marginal, but colossal. There are few of us, and many of them. We have far more than what we need: and they, far, far too little. It is essential to unbroken patterns of efficiency and power in this land that a moment of recognition of this kind should be containable in clinical terms and manageable in any social context. The first context we encounter, outside of our home, is public school, and in the public school we learn *before all other lessons* how to manage, how to label and contain the first signs of an ethical unrest.

The price paid for personal surrender on this scale is seen in its most bitter form when we are in a situation to perceive the subsequent evolution of a student of the kind that I have just described. The most disheartening part of all is to observe with what great ease a student, once "drawn back discreetly" from that precarious and unfamiliar place of ethical upheaval, can come to have a sense of vested interest in defense and justification of the kind of life that he has chosen to accept. It is not a long journey, after all, from the place of compassion overcome to that of cold self-interest justified. It is not long before the vested interest that we feel in the need to justify a moment in our life that seems to us most like a moment of capitulation is turned into a manner of alienated intellection, of icelike separation from our own most deep and passionate convictions. From decent children troubled and failed, we learn how to be reasonable grown-ups: muted, well-adjusted. Once dreaming of Gandhi, and once yearning for the kind eyes of Saint Francis, we end up sipping sherry with our old professor in his pleasant home off Brattle Street in Cambridge, or sharing "innovative notions" with the folks from I.B.M. and Westinghouse. The forces of adjustment have been able, at a certain price, to cure us of our conscience. Now can they cure us also of our emptiness?

There are these words in the Bible: "Where there is no vision, the people perish." In my view, it is the business of the school to neutralize the dream and to indemnify the child against the dangers that may otherwise be inherent in his future decency. To institutionalize ecstasy, universities channel poets into the explication of their metaphors. To rectify zeal and to contain the vision of a generous or impassioned child, we construct school systems. Friedenberg writes of this, but never with sufficient power or with words that do not undermine, by cleverness, the pain that ought to have been present. We teach children to adjust to evil carried out in their own name. We teach children to look on at misery without rage.

We teach children *not* to vomit up the lie that poisons their own soul. The first moment in all of this process is to plant in each of us a simple and straightforward bias against ethics.

Even in the Intellectual Left, a lifetime of indoctrination sinks in deeply. Few, if they can possibly avoid it, will admit to doing something out of motives of compassion. Instead, we try to fabricate a good, "hard-headed" reason for our actions. To do something because "it makes sense" is a more attractive reason than because someone is in great pain. The U.S. government, in much the same way, used to justify the Job Corps on the grounds that it is easier to "train" an eighteen-year-old black man than to pay for his electrocution or incarceration in a prison. This is the tough, no-nonsense logic that the U.S. Congress finds unsentimental. Well-indoctrinated students learn the lingo too.

In preference to the child who predates, by his rebellion, someone like John Brown or Malcolm X, we look for models of acceptable behavior to those who are prepared to understate their ethical intentions, imply a kind of "quiet sense of decency" that they do not like to boast of, and demonstrate instead a "realistic" capability for candid deprecation of their own worth. In intellectual terms, the highest goal is taken to be adept articulation. Cogency, even in the service of injustice, is granted more esteem than open advocacy of fair play. The ideal "mix" within the social setting is a certain quality of good intent, watered with realism, spiced with a drop of cynicism, stated with humor, believed in only with graceful reservation, and enacted only if absolutely necessary at pistol-point or in the full face of public desperation.

I suspect that many people who have had their education in the same time period as I, will recognize the sense of personal defeat I have in mind. We learn to tolerate, like a low flame on the fire or like a low fever in the body, a "reasonable temperature-level of admitted cynicism." We learn to feel that it is not intolerable to "be" self-compromised if one is open and amusing in discussion of the matter; or, again, that cynicism, charmingly admitted-to and interestingly described, in some sense cancels itself out. It is not corrupt to "be" corrupt so long as a person is perceptive and articulate concerning his corruption. At this point, as we know, the word itself becomes a distant and quite bearable designation, one scarcely having to do with our own being any longer, but a label identified rather with some interesting character of our late-at-night imagination.

Few people end up totally cold and icelike and removed from their own feelings of self-accusation, but it is a type we strive for and it is a model to which we often gruesomely aspire. It is this, that we should strive with all our hearts to find such desert regions, that appears to me most frightening and most horrible.

XIV. RESEARCH

"Alas, there is in every man a power, a dangerous and at the same time a great power. This power is cleverness . . . Now in the inner world a man uses cleverness in a ruinous way, in order to keep himself from coming to a decision . . ."

— Kierkegaard

A SPECIAL ISSUE of The American Scholar (Autumn 1969) is devoted to the topic of black anger and the youth revolt in the U.S. Nothing in the full length of the issue has the strength and passion of its outside cover: one which bears the four straightforward words, "Revolution on the Campus." It is as if four words were to bestir a sense of history and hope which something like two hundred pages of grim, gutless and reiterative prose were then to learnedly sedate.

One of the most conspicuous pieces in the issue is contributed by Daniel Moynihan. His emphasis falls upon the need of government, the universities and such to "learn" a great deal more about the intricate problems of the black and poor before we dare to start to deal with them. "The worst, the most corrupting of lies," he writes, "are problems poorly stated."

The statement, quoted out of context from Bernanos, is, of course, untrue and, we might add, corrupting in its own right: above all if we have in mind some of the manifestly gruesome lies of recent times, lies which had nothing to do with anything so charming and so indirect as "problems poorly stated" but with sheer and unadorned mendacity; lies, for instance, of three Presidents in sequence and their numerous, dishonest and well-educated spokesmen, in their efforts to conceal atrocities initiated by young soldiers under their command in villages of Southeast Asia; not even to speak of those more subtle, but no less corrupting, "lies" of problems *excellently* stated and *adeptly* phrased, but whose adept articulation in itself was carried out, not to advance effective action but in order to postpone it.

It is the truth that, in some situations, problems "poorly stated" can delay some processes of social action, change or legislation. It is also true, however (and a great deal closer to the point at hand), that the social scientist, in many situations we confront today, has very great vested interest in extending, for the longest possible period of years, the time it takes to give to certain problems their precise and proper definition. In the years it takes to learn to state "the problem" clearly, to gather information and at last to instigate some concrete course of action, the research scholar can buy for himself an awful lot of handsome and expensive items: excellent food, attractive clothes, companionable friends and privileged distance from the stench of pain and shriek of fear that he researches.

It is essential that we have the boldness to be candid on this score, above all since the research exercise is now purveyed, with great sophistication, at the grade school level. The actual function of most research in the social sciences today is not to settle on the proper steps that must be taken to initiate a realistic plan of action, but rather to keep a number of intelligent people busy for a reasonable period of time with a plausible sense of honorable intention yet, at the same time, to maintain them with an ample source of cash with which to go about the course of their conventional existence.

The key deception in the brand of research now becoming popular in public school rests in the essential issue of original selection: Who gets to pose the questions which we have the license, time or resource to research? The most intense and honest course of research can be well-accepted by this social order so long as it is kept within a set of boundaries no one cares about. The education-innovation organization, E.D.C., now makes a skilled profession of inducing children to do "free," "wide-open" and "unstructured" research into such dangerous areas as the life-struggle of the Netsilik Eskimo (long-since destroyed) and the life-cycle of the mealworm. So long as children are prepared to limit their irreverence to such low-key and non-controversial realms of knowledge as the Eskimo and mealworm, they are allowed all freedom of decision.

"I don't care who does the electing," Boss Tweed said, "so long as I can do the nominating." E.D.C., the Carnegie Foundation,

I.B.M. and S.R.A. can paraphrase Boss Tweed in these terms: "It doesn't matter to us what kinds of bold, irreverent answers children give — so long as we can be the ones to pick the questions." There are, of course, whole sequences of detailed ritual involved in getting children to believe that it is *they* who come up with the questions.

There is a second level of dishonest research carried out in public school. This second level is the implantation of a crippling sense of self-distrust in face of things that seem to us at first to be quite clear: "Whatever we know, or think we know, is probably suspect." The presence of an overwhelming body of persuasive information, by automatic reflex, comes to be the justification, not for action, but for the redoubled exercise of research-labors. In practice, the more powerful and more persuasive the existent body of raw data and hard evidence, the more inexorable our obligation to go back and start again at Intellectual Zero.

Little respect is paid to research carried out and documented by the most respected scholars. Each adult, each small child, must re-run the information-gathering exercise on his own time: "We are about to spend the next few months discovering how to gather and assess materials. We are going to attempt to ascertain the level of racism in this nation. We will try to find out whether it has power to intrude *within* political structures — Congress, the Judiciary, State and local organizations — or whether it functions only on an intermittent and external basis. In seeking to work out a balanced point of view, students are expected to make use of several documents . . ."

It would not do to start out at the point at which six Senate subcommittees, The New York Times and the last ten studies by the U.S. Civil Rights Commission have left off. It would not be a part of the convention for young people to accept, to start with, after all these years, and all these speeches, all these hundreds of "conclusions," "studies," "National Investigations" and the rest, that they did grow up in a racist nation, under a President twice-elected by a racist vote — one who then pursued a series of domestic policies calculated to consolidate a racist base for his successor. It would not do to start with some of the hard facts. Instead, one must strive *toward* them.

The fraud in operation here seems evil in direct proportion to the actual knowledge of the individuals involved. The fraud depends upon the willingness to live, and to behave, as if we did not know some things which we *do* know and which our teachers also know but cannot bear to recognize head-on: "We do not yet have in our hands sufficient information to explain these economic disproportions. If we could just get hold of certain items of additional information — and, for this purpose, just another quarter-million dollars to enable us to study and assess the implications of this added information — *then* we might well be in a position to determine how, or whether, or by what realistic course, we might be able to reduce these disproportions, or else render them less painful in their implications . . ."

The third essential stage in research carried out in public school involves a sequence which the handbooks call "the search for diverse sources of raw data." Teachers invite pupils to believe that they are in a situation to draw freely on the broadest possible spectrum of available resources. The breadth at stake, of course, is scrupulously contrived. The children choose between the data which is present in World Book, Collier's, Book of Knowledge, Encyclopaedia Britannica, Time-Life booklets, similar (if less costly) publications packaged by the Reader's Digest, hand-outs from industry, the A.M.A., the N.A.M., the various private lobbies, filmstrips from E.D.C., sound-tapes from Westinghouse, packaged "resource kits" from Xerox or from S.R.A. (i.e., from I.B.M.), Hip propaganda from Junior Scholastic and Scholastic Scope, exciting paperbacks prepared by Little, Brown (i.e., Time-Life), "learning kits" from Ginn and Co. (i.e., from Xerox), special issues of My Weekly Reader (owned by Xerox too), the local papers (owned most often by one of a dozen chains), in liberal schools the teacher's copy of The Sunday Times, in super-liberal classrooms New Republic, in counterculture classrooms Whole Earth Catalog . . .

In certain of the more experimental schools, the range of data is extended to the total neighborhood or town. There is by now, for visitors such as myself, almost a standard "pitch" in this regard: "We are learning to be social scientists. We are learning to do independent research." Children learn to parrot the same phrases;

often they go home and say the same thing to their folks. Sometimes now the teacher goes still further in his claims:

"We won't only use the press, T.V. and magazines. We'll use them too, but we'll go out as well and interview *real people*. We'll talk to doctors, lawyers, writers, bankers, engineers. We'll talk to the Mayor and visit the newspaper and explore the local Ford assembly plant, visit the airport, hospitals and housing offices and T.V. stations. We'll ask tough questions. We'll elicit honest answers. We'll bring our cameras, notebooks, tape recorders. Then we'll come back and do our background reading and work out the patterns and attempt to come to reasonable conclusions. Indeed, we may well ask some of these doctors, writers, lawyers, T.V. editors, to come right in and *visit in our school*. The class will go out into the world. The world will come back into the class. This is the way we learn to be researchers."

The teacher who conducts this complex labor is working, without question, at a more high-powered level than the old-time teacher. At least he offers children access to more substance. They move their legs, and dial their phones, snap their cameras and turn on and off their tape recorders. It is obvious, however, that without the conscious and provocative *intervention* of the classroom teacher, of another adult or else of an exceptional, defiant and incendiary child, there is no more likelihood today than thirty years before of serious conflict of opposing views, of serious confrontation of ideas, indeed of anything of any sort that might subvert the basic purposes and patriotic guidelines which are built into the steel and stone, the glass and girders of the U.S. public school.

What, after all, have we achieved when we depart from the homogenized indoctrination of the old-time text and turn instead to the more variegated indoctrination of mass magazines and T.V. news? Still more, what do we really think we have achieved when we put on our coats, lock up our classrooms and head off into "the world outside" to carry out our research-labors? Do we achieve a serious form of intellectual emancipation when we throw out the old, outdated vehicles of printed text and published lie and turn instead to those who have themselves been so well-trained and thoroughly indoctrinated in the course of twelve or sixteen years by just these documents? Is it to be supposed that children will, all on their own, and quite by chance, seek out and ascertain the voices of dissent? If they do, will they find real dissent or will they find, instead, those voices of agreeable (because innocuous) dissent which offer us the semblances of dialectic and dispute — with neither the pain, the passion nor the risk?

It is conceivable that Eighth Grade children in an innovative and experimental junior high *might,* in course of "field work," hear at least a couple of divergent views on urban problems, welfare, trade, taxation, voting age. They will hear, perhaps, from those who favor low-cost housing, those who feel that water-fluoridation is a good idea, and those who think that smog is a bad problem. They will hear from Democrats. They will hear from Republicans. They will hear from liberals, from moderates and from conservatives. They will hear from those who favor health insurance as a national priority, and those who think the whole thing can be handled better by Blue Cross and by Blue Shield. They will hear of "know-how," "input," out-put," "programs," "structures," "systems."

What we must ask, however, is what they will learn about starvation? needless hunger? conscious exploitation? purposeful injustice? What will they learn, not of the friendly Mayor and City Council, but of real power? What will they learn of the accountability of public officers to those in corporation offices and private-interest lobbies, "funds" and "fronts," whose cash donations make their re-election possible? What will they learn about the power and control of schools *themselves* and of the ways in which the schools, the publishers and educational consulting-firms labor together to expropriate the candor and the courage of the pupils who are locked within those schools? How much of *this* will get to children, unassisted, undirected, unprovoked, by "random" accident of "open" access and untutored inquiry? I think we know when we are in the presence of overt deceit.

The rituals described above function in tandem to construct a clever formulation: "WE DO NOT KNOW ENOUGH TO MAKE DECISIONS OR TO SET OUT ON A CONCRETE COURSE OF ACTION. WE DO KNOW JUST ENOUGH, HOWEVER, TO KNOW HOW MUCH INFORMATION WE STILL NEED TO GATHER . . . HOW LONG IT WILL TAKE . . . AND HOW MUCH IT WILL COST."

Even, however, if the students should be able, by some means or other, to assemble much more powerful and more authentic sources of raw data, and to overcome the multitude of other limitations which are set up in advance, there is little likelihood that they will end up, after all their work is done, with anything that constitutes a real "conclusion." Instead, it is more likely they will end up at a plateau which can best be labeled as Conclusive Indecision: "Either of the following two ideas might well resolve this problem. We do not yet, however, have sufficient information in our hands to know which would be *best*. The task before us, therefore, or the task before those others who may next approach this problem (after they have re-run all the work we have just done) is to study *both* these interesting options . . ."

There is, in 1975, a standard form of this postponement tactic. Weeks of research into that large area of human desperation, still so timidly referred to as "The Racial Situation," lead out, after all the obstacles have been transcended, into a "class report" which states that "some black people seem to favor integration, while others favor separatist development under community control." It is, in all respects, a serviceable conclusion: one which grants entire amnesty to those who, if they had been told which option of the two the largest numbers of black people choose, would still not dream of turning their own day-to-day existence upside down to *act* upon it.

"White people," says the final paper, "now must gather further information from all sources to determine which of these directions will receive the best acceptance in the black community . . ." In such a manner, child or adult (for it is done in very much the same way at both levels) is spared the anguish of a direct confrontation with the painful fact that either option, put into immediate effect, would make a massive difference in the lives of millions of black children and that the only thing white people ought to dare to "research" in this day and age is how best to raise enough Hell to bring *either* of these options into operation.

The purpose of research, however, as we know too well, is not to teach young people how to raise Hell. The purpose is to teach them how to sit still in their places, how to be "good children," how to be benign, inactive, terrified, respectable. The purpose is to teach them how to gather information, not in order to take action but in order to increase the body of material that they possess already. The goal of research in this context is not ethical action based upon reflection, but a self-perpetuating process of delay.

In conversation with a group of high school pupils in the Midwest, I present a number of questions in regard to the end-consequences of a year-long research-project into "Urban Crisis and Race Turmoil in the Nineteen Sixties." I ask these questions: "What was it for? What was the object of the research? What were you hoping to achieve as a result? What form of concrete action did it lead to?"

One student answers: "Frankly, what I hope it leads to is an A in Social Studies."

A second student says: "I think the knowledge of these problems makes it easier to draw intelligent conclusions. It helps to broaden out your mind and make you a less shallow human being."

Another student offers this reply: "Concern — awareness — comprehension — this, I think, is what it leads to. I think this is important for all people."

I press the issue with a more specific point: "In actual consequences, where does this year's research *lead* you? What does it modify or alter in your own career?"

The same boy who has just replied answers again: "The consequence is — we *understand* the problem better. We recognize the ways in which discrimination works. We gain an overview. In schools, in hospitals, in jobs, we see the same routine. Some people are held back and crippled their whole lives. Others can move on to guaranteed success."

I stop and listen to the words that he selects. "Some," he says, will be held back. "Others" can move on. I ask him, therefore, a still more explicit question: "Exactly who that you know will be held back? Who is most certain to be able to move on?"

He pauses, stammers, seems unsettled by my question. "Look," he says. He breaks into a hesitant, yet "realistic" grin, one which is familiar to me now from a number of other conversations of this kind. "Look," he tells me . . . "Everybody knows the answer to that question . . . I'm the one . . . We're all the ones . . . We know that very well. We're the ones who get the good end of the deal. The losers, those down at the other end — let's face it —

they're the ones who work for people like our mothers and our fathers." His smile grows, little by little, into a still more awkward and more "realistic" sneer: "We talk about things we don't intend to change. Why change a situation which puts us right where we want, and other people that we never need to see, so far away we never even need to know that they exist?" His glazed smile seems, in this instant, to be made of two equivalent emotions: confident sneer and endless self-contempt. There is dead silence from the other members of the class.

The teacher interrupts at last to demonstrate his irritation: "In all frankness, Mr. Kozol, I don't think that you are being fair. Is there a point in forcing answers of this kind? The work these children did this year was serious and strong. For some, it might well lead into the Peace Corps . . . Others might well go into some forms of volunteer work . . . Three of our students have already been devoting weekends to the Halfway Houses . . ." He pauses. Then he speaks those words which, by this time, for me, subsume and crystallize all of the rest: "I think the very fact that they *write essays* for their own school-paper on the subject of their independent research — this, in itself, is one quite honest means of taking action. Other actions, the more belligerent and less reflective kind you have in mind, these things can wait until these kids are somewhat older . . ."

I go out to have coffee with one of the less defeated and less broken teachers working in the school. "Listen," she says, "I do the college applications for the senior class. The colleges love to see that stuff about the Independent Research. They like it most when it ties in with something like the Urban Crisis. It looks so good! It knocks them out. It sounds so noble and so idealistic . . . and so safe . . . so unimportant!" She smiles — not at all, though, in the same cold and denatured manner as that "realistic" and self-hating student in the class: "Think what they say at Yale and Wesleyan and M.I.T. when they find out how much our kids are like their own professors!"

SUNDAY MORNING, NOVEMBER 1969. I come upon an essay-interview in The New York Times that deals with urban crisis, hunger, malnutrition, childhood starvation: "In a plush restaurant around the corner from the White House, Daniel Patrick Moynihan, counselor to the President on urban affairs, removed his double-breasted . . . brass-buttoned blazer (Taylor and Solash, London) and draped it respectfully over the back of an empty chair . . . Ordering a Scotch old-fashioned, then another, then a sirloin, New York cut, medium rare, and a bottle of Bud to wash it down, Moynihan sighed happily: 'If it weren't for Saturday lunch, I don't think I'd make it through the week . . .' "

In words that follow, Moynihan goes on to detail for a listening reporter his ideas, his theories and his suppositions, in regard to sickness, urban crisis, hunger, malnutrition and, in general, to address himself to the entire syndrome of despair, of racial bitterness, of exploitation and discrimination, of those among the black, the Spanish-speaking and the urban poor whose advocate he is supposed to be within the highest councils of the nation. In the time it takes before he comes to the tail-end of lunch, one that winds up with a glass of brandy and a good cigar, the President's chief adviser on the problems of the urban poor has run through a number of intriguing notions for the possible alleviation of the sense of desperation in New York, Chicago, Boston — and has, in addition, spent, either of his own or else of the reporter's funds, just about the same amount of hard-negotiated cash from which poor children in New York and Boston are expected to derive all food, all clothing, shelter and all health care, in the course of *fourteen days*. The fact that he does this with so little hesitation, the fact that he finds it possible to do so, incurring thereby neither the scorn and indignation of his enemies nor even the ironical condemnation of his friends, is one vivid instance of the real success of public education in this nation.

The issue here is not one of a strange and unexpected cynicism in a cruel, vindictive and peculiar human being. Moynihan here does not do something odd. He does, instead, something both comfortable and sane. He does his work. He draws his salary. He eats his meal. He lifts his fork. He manipulates his knife. He carves into the beef. It is so normal, so amiable, so hearty, so routine, to speak about starvation over a forty-dollar lunch, and to sip a glass of brandy, while developing the details of a malnutrition plan. Even the wish to draw attention to a situation of this sort appears a bit

preposterous or, at the least, "uncalled-for." We live in a land in
which this type of direct and sophisticated exploitation has, by now,
been institutionalized as "rational self-interest." It is not reprehensible to research pain or to investigate despair while living in the
town-house of the man who draws advantage from perpetuation of
those evils we research. It is not reprehensible to speak of pain,
starvation, hunger, over good rare beef, a glass of brandy or an
excellent cigar.

"Now . . ." writes the reporter for The New York Times, "satisfied with his steak, his brandy and a Presidential position on welfare, Moynihan savored them all . . ." There is a moment's pause for
recollection of a sentence, spoken by the President, which Moynihan
enjoys. Then he proceeds: "Isn't that a nice phrase — 'enlarged
democracy?' " Reaching over to his coat, says the reporter, Moynihan "withdrew an impressively long cigar. From his wallet he
slid a double-edged razor blade and delicately sliced off the cigar
tip . . ." Then, lighting up and drawing on the aromatic smoke, he
leans back in his chair to keep on with the conversation.

It is with the same precision, coldness and efficiency of motion
that all men and women of a certain economic class and intellectual
position, once prepared for self-protection in the U.S. public
schools, learn to divide the words they speak from the real lives they
lead, and to divorce the ideals they espouse from the behaviors
which they foster, demonstrate and learn to live by.

XV. THE EXAMINATION OF DISSENT

"Do not ask a screaming student what he hopes to gain. His is a holding action on behalf of humanity . . . When this nightmare is over, the quickness of his compassion will have survived. It is the rest of us who will have slipped imperceptibly backwards into deadness."

— Charles Hampden-Turner

WHEN ALL ELSE FAILS, schools and universities are often able to defuse rebellious students by a method that I call Examination of Dissent. The process takes place in direct association with much of the liberal press and with some portions of the medical profession too. In this situation, it is not so much that students learn to *compromise* their views. Instead, what they consent to do is place their judgments and intentions *on display* for "reasonable analysis" and "explication" at the hands of the official representatives of the adult world: scholars, sociologists, T.V. reporters, college deans. In effect, though he may not perceive it in this way, the student makes a compact with the adult world to transform his direct intention, rage or vision out of the status of insistent need, mandate, vocation, into the status of "appropriate subject-matter" for examination, scrutiny and explication.

There is a certain pattern and routine by which this ritual takes place. The students agree to put their views on record. The adults agree to "listen and report" on what the students wish to say. There is no evil in the process of communication; there *is* some evil in the purpose that the process holds. The purpose is not to nourish or to reinforce a person's ethical intention. It is, instead, to situate him, from the first, at arm's length from his own original idea, to lift him up and set him down outside the role of active or creative agent of a social transformation, turning him instead into the role of "interesting object" (clinical topic) for somebody else's interesting views.

Keniston, in his book *The Uncommitted,* describes the power of the "over examined action" to undermine our sense of agency and authenticity. There is a sense today, no matter what we do, that every word or action we contrive will have been predicated, understood and explicated, in somebody's book or research-paper, long before we ever start. It is remarkable, in this regard, how many books of "observation of the nature of dissent," and even of "the make-up of the radical dissenter" have been published in the past ten years. The radical student offers changes, commentaries and prescriptions for the social structure. Simultaneously, and with a rising fervor of momentum, he is reduced to object-status as the target of prescriptive diagnosis by the world of teachers, counselors or college doctors.

Many of the titles of the books I have in mind are prominent still in bookstores in the Nineteen Seventies: *The Agony of the American Left, Radical Man, A Prophetic Minority, Young Radicals, The Uncommitted.* Each of these books is one that has been of some personal value to me in my life; all are books that I admire. It is not the excellence of the work which is at issue. It is the social function of the genre. In olden days these kinds of books were almost universally historical and retrospective. If written at all, they were composed once those they spoke of had prevailed and triumphed — or withdrawn from battle. Today the radical student comes to be the topic of concern, analysis and in some cases eulogy, prior to death and long preceding potency. His ardor alone becomes a matter of intrigue, analysis and comprehension.

The literature of social justice thus becomes, in large part, not a literature of provocation, but a sociology of dissent. We do not *profess.* Instead, we "understand" the motives which bring *others* to the moment of profession. The focus is not upon the *agon* of the confrontation, but upon the diagnosis of the *agon.* Students at the university protest the war. Their professors and their teaching-fellows go into debate for two months to decide "the proper nature of their own response to protest." The one gropes, struggles, suffers deeply for the real thing. The other deals with the less urgent matter of the "implications" of the groping, struggling, suffering of the first.

During student protests that developed in response to the invasion of Cambodia (spring 1970) the exercise of The Examination of Dissent attained the character of national apotheosis. For just one hour, as it seems, the real thing is *right there before us* on the screen of consciousness: eyes of dying child in the ruined village, mother's cry and father's echoing scream, U.S. soldier with his hardened eyes and U.S. rifle underneath the sickening banner of our nation. Few days go by before the screen no longer holds the eyes of dying children, but the words of clever people. The loss of the real thing takes place by several stages. First, we perceive the war; then we respond with words to things that we perceive; then others speak about "the nature of the rules and regulations" of appropriate response, and we agree to settle on the ground rules for responding. At last the editorial writers, authors, scholars, politicians and physicians set forth to define the "quality and character of our reaction" and to ascertain its final impact on the mainstream of the population.

"Young people, increasingly, are lashing out . . ."

"The student response is rational and sober. In the long run, whatever the disruption we now suffer, we shall have gained a good deal from this period of discussion and dissent . . ."

"The concern of youth is, in some ways, commendable . . . Their self-restraint is in all respects impressive . . . Their lapses into irrational behavior have been both rare and unintentional . . . Their ethical concern would have been inconceivable ten years before . . . We should be grateful for their decency and courage . . ."

Laudatory or not, the response to a response is distant, by at least one stage, from hard reality. "A Sane Look at [Student] Dissent" reads one newspaper headline on the way in which Supreme Court Justice Burger speaks about the ways in which the students speak about the war. A conference of concerned physicians, held in Boston, hears one of its members recommend that they, as doctors, must speak out against the war in Vietnam because of what the war is doing to our mental health. The war becomes appropriate subject-matter for discussion at a medical convention only if its impact on the comfortable numbness, alienation and sedation of our population is considered harmful to our own internal health. No mention of the "health" of dead and non-white Oriental infants under the muzzles of well-manufactured U.S. instruments and by the trigger-pressure of our football captains and debating champions. A "sane" look at student dissent to documented genocide is a bit insane to start with. *Sanity lives in dealing with the first thing.*

This is, of course, the heart of the whole business. To deal directly with the first thing is, in all respects, more painful, and less easy to dismiss in time for drinks and dinner, than to look upon the matter through protective lenses. Blue vein bursting in the frail young forehead of a dying child on a college campus in Ohio is of a more relentless and, in certain ways, less postponable intensity than "a sane look at the current patterns of disruptive protest" might, by word or flavor, signify. *The Agony of the American Left* is a fine piece of writing; but it is a safe bet that the agony at stake in this compassionate and even partisan work is of a lesser degree of import, urgency or — for that matter — "agony," than those imagined and now barely recollected agonies of the helpless and the poor whom the Left are said, in this book, to be agonized *about.* Hunger, war and death are real things. Ruined skull of aged woman shot by our old high school classmate is a real thing. Hospital corridor is real and widow's terror in the evening light is rather real. Alcoholic dying like a dead dog in the Boston winter, red hands frozen fat with death, thick nails curved-in and yellow, big feet, arms and wasted body freezing slowly into cold accretion on the gutted sidewalk: there is enough real provocation here to warrant someone's pure and undeflected passion of response and purchase.

Not to address these things head-on, but to deal always with concatenations of such matters, is to assign ourselves respite from pain and amnesty from bad dreams. A nation confronted with the painful fact of a dehumanized, cold and terrifying Army, educated for twelve years in its own schools, nourished to kill with innocence in its own culture, blinded to any sense of moral mandate but the mindless brutalism of its own dishonored flag, does not for long, nor with a willing vision, look into its actions, values and behavior. To make a compact of disjunctive intellection, to speak of "serious problems of dissent and intellectual upheaval," while sitting in the safe and unappalling parlor of a rich man's home or spooning in the cool lime sherbet in the college dining-hall, is to deal forever with the second level of *response to pain,* but not with pain itself.

It is, for this reason, to escape forever from the burdens and responsibilities of intervention.

It is naïve to think that we can ever totally subvert this etherizing process — not, at least, so long as we remain within the context of the school, or prior to a full-scale economic and political rebellion. It *is* within our power, I believe, to learn how to exist and struggle as "internal rebels" — above all if we can contrive not to be fired, or suspended, prior to the time at which we have been able to have left a penetrating impact on our students. In such a way, we have the opportunity to shape, and leave behind, a concrete precedent not only for *our* struggle but for *theirs* as well: one which cannot be distorted or diluted into meaningless consensus, nor one which can be turned into the topic of a learned disputation for clinicians.

The only way I know, for now, by which to do this is to learn how to transform our deepest values and beliefs, by direct actions, into concrete deeds. Student boycott in the face of school indoctrination, as described within this book, is one explicit form of struggle which cannot with ease be neutralized into polite miscomprehension. The ten-day fast of sixteen-year-old children, in protest at the operations of the C.I.A. and of its unjust and illegal murders and manipulations — this also is a brand of action which cannot be "comprehended" in one hour into bland and meaningless consensus. Sudden refusal, on the part of hundreds of young people, to share those medical services which can be purchased for them by their mothers and their fathers, but *cannot* be purchased by the parents of those black or poor-white children whom they tutor, teach or work with during summers, evenings, free semesters — here too is a form of action which cannot be undermined, or talked away, or clinically dissolved before it has begun to take effect.

The conception and creation of a strong and vital Free School of the kind that I have worked with in the past six years — this is another form of piecemeal labor to which both students and adults can bring their energies and dreams before the ritual of instant playback can begin. A project like a Free School or Street Clinic is of special value, in my own belief, because it does not lead to just one moment of apocalyptic thrill and revolutionary exaltation but leads us rather into an entire landscape of intelligent rebellion and sustained revolt. There are dozens of other forms of concrete action. Some are of a much more private and less obvious kind. It is the fact of visible action and sustained exhilaration that seems most essential. It is the fact, as well, of something that involves at least a certain portion of risk-taking nerve.

If teachers and students cannot summon up bravado of this kind, I do not think that they will ever find the leverage to transcend the all-forgiving vision of the adult world. If they can do no more than weep and tremble for the passions that they feel, then the "kindness" and "compassion" of the adult world will go, in every case, not to those real conditions of injustice, outrage and specific desperation which provoke this tremor and these tears, but rather to the tremor and the tears *themselves*. Concern itself will be the *topic* of concern, and mirrors within mirrors will forever take the place of blood-filled images and of unfalsified perceptions.

In The Boston Globe, one morning, I begin to read a full-length essay by John Rockefeller, III. For six long columns he discusses the intriguing aspects, pro and con, favorable and less so, of the current period of youth revolt, argues for student-industry cooperation, warms us alike (as if he were in no respect involved) that we must be quite careful lest "we play into the hands of the extremists," and quotes from one of his co-workers in the banking world those words that crystallize the heart and center of the whole disjunctive process. "Whatever the causes of . . . rebellion," Mr. Rockefeller's fellow-businessman observes — business and youth "had better get together."

It is only in his next-to-final paragraph that Rockefeller feels impelled at last to mention the idea that, if we can persuade young people to tone down their condemnation of the old, and if we can persuade the business world to be less hostile to the young, perhaps "we would make progress" on some of those "issues" that confront us. The likelihood that one of those imagined "issues" might be Mr. Rockefeller in and of himself — and the vast inheritance that each of his own children will receive to guarantee their own capacity to buy town-houses and to pass on to the subsequent generation of *their* children — is not mentioned in this essay. The essence, indeed, of the entire ritual of The Examination of Dissent is the willingness, on both my side and yours, never to speak about The Most Important Point. To do this is considered in bad taste.

It isn't only in mass publications that these processes take place. In the New York Review of Books one day, I find a piece that bears the very near apocalyptic title: "Jason Epstein [writes on] Martin Mayer's Ocean Hill," It is like wrestling with the Laocoön to stop here and to remember for one hour that Ocean Hill–Brownsville does not *belong* to Martin Mayer: that, whatever his entrepreneurial genius, or that of Jason Epstein, or of Robert Silvers for that matter, none of these three is in a position to own, appropriate, buy, sell or merchandise Ocean Hill–Brownsville. It takes, in reading essays of this sort, almost a Herculean leap of the imagination to recollect that at some point beyond these internecine feuds of pen and power and public renown, which bring at once both cash and delectation to all three good intellectuals involved, there is a specific census-tract of actual people and imaginable structures of steel and concrete which is, purportedly, still there, still trembling with havoc, still burning with its now-almost-irrelevant, almost-forgotten fires.

Three years later, in another issue of New York Review, I come upon a sensitive piece of critical response, on the part of writer-scholar Christopher Lasch, in which he condemns the views and the assumptions of a recent book by Harvard scholar Oscar Handlin: a book, in turn, in which Professor Handlin offers *his* response to ways in which the radical students at the universities attempt to offer *their* response to what they view to be the university's inadequate response to something which, somewhere, somehow, far in the back of all of these disjunctive hinges, is still reported to be a real world of specific needs of actual human beings in genuine pain and in believable ordeal.

The exercises in Examination of Dissent which I have just described may seem, in certain ways, innocuous. They are, however, far more dangerous than some of us would like to think. In much the same way that the risk of intellectual co-option tends to lead young men and women to co-opt *themselves*, so also many students nowadays learn how to "explicate" and to "report" their own intentions and ideals even before the social scientist or T.V. camera can arrive. In high schools, students and teachers often "rap" (as it is frequently described) of what they think to be the issue of "The

War," "Racism," "Urban Problems," when in reality what they discuss, debate, consider and conclude, all has to do, not with the war, racism or the poor, but only with the way in which one ought, or ought not, to respond, or how one should or should not "feel," "relate," "react," to what he takes to be, and still vaguely recalls, as some sort of outside "issue," "stimulus" or "truth:" i.e., BLACK INFANT, RACIST COP or GHETTO HOSPITAL.

Dozens of books, now present in the public schools, "mediate," much as oldtime teachers used to do, between the truth of need and pain, on one hand, and concatenations of such need, truth, pain and devastation on the other. There is a book I have before me now, one which bears the vigorous and inviting title: *Challenges For The Nineteen Seventies*. It is published underneath the imprint of the U.S. Congress and is found today in common use at junior high and high school levels in large numbers of the U.S. public schools. The work consists of nine extensive sections, each of which purports to deal with major social issues. Out of these nine, one deals with "ecological" dilemmas, one with the role of science in our lives, one with the labor market, one with space missions, one with the military. The other four sections represent ideal examples of the exercise I call Examination of Dissent. In theory, each sub-section deals with basic social or political dilemmas: hunger, sickness, exploitation, segregation. In truth, however, they do not deal with these subjects but deal rather with reverberations from (reactions to) these areas of anguish and ordeal. The four sub-sections start out with these topics: (1) Rising Dissent, (2) Street Crime in America, (3) Conflict Resolution, (4) Discipline in Public Schools.

The section on Rising Dissent speaks of the Nineteen Sixties in these words: "Red guards brought turmoil to China . . . Students in Mexico City embarrassed their government . . . on the eve of the . . . Olympic Games . . . Months earlier, student-led demonstrations in Paris weakened the French Government . . . Masses of war protesters, most of them young . . . battled police during the 1968 Democratic convention." The page concludes with this exhausted statement from George Kennan: "The world seems to be full, today, of embattled students." He does not tell us (possibly because he does not like to know) that the world is also full of starving children, desperate men and weeping women, hungry blacks and migrant laborers, limbless orphans in Vietnam and brain-damaged infants in New Orleans and Chicago. Kennan's concern — consistent with his own successful national career — is not to deal with torment, hunger or starvation but solely with those *consequences* of such torment as might cause too loud a noise outside the parlor of his pleasant, sheltered, segregated farm in Pennsylvania.

The section Discipline in Public Schools again shifts emphasis from pedagogic lies, deceptions and oppressions to the end-consequences of these prior provocations in the actions and reactions of school children. The nation's public schools (the text reports) now face what may be — or become — a critical year. "The private schools will have their troubles, too . . ." Yet, as the text reports, the private schools are still in a position to select and choose, as well as to suspend and to expel. The public schools, in contrast, must expect a difficult time. "The most immediate problem . . . can be summed up in two words: *student unrest.*"*

This, in my belief, is the one basic point which must be stated and restated: The exercise itself, the very presence of the "field" of observation, explication and examination, with its own pervasive power and apparent sanity — this is the greatest danger which the rebel-conscience must confront. Most young people are quite unprepared to recognize the danger which is instantly at stake both in the generous eyes and in the liberal manner of the man or woman who consents to "understand" them. More often, they are flattered and exhilarated by the interest and attention they receive. It would be naïve to think that a result like this is accidental. It is the planned and conscious object of an unjust social order that serious children should be held back by devices such as these from head-on confrontation with the evils they ignore but which their mothers and their fathers do not hesitate to turn into good houses, ample meals and high-tuition college education for their kids. "Get out of the world and get inside your head." When youth itself can be manipulated to perform its own self-explication in this way, the adult world has carried out a very impressive and successful action of mass-alienation.

In high schools, as in university circles, there is far more talk right now of "how we learn what we perceive" — still worse, of "how

* My emphasis.

we learn to find out what we think we feel when we perceive" — than of the real thing which is somehow still there, at the long, long end of the extended telescope of our disjoined and neutralized perception. "Interesting things about the state of being known as RADICAL, LIBERATED, FREE" become far more important than those things that we are radical *about,* or liberated *for.* Little by little, we learn to remove ourselves from the immediate field of forces, actions, options or intentions, on which we have briefly stood, but always and forever at its indecisive margin, and situate ourselves instead upon a safe and sober ledge from which to look down on the action. It is as if the explication of the text were to precede the composition of the poem: still worse, as if *we* were to be the explicators. When we end up at the point of explication of the poem we have not written, and no longer dare to write, we have come to that point of ideal alienation at which we qualify for academic tenure, intellectual respectability and decent income.

There is a certain moment when the erstwhile revolutionist, the one-year radical, is seen slightly behind, or just *beside,* the portable T.V. camera which records a campus action. He stands there now, relaxed, full-bearded, uninvolved, commenting for the edification of a sympathetic T.V. newsman on "the way things seem to be developing this year" and on "the specific character of the demands of youth." He is, himself, just twenty-three years old. He was the campus leader only eighteen months before. Today he stands: narrator, viewer, commentator, on the scene of his own never-consummated vision.

It is tragic to be forced to say this; but, in my belief, this is not unexpected. It is the norm. It is the goal and destination. The poet must be dissuaded from his vision. The rebel must be transformed into participant, informer, counter-agent, in the process of his own domestication. The ritual-exercise of the Examination of Dissent is only one of several ways in which an unjust social order can reduce to size the vehemence of the rebel and contain with clinical insight the potential fury of its most audacious children. We are innocent indeed if we attempt to tell ourselves it does not have grave power upon us.

XVI. THE OBLIGATIONS OF THE READER AND THE WRITER OF THIS BOOK

"My job is teaching Ethics, Education and their point of intersection. It's someone else's job to put them into execution."

— Professor of Religion at a
Catholic College in Wisconsin

TRUTH, in my belief, is something which occurs when actions take place: not when phrases are contrived. Truth is not a word which represents correct response to an examination, nor a well-written piece of prose. Truth is not a "right word" which can be printed. It is (it only is) a "right deed" which can be done.

In school, children learn that truth is something they must learn to *say*. What if, instead, we were to teach them it is something that cannot be said, can never be said, but only can be done or undertaken: "Oliver — are you telling me the truth?" What if, instead, we were to ask him if he dares to *live* it?

Teachers, if they are not seriously committed to subversive action, cannot dream to speak in words like these. School is posited, as Whitehead long ago observed, upon the pre-planned domination of Inert Ideas. Students learn, very early in the public schools, that anything they think, or feel, or long to undertake, of even the most restricted and tangential character, so long as it is touched with ethical potential, but no ethical *event,* can bring substantial profit. The child who takes the extra step of concrete deeds will learn a different lesson. The admiration that accrues to ethical ideas decreases in direct proportion to their concrete application. Most children that I know in public school learn, without words, the magical cut-off point, and stop at least one hour this side of justice.

In place of concrete action, school instructs our children in a false form of "behavior" called CONCERN. Children are trained to look upon the cost-free exercises of "compassion," "care," "concern," as if they were real forms of ethical behavior. They take on the illusion of completedness. Little by little, they begin to stand-in for their own intended end-results. "In any event, if we do nothing else, the very least that we can do . . . is care." I have heard teachers talk like this in course of classroom visits in all sections of the nation. There are a number of consistent clues within these words of childlike and sentimental absolution: mellowness, relaxation, resignation (though of a melancholy kind), the nursery-lilt, the singsong note of recapitulation, the sense somehow of final resolution.

There is good reason for this note of mellowness and resolution. There is a reason also why it crystallizes quite so much of what is anti-human in the process of our public education. The expression, in its common use by decent, liberal, yet ineffective classroom teachers, is a phrase that means the diametric opposite of what it seems to say. The teacher says it. We say it to ourselves. In later years we pass it on to our own children. The words soon take on the aroma of a genteel benediction; yet the benediction, in the last event, is not for others, but ourselves. We do not bless *others* by risk-taking action. We bless *ourselves* by extrication of our conscience from a world of truth and pain.

"The least . . ." "At least . . ."

These phrases ought to be perceived by us, from this point on, as signal flags to warn us of the presence of a code-expression. The code-expression needs, for its decodification, to be restated in this form: LEAST means most. CARE means self-consolation, amnesty and exculpation. CONCERN means lies, hypocrisy, surrender. The sense of "unreal talk" which is, by this device, conveyed to children, leads child and teacher both, by an inevitable progression, into a longer series of dehumanized expressions. Freire speaks of the entire word-set which evolves, within the phrase Narration Sickness. The language is capable of speaking *to:* not *into.* The word has power to circumnavigate a point of view: not to possess it. The word, in Freire's phrase, becomes an "empty" word. It cannot celebrate the world. It cannot challenge or subvert the world. It cannot possess, invade or reconstruct the world. This is the definition of Narration Sickness.

"Children . . . if you do nothing else tonight before you go to sleep, I want you to think for just a little while of those who are less privileged than you. I want you to close your eyes and think of those who live within the hot and crowded ghettos of Chicago and New York, children who do not have warm clothes, and comfortable houses such as yours, or schools like these. I want you to think of those who live in Harlem or the Bronx. I want you to think of all the children that we heard of when we did our research-project on The Black Experience . . .

"Most of us have read the book about the little boy who lives in East St. Louis. We remember also what we said to one another on the day that Dr. King was killed. So there is another thing that we can think of when we close our eyes before we go to sleep . . . The little children in the cities, in their crowded tenement-houses . . . so many days, so many nights, when they do not have food to eat . . . places to sleep . . . or games to play . . . parks where they can walk out in the air . . . It may be you will never know those children in the Bronx or in Chicago. It may be there is nothing you can ever do to show those children what you think, or how you feel, about the lives they lead. It doesn't matter. There's something else within your power. You can feel *kindliness* toward children who are not so privileged as you. You can *care deeply* what becomes of those poor children. You can grow up to feel concern about those children. You can teach other children that they also can experience care and concern."

Words spoken thus, not in order to define a realm of Ethical Aspiration we intend to enter, but rather to describe a kingdom of complex intensities from which we have forever taken exile, denigrate our spirit and deny the possibilities of love and power that exist within us. What is the purpose, what is the pedagogic goal, of working for twelve years to build a kingdom of new words within a child's mind if he is then denied the right to crack just one of those words open, and release the invocation to effective action that it might contain?

The concept of Inert Concern which is at stake in this is separate from the brand of self-deception present in the Myth of Research. It is not so much, in this situation, that "care" or "concern" postpones behavior, but *replaces* it. Inert Concern, quite in itself, is advertised to children as one form of ethical event. To comprehend the situation of the black and poor, while we enjoy the unjust proceeds of the disproportion which exists between us, is held to be an honest substitute for having taken steps to *lessen* pain or to *reduce* that disproportion. Children learn to think of the idea of an "intelligent decision" — and, therefore, the whole process of Inert Concern that goes with such "decision" — as something so much like a real deed as to render differences inconsequential. Schools, moreover, go still further, and inform us, softly, quietly and almost parenthetically, that there is at least one definite advantage in the "higher" activism of reflection, as opposed to visible event. The first, as children are advised, is seldom flawed by unexpected outcomes. The latter bears the risk, in every case, of possible harm to other human beings: a risk which is, of course, at all times present in the realm of the real world. There is little danger of an unanticipated mishap when all of the action takes place in the tortured mind and introverted soul of one who never leaves his desk or lecture hall.

The key to it all lies in the exercise of calculated substitution. The passage of sub-muscular intellection which transports a person from one point of impotent advocacy to another — to change opinions, to arrive at an unusual position, to decide on something different from before and then to be willing to announce that new decision to the world — develops the aura of a visible occurrence. It seems to us as if, by recommending justice and propounding social transformation, we have advanced the one and staked our conscience for the other. It is an efficacious lie.

In setting down these words, I have in mind a man whom I have known for more than twenty years. This man, gentle in speech, shambling in style, now in his middle fifties, is a scholar long associated with a college close to New York City, a man known first for work in welfare, then for research into race discrimination in the field of social medicine, best-known, however, for his work in education and in school-desegregation. Starting in early 1964, he spends one year, then two, then three years more, in carrying out investigations in the public schools, inquiring also into housing patterns, rent discrimination and police behavior, medical and psychiatric treatment-inequalities. He gathers statistics, arrives at length at certain end-results of seemingly irrefutable force, puts it all together in an excellent monograph directed at his friends, then, as the material expands and his conclusions grow into a larger theme, develops the work into a book that reaches print within another year.

He arrives, as a result, at the first plateau of financial safety in the course of fourteen years, buys a pleasant home outside New York, within a largely segregated section of Long Island, sends his younger children to the local (segregated) public schools, an older son to a (more segregated) prep school, his daughter to a (still *more* segregated) Summerhill. In medical need, he turns, without particular hesitation, to a competent physician who lives nearby, in the next town. He sends his older son, in time of turmoil, to a psychoanalyst ensconced in an impressive office on the West Side of Manhattan, a man with whom he went to college many years before. He pays his taxes to support the Asian war, though he is now at work on an extensive essay to explore the question of withholding taxes that support this *kind* of war at some time in the future. He keeps his residence in a secure and upper-class community, enjoys the benefit of legal apparatus and proceeds of war economy (even while he defines the evil of all three), distrusts T.V., but owns three sets (two for his kids) and makes a brilliant presentation on a number of national discussion programs every year.

The power of his convictions does not lessen as the years go by but grows, if anything, more vital. In public, during special year-end seminars at universities and on T.V., he speaks, time and again, of medical discrimination, psychiatric treatment-inequalities, the virtual absence of pre-natal service for poor people. In spite of this, he sends his wife to the best obstetrician, takes himself and his young children to the finest oral surgeon. Ironically, he pays the bill for services like these (the denial of which to people who are poor he finds "unconscionable" and "unacceptable") with royalties he earns from publications on these very issues — if they are not covered by the pre-paid health plan at the university in which he leads a seminar on the same topic.

The point is not that he is hypocritical or insincere. He simply does not feel it is the obligation of a decent person to exist as witness to his own beliefs, and feels somehow that it might even be unsound, "neurotic" possibly, distasteful in whatever case, to place himself, his wife and children, in a vulnerable role. To sit with wife and child, for example, in a crowded, inner-city clinic, to trust to marginal services for psychiatric treatment of his son, to move into a poor or a "degenerating" inner-city block while giving his own home, at low rental, to a family from the inner core and, by this trade-off, granting to the children of poor people the mechanical advantage (if no better) of efficient public schools, trusting for the education of *his* children to his own capacity to make up in the evenings what they do not learn within the public school (or else to counteract that which they *do*) to do real things, participate in real EVENTS, to take such actions even as these few symbolic gestures outlined here, appears to him to be (1) unimaginable, (2) needless, (3) possibly unjust.

Would it be "fair" to his own wife and children, after all, to force them to suffer for the consequences of his sense of justice to the same degree that they now profit from the proceeds of his expertise and marketable skills? Then, too, can he be sure that it would really help poor people to have been so curiously transplanted to an alien neighborhood they do not know and might not understand? Is it known, for instance, how much research is already extant in this area? Have studies been made? Are studies now in progress? Is it even known if these imagined poor would *wish* to be so benefited, condescended-to, "rewarded," or whether poor folk living in the inner core would be prepared to have him and his wife and his own children as *their* neighbors?

The dangers inevitable in any course of action whatsoever, and the likelihood, in any case, that all specific transformation in the lives of those he chooses to "assist" will be quite strictly limited in range, with little spin-off on the total population-group at either end, both these realistic inhibitions, strengthened by a lifetime of indoctrination — the stigma, for example, that attaches to conspicuous acts of unsophisticated ethics, the "counter-productive" character of dangerous (i.e., "extreme") behavior, the distrust of unique acts and unique ideas in contrast to consensus viewpoints, the need for research of extensive nature, of research most of all in situations where strong actions seem almost beyond dispute, the likelihood that guilt may be neurotic and self-sacrifice inherently suspicious, added-to by our capability to think, or to pretend, for very long periods of time, that those we do not know, or see before our eyes, may not in fact exist, and by our inclination to believe, as well, that change, where necessary, will take place in its own good time without us anyway — all of these inhibitions come together in the situation of the scholar I have now in mind, a man, in any event, who has before him at all times the complex and persuasive richness of his more-than-ordinary earnestness, compassion and concern, and research which comes closer to the gut and bone of life than that of nine tenths of his peers.

Ethical aspiration, in effect, becomes his form of action. It takes the place of visible behavior and grows, for him, into a credible substitute for realistic transformations in his manner of existence. Moreover, in the eyes of many, he appears heroic (and, from a certain point of view, he is) merely for the words he still can speak out of a conscience which, unlike that of his neighbors, still gives voice to even febrile benedictions. In the long eye of history, or from the viewpoint of an eagle circling the city, he knows very well that he will look no different from his neighbor in the Birch Society, or his neighbor who supported Richard Nixon and who made his money by the manufacture of defoliants and napalm. He *does* no different but, in the words of Thoreau, bids "God-speed" to the right as it goes past him. Yet he *feels* different. At least, he says (and others say it to him, too) he "cares." He is a concerned man: serious, not shallow; reasonable, not headstrong; ethical in intention, earnest (if immobile) in inaction. He is, in a sense, the North American version of a "decent" person. In any event — and by comparison with men like Moynihan and Hook — he is the upper-academic version of a saint.

"Earnestness," writes Kierkegaard: "to listen in order to act." It is not possible for most of us, once trained by public school, even to dare to look without alarm on words and syllables like these. We listen, not in order to act but, rather, in order to assign, to slot, to profit, analyze or publish. We listen in order to find out how *this* recent item of our intellectual appropriation fits in with those ten *other* items we possess already, then how it may be of use in perpetration of our wishes, purposes and acquisitions. Each item of new information can be drained of passion and provocative implication and transformed into some form of gain. Hunger of infants becomes a "rather interesting" essay for New York Review. Torment of mothers is transformed into the qualifications for a Ph.D. Ethics itself can be back-alchemized from the high stakes of Gandhi and the high risk of Martin Luther King into the thin and low-grade metal of foundation grants, book royalties, East Side prestige and West Side cocktail parties.

I find myself, of course, endangered deeply by the kinds of statements I am making here. I am a writer. This is a book. A book consists of *words*. Words on an ethical issue which do not compel to action are: inert, non-earnest and dishonest. For all my efforts, stretching now across the course of ten complex and inconsistent years, I still do not divorce myself, to a degree which seems both ethical and clear, from just that realm of compromise which I condemn. Then too, in order to obtain some periods of isolation at some of the crucial times of labor on this book, and to escape the guilt of letting down close friends in need, I am compelled to seek out and accept financial aid, even in small amounts. I try, as best I can, to cope with this in my own mind. I tell myself that all funds in an unjust social order are inherently corrupt and that the only real choice is with what integrity a person puts to use, and in all possible cases, *shares*, what he can manage to obtain.

Thus in the last event I live, like some of those whom I condemn, with multiple contradictions of the views I hold. There is no way I know by which to lead a totally just life within an unjust land. Yet I dissent with those who would accept this statement, or restate it on their own, without (1) genuine anguish at the fact that we are all caught up, one way or other, in an evil apparatus of this kind, (2) a constant struggle to reverse the tide and to transform the odds in every way we can, (3) unceasing self-examination as to what one really needs in order to maintain the economic base and personal sticking-power to survive the struggle longer than those three or four years people tend to stay — before they "settle down" to what are called "more reasonable lives."

Even to state, as I am stating here, this sense of deep dissatisfaction with my own as-yet-unfinished resolution of this problem is by no means to confront it, to deal with it, but only to speak of it, to address it, and (ironically, therefore) to turn it into profit, to exploit indeed my very indecision, to "sell my agonies" on the common market. It is the heritage of many years of privileged indoctrination and reward to know the way to tell ourselves, at least for manageable periods of time, that words *are* deeds and that intentions are the "early stages" of perceptible events.

The constant object is, above all else, that our own routine lives shall not need to be changed. The facts that we have gathered in regard to schools of Harlem or the Bronx have nothing to do with where we send *our* kids to school. The timbre of the voices in the college dining hall remains the same . . . We take our General Exams in senior year, drive out to Hartford for an interesting luncheon, fly to Toronto to discuss another interesting issue with *another* interesting friend . . . We speak now and then, with fervor of a certain reasonable kind, of serious matters which "disturb," "unsettle" or "concern us deeply." We draw on our pipe and speak of revolution, press fingers to the nose-bone and remark upon ordeal. The words come into the room without the pain. Integrity is here, but passion is not present. Liberal intention is in evidence, but risk and venture in a form that has the power to transform our lives are not a portion of our ethical vocation.

It does not seem honest, in discussion of this point, to seek to demonize the grade school teacher. Teachers are perhaps the least explicitly corrupt of all the self-defrauded citizens within this land. The teacher has few of the sophisticated methods of the university scholar, the high-level social scientist or author, traveling about the major colleges of the land with briefcase in his right hand and consultant's payment in breast pocket, explaining to people in various well-fitted rooms, and at elaborate convocations, that the problem we now face is not one of sheer exploitation and gut-level greed, but only one of "insufficient definition" of appropriate goals, and reasonable avenues, and proper sequences:

"It is important that we come to understand and to espouse a sane, responsible and reasoned point of view. Our first responsibility is to define the problem with some minimal degree of clarity, next to settle on our long-term goals. Inept definition of the situation and head-first activism might well prove to be our greatest errors. Indeed, they might well prove to be more dangerous than doing nothing . . ."

It is impossible, at least within the terms by which we teach and learn today, for men and women to come out and say to one another what it is they really mean: "Ethical actions belong to other people, other places. Serious transformations of society, along straight ethical lines, are not in the stars for ordinary men and women such as you and me. The least — and most — that you and I can do is care. Impotent advocacy, tinged with kindness, touched with irony, decorated with compassion, is a reasonable goal for moral paralytics in a land of drought."

There is one social studies teacher that I know, a woman still working in the public schools, who has been able to maintain a vital, honest and subversive concept with her students. Children are free, at least within the pre-set limits and perimeters of U.S. media control, to advocate whatever views they hold, to take original positions, to follow a unique direction of irreverent research or investigation, to come up with conclusions and announce them, if they choose, in form of written word, essay or such. There is, within this class, one rule, and one rule only: Any idea a student genuinely believes, and feels to be his own, must be *enacted, executed* or *applied* within the realm of the real world.

This does not mean a three-dimensional poster in the hallways to be given false praise by the principal and supervisor, then to be fawned on by the P.T.A. It means some visible form of concrete deed, outside the school, outside the semester and beyond the realm of blackboard, chalk and flag. The action, moreover, no matter what its final form, cannot be one of those pre-flawed and predoomed endeavors which I have described above. Each action must possess realistic possibilities for visible success. The only rule is this: A point of view, once taken, must be given execution. If not, the student does not pass the course.

The rule has had some obvious repercussions. Kids who come to strong conclusions in regard to slumlords, housing covenants or racist realtors, lawyers, doctors in the neighborhood in which the school is set, have launched attacks, begun with words, gone on to visits, tabulations, press-campaigns, a picket line and blueprints for a boycott in those situations where a boycott has a chance to work. Other plans are still in stages of class-formulation. Hunger strikes, extended fasts and carefully stage-managed interruptions of expensive dinners at the local country club or in the homes of certain people who live nearby on the profits gained from exploitation of the poor — these are all among the present or projected consequences of a single rule: IF YOU BELIEVE NOTHING, SAY SO. IF YOU BELIEVE SOMETHING, TURN BELIEF INTO A CONCRETE DEED.

The regulation has not led, up to this point, into a head-on confrontation with the school administration. There is consensus, however, among students in the school, that the teacher's tenure is not evidence of backing from administration, but only of the slowness with which news can travel in a large school system. It is not easy to believe that mothers, fathers, School Board or the P.T.A. will look with favor, or respond without alarm, in face of a rule which forces children, in the fullness of their years, to take specific and sometimes disruptive action, based on research drawn from periods of serious reflection. It is difficult, indeed, to think of any tactic of "in-school" rebellion more specific, more precise or more subversive of the deep, dehumanizing function of those exercises of Inert Concern, as now purveyed to young men and young women in the U.S. public schools.

XVII. COLLEGES AND UNIVERSITIES

> "Since our Tenth Reunion my life has developed a certain
> consistency . . . After two fun years of owning a house on
> Beacon Hill we decided the country was for us. We pur-
> chased a small farm in Hamilton . . . Business, as they say in
> the trade, 'has been good. . .' This, coupled with a 'little oil
> in Texas' keeps me on the road more than I would like but It
> has given me a chance to keep in touch with . . . classmates . . .
> Last year saw me ski in Taos . . . play golf in England . . .
> shoot quail in South Carolina . . . and sip a little rum . . . in
> Nassau . . . On the more serious side I have stayed active in
> the Army Reserve, graduating from Command and General
> Staff College, Ft. Leavenworth, Kansas, in 1971 and commis-
> sioned a major this last June . . ."
>
> — Harvard Class of 1958
> Fifteenth Anniversary Report

THE UNIVERSITIES have come today to represent one basic portion
of the U.S. public education apparatus. There are at least two obvious reasons for this claim:

(1) The greater numbers of our universities receive large sub-
sidies of State and Federal funds, including military funds, and therefore represent a literal extension of the public-funded education apparatus. (2) In a much more obvious respect, it is a simple fact that
college, for most kids, is designated as the only logical and impressive
endpoint for the lower levels of the education process. Whether
a student does, or does not, head on from his high school years
to four more years of intellectual incarceration, the fact of college
admission or rejection comes to represent the primary index of his
self-esteem. It also represents his parents' major grounds for satisfaction or for disappointment. It is, then, not surprising, when we
look into those inhibitions, loaded arguments and covert ideologies

which dominate in upper academic circles, that most of the values foisted on our kids in public school are present here as well.

The concentration, in most university apologetic, settles on the fiction of a neutral territory of enlightened aspiration: a plot of land, a pile of mortar, stone and brick, that constitutes an island of un-biased, non-political and value-free discussion. This self-descrip-tion, cherished by the liberal professor, seeks to perpetrate the image of a world of pure and learned rumination, uncontaminated by those raw-boned men who run the businesses, govern the armies and dictate the course of nations. The idealistic and non-critical character of this self-description represents a yearning back, or a nostalgic gravitation toward, the Middle Ages — a beautiful Gothic and Episcopal construction, hours and days associated with pure learning, inquiry, reflection in tall Medieval towers. It is a pleasant and disarming frieze, one that people here in Cambridge, as in Boulder, Berkeley, Palo Alto, do their best to foster. It is a consol-ing recollection too: pre-modern, pre-catastrophic and pre-Ausch-witz. It is all of this. It is also whole-cloth fiction.

The university is not exclusively, nor even for the most part, a context of toil, within which eloquent women and reflective men earnestly yearn, patiently seek and generously extend the bound-aries of pure knowledge. It is instead (or it is many times more often) the place above all others where the graded, numbered and cre-dentialized end-products of the previous twelve-year interlock of public school turn in their credits (hours and years of heart's humil-iation, proven rectitude and inept moderation) for *better* credentials, *higher* numbers and *more* excellent rewards. It is the place, as well, in which these men and women are protected by complete and cost-free medical insurance, enjoy unprecedented social benefits, pur-chase well-tailored clothes, shop in expensive stores: all of which benefaction is consistently denied not only to the poor slum dweller who did not attend the public schools of Evanston or Great Neck, Wheatridge, Darien, but also to those people in far-distant lands who live and die so frequently beyond our credence, recognition or imagination, yet work their whole lives to produce the wealth from which our corporations draw their profit, and our universities their building funds and their endowments.

The university is built on blood and nourished by injustice. This has not changed. It has not lessened but, with passage of the years and with the escalation of exploitative wars and corporate predations, it has steadily increased. Each privileged young man who walks each afternoon across the ivy-covered lanes of Harvard College, or sits down in the pleasant, sheltered stacks to pore into his Chaucer or to explicate Rimbaud and Baudelaire, is living his life and building his career upon the ruined hopes and broken dreams of other people every bit his human equal, yet who — for reason of no greater sin than non-possession of the proper ticket of admission — will never be able to live as he now lives, stroll as he strolls, through ivy-covered lanes, across diagonals of ancient stone between the sheltered space of shaded courtyards and old red-brick Georgian walls.

There are ten times four thousand students in the black, poor-white and Spanish neighborhoods of Boston, Cleveland, New York and Chicago who would be effective competition for the students now enrolled in colleges like Harvard, M.I.T. and Yale, but who will never have the chance to stand or struggle, perish or prevail, all for no reason but the accident of color, cash and birth. Those, however, who partake of opportunities like these do not dare confront the fact that what they now perceive as their ascent is somebody's decline, that what they recognize as their participation is someone else's cold and inexplicable exclusion.

This, then, is the university version of the myth I have described above as No Connections. It functions well: both to sedate the lives and to protect the conscience of the university population, to insulate the College Common and the paneled dining quarters of the college faculty and deans from either knowledge, memory or recognition of the pain, the desperation and the devastation of those tens of thousands who live just beyond their reach and recognition. The air-conditioned dining room in Princeton, Cambridge or Ann Arbor cleans the surface of the scholar's conscience with the polish of good manners, decent bearings and appropriate understatement of his discontent. Clean silver, cool sherbet, slivers of lime and fabric of seersucker, ladies and gentlemen slender and adept: They learn to be the managers of their own self-examination. Should they become intolerably disturbed, someone in the Mental Health Department of the pre-paid medical plan will tell them that their guilt is of neurotic origin and ought not to be given opportunity to distress them. Guilt, in any case, they will be told, is not productive. Even worse (they will be told) it would be "counter-productive" of real benefit or of important transformation. Skull of infant, blood and bone, the desperation of young mothers in the back-street clinic of a Memphis slum: It does not go with sherbet and seersucker.

There is a second myth which functions also in the upper echelons of these prestigious institutions. This is the myth I call the Fiction of Hard Work: "proper pay for quite unusual extremes of toil, labor and responsibility." The student learns to think, incant, believe (so also do his teachers, tutors, deans) that intellectual work is, in itself, exceptionally oppressive. There is, indeed, a quite pervasive myth, not often questioned within academic realms, that labors like these are possibly *more* difficult, *more* burdensome and *more* exacting than plain physical day-labor. University professors really do believe that this is difficult work. They say not only this (i.e., that they are working "hard") but even that they work much harder than most other people do.

It is difficult to know how this conclusion is arrived at, by what criteria the scholar measures work, exhaustion, anguish, physical endeavor. The truth, of course, is different from that which these scholars advertise. Millions of poor people in the U.S. work for longer hours, at lower pay, in far less comfortable situations, at labor many, many times less pleasant and secure, finding their nourishment in food less wholesome, going to sleep at last to dreams less hopeful, waking again to lives far less rewarding.

The father of one boy I know quite well works as a janitor within an office-complex. He works for ten, sometimes for fifteen hours, every day. His job is in an unseen "second basement" underneath the regular sub-basement of the tallest skyscraper in Boston. He works so many deep and sunless meters underneath the level of the lobby floor that he is sometimes underneath the level of the turnpike that runs *underneath the building*. I talk with him often in the evening hours when he returns from work, coated with dirt and broken with exhaustion. I am aware not only of how hard he works but also how disheartened he becomes.

This man, born in South Carolina, is now fifty-six years old. In this, his sixteenth year of labor for one corporation, he takes home seventy-four dollars every week. He lives beside, and almost underneath, the elevated railroad in the poorest block of the South End. He eats left-over cold cuts, bread and pastries brought home from the corporation cafeteria, drinks (when he has cash to drink at all) the cheapest red wine. He gets no health insurance and no benefits for overtime. He has two weeks of paid vacation every year — is forced, however, to work Christmas, New Year's and Thanksgiving.

The contrast between this bleak, unglamorous and underpaid employment and the familiar pattern of low-pressure labor and reflection, both expected and enjoyed by college dean, professor and the rest, is no simple matter for the conscience of a serious intellectual to handle. University people, therefore, learn to lie, first to themselves, then to one another, in order to continue with their routine lives without remorse. If they did not, they could not possibly explain or justify the relative ease, delight and satisfaction of their own well-fed careers — and the relative penury of those who sweep the basement floors and clean the toilet bowls and set the tables in the dining hall. The contrast is bitter: the interposition frequently unbearable. It is for this reason that the Fiction of Hard Work ("higher endeavor," "more noble, more exacting, less forgiving aspiration") has to be fostered, advertised, believed, by those who are the functionaries and the beneficiaries of the college Common Room.

There is a third point which, like the preceding two, is an extension of one of the basic myths of public school. This is the myth of "open education." The university version bears the label: "Civil Liberties." It is the myth which liberal jargon calls "the open market of ideas." The point is of exceptional importance at this time in history. Intellectuals write often, and with considerable alarm, of those within the Left who seek to "undermine" the so-called "open conflict of competitive ideas." Even in those sub-sections of the major universities — Law, Medicine and Business — where straightforward economic self-perpetuation of the ruling class seems to hold sway, efforts still are made to propagate the fiction of (1) ethics and (2) freedom.

Harvard Business School makes use of what it labels "innovative methods and ideas," in order that its students may consider (as they

think) with honest, open and unbiased minds, the issue of expropriation of U.S. investments by insurgent elements in Colombia or Brazil. They speak of it, however, only from the point of view of
finding out how best to minimize their loss of profit, never from the
point of view of finding out how best to help a desperate population
to drive out a parasitic class of U.S. businessmen and covert C.I.A.
officials. The question is forever how they can get Sheraton or
Hilton out of Bogotá or São Paulo before the masses can invade
the lobby. Never do they struggle with the more humane and serious
dilemma of how to turn a modern luxury hotel for North Americans
like you and me into an orphanage, a hospital or a pre-natal clinic
for those people who are victims of our international predation.

Teachers that I talk with at the Harvard Business School seem
earnest, serious and not corrupt. Yet there is no way to work around
the painful fact that what they do is not to open up real options
or to broaden out the possibilities of serious alternatives, but only
to adorn their profit-hunger with the trappings of an innovative jargon
and to decorate their sense of cold self-interest with the glamorous
aura of a set of phrases redolent of Summerhill and Civil Liberties.
This, then, is the upper academic adaptation of the pretense of
Free Options which is given prior application in the Fifth Grade
of the public school. The process is open, but the options are not;
and the goal is pre-determined. It is a fraud, because The One
Important Thing (our ethical position, in this instance, as a nation)
is not questioned — or, indeed, considered worth the asking.

In terms, of course, of sheer sophistication and detail, the pretense is a great deal more complex at Harvard or at M.I.T. than in a
Fifth Grade classroom; yet the center of the myth remains unchanged. "Free expression," "open market of ideas," words of
this kind are stated and restated in the publications and the speeches
of such men as Handlin, Hook and Nathan Glazer, with all the zeal,
reiteration and hypnosis of the most expensive media-promotion.
Phrases like these, and their summation in the single formula of
Civil Liberties, assure us all the right to speak our minds or act upon
those views which we *believe to be our own*. There is, however,
one essential item absent from this presentation: Intellectual license
is not serious or substantial — certainly it is formidably circum-
scribed in its results — if, prior to words and long-preceding

deeds, our yearnings themselves are in such firm constraint that we no longer even wish to do that which, if we *could* wish it in large numbers, colleges would then assuredly forbid.

It is not necessary for this social order — nor for any institution that provides the basic training for success and for survival in the field of forces that it represents — to withhold from its students many forms of free expression. The greater numbers have already handed in their most important forms of liberty long years before: those forms that have to do with hopes and wants, wishes and dreams, ethics and aspirations. The student or teacher who, in course of hours, days, semesters spent in public school and university, and many hours too of massive onslaught from a steady wave of media-control, learns how *not* to desire that which this social order does not wish him to desire (or else, desiring, no longer feels that his desires are the proper starting point for concrete deeds), a student or teacher trained *not* to believe that he is living in an intellectual prison, who does not know therefore that there are other worlds beyond his window, this student or teacher does not need to be forbidden many forms of freedom. Intellectual license, under such conditions, may well be official luxuries of every scholar. Words and deeds can be quite unconstrained if there is no danger, or else very little danger, that they will be generated by untrammeled minds or by unmanacled imaginations.

Nations which do not know how to get down to the roots must settle for the branches. Thus, in nations that our textbooks call totalitarian, strict controls obtain concerning press, T.V., public debate. These societies are like bad gardeners who spend whole days out in the hot sun pruning bushes, doing their best to cut down hopeless growths of undesired ideologies, because they do not yet have skillful means for poisoning the soil. Because they are old-fashioned, and are forced to strike with crude utensils at the full-grown foliage they did not know enough to poison in its bed, we are entitled to decree that they are brutal and undemocratic. By implication, we discern ourselves to be more civilized. The truth is that we simply know a better way to tend the garden.

Professors at our universities, with rare exceptions, are granted the theoretical right to advocate rebellion, to develop and reflect on Marxist ideologies, to argue for an end to private ownership of land, homes, factories and means of transportation. In the same sense, editors at Newsweek or The New York Times are free to view the Cuban Revolution as a positive step forward for humanity. It is a clever North American deception to allow professor, scholar, editor alike, to say what they please when we know well that what *they* please is what *we* like. When wishes, ideas and dreams themselves can be confined like this, words can be free. The bulls, once surgically restrained, receive all barnyard privileges. College professors, in the aftermath of proper preparation, are allowed their Civil Liberties.

To many, the views I hold in this respect will seem not only lacking in conventional politeness but lacking also in substantial precedent. The first is true. The second is an error. The same ideas have been expressed in every generation for a hundred years.

Charles Sumner, firebrand senator from Massachusetts who took to the U.S. Senate floor to launch a direct onslaught on slaveholders and their representatives in power, was judged unfit to teach at Harvard Law School. He recognized the reason and described it clearly in a letter to his brother: "I am too much . . . reformer . . . to be trusted." Wendell Phillips, the courageous lawyer who supported Garrison in face of mob attacks in Boston Common, denounced not only the dishonest stand of Harvard on the subject of slaveholders, but also its manipulation by the dominant business interests of the time. Garrison himself was dragged through Boston and came close to being lynched by State Street lawyers, business leaders, corporation heads, whose ethical preparation was delivered and received at Harvard College.

Emerson also had some memorable words to speak in this regard. "Harvard College," he wrote in 1861, "has no voice in Harvard College. State Street votes it down on every ballot." Everything is permitted in the university, he said, so long as it adorns the elegance of Boston. That which implies an ethical provocation is not given voice. Generosity of thought within this university, he said, has a bad name: "The youths come out decrepit citizens . . ."

The strongest statement of them all is that which Upton Sinclair set down in a volume called *The Goose-step,* published first in 1923. Sinclair had no fanciful illusions in regard to the realities of power

and class domination.   In each of the major universities which he
described, in aftermath of a cross-country tour in 1922, Sinclair
situated the real source of power in the largest local corporations.
Reed, in Oregon, was honored with the label of the college of "The
Lumber Trust."   Columbia received the title of "The House of
Morgan."   The University of Pennsylvania was described, in se-
quence, as "The House of U.G.I."   (United Gas) or else "The
University of Morgan-Drexel" (railroad and stockbrokers).   The
University of Idaho was called "The University of Anaconda."
Individuals die, he wrote, but the power of the ruling class goes on.
It is necessary too, he said, that new generations should be broken
for its service.   It is for this reason, above all, that colleges exist.

Sinclair saved his deepest vehemence for Harvard, an institution
which he labeled as "The College of Lee-Higginson" (investment
bankers).   We are told of Harvard, by its loyal friends, he wrote,
that it is liberal in its education policies.   Is it liberal also in the
policies by which it governs its investments?   "Do you suppose,"
he wrote, "the votes of Harvard . . . are . . . for policies of justice
and democracy in enterprises it exploits?"   If you suppose that, he
replied, you are naïve.   The votes of Harvard are cast, just as the
votes of any other business, for the largest dividends for Harvard.

With the same irreverence, Sinclair scrutinized the bias of the
course of study.   He spoke without much kindness of the so-called
"open market of ideas."   Course-study at Harvard, he observed, is
governed by "class ignorance, class fear and class repression."
Harvard, he said, proclaims its doors are open to all classes.   It
"sets forth statistics" to confirm that it is not a rich man's school.
Yet the bias of its courses — as much that which is kept out as that
which has been retained — reflects the wishes of the Harvard Corporation.   The revolutionary struggles of the present period, he wrote,
are not presented to the students: "They go out ready to believe the
grotesque falsehoods which are served . . . to them . . ."

Time seems to make few changes.

I have in mind a day, about six years ago, when I returned to
Cambridge late one afternoon in May to visit with an English scholar
who had been one of my teachers when I was a senior.   I remember
that I spoke to him that day about the sense of vested interest men

and women in the university inevitably feel in the denial or non-recognition of those very disproportions and unequal opportunities for economic self-promotion which they presently enjoy. I spoke, for example, of the overwhelming gulf between the elegant room in which we sat and spoke that afternoon, the garden outside, the street beyond, the mood and atmosphere it all conveyed — and those more bitter and far less consoling streets of turmoil, need and devastation that he seldom saw, traversed or even thought of.

He was polite, relaxed, attentive and unhostile. He nodded, reflected, took off his spectacles, put hand to chin and studied me a while, knocked out his pipe-ash on the round cork knob within the center of a pewter bowl, looked out the window with a weary sense of aging decency, pressed thumb and finger to his brow in old and practiced sense of sorrowful exhaustion. He said to me: "Of course it's so . . . Of course it's not correct. It isn't right for some to have so much, and others have so little. It isn't right. It isn't necessary. We don't need all this surfeit and excess."

He sits and speaks. I listen and I hear. He says he does not need what he now views, possesses, holds, enjoys, depends on; yet the truth, I think, is that he *does*. He does need life set up, protected, ordered, in this way. He cannot live without it. Still less can he emancipate himself from the remarkable belief that his career, his work and his reward exist *in vacuo;* that little or none of it is tied to hunger, need or devastation of those children, men and women whom he cannot see and does not know; those, for example, who have been consistently excluded from that competition in which he was victor only by default. Nor, to be candid, do I think that he does literally believe that all those needs he hears of, and those abstract agonies to which his syllables of decency reply, are *genuine* needs and *actual* and *unquestioned* agonies. I do not think that he believes it. I do not think that he can dare to give belief to this. If he did, I think his whole world would begin to crumble. He would be forced to take his children out of segregated private schools. He would be forced to question his own right to two homes: one up in New Hampshire, one here in this perfect shaded lane, off Kirkland Street. I ask myself: Could he survive these kinds of questions, self-imposed? If so: What answers could he summon forth?

He sits here now and looks out, thoughtfully, into the courtyard.

The sun reflects and shivers in the garden window, patterned with small panes behind his desk. The glowing space of light and warmth within this room, along the book shelves and above the desk, summon for me a wealth of English recollections, olden days in ancient places green and golden, many good hours of secure existence. I think of this also: lead-paint plaster, roach-invasion, rat-infestation of those tenement-quarters on the other side of town in which ten thousand black and Puerto Rican families lead their hungry, hot and agonizing lives. I ask myself: Is it for this, for disproportions on this scale, that all his labors, dreams and hours were exacted and expended? Is it for this that he has given thirty years to the analysis and explication of the work of Mann and Kafka, Auden, Eliot, John Donne?

Gandhi, asked once what it was that made him the most sad in life, is said to have given this reply: "the hardness of heart of the well-educated." The genteel English scholar in his sun-bathed study does not seem to go with words like coldness, emptiness of love or barrenness of soul. Gandhi had in mind perhaps a less benign and more Imperial prototype; yet there is a form of unresponsive love and of Inert Concern which blesses no more, and damages no less, than straightforward cynicism. Quiet compassion and relaxed (i.e., controllable) self-accusation are no less evil in their end-results than those more blatant actions of the redneck cop, ill-educated soldier, ice-cold corporation leader. Different in temper, intellectual dispassion of this kind is nonetheless the same in faithful service of an unjust social order. Less explicit in form, it is no less brutal in its operation. Covered with ivy, and pronounced with low-key, understated intonations, it is no less final in its ultimate exactions.

XVIII. INEXORABLE DECISIONS

"Those who profess to freedom . . . yet deprecate agitation
are men who want crops without plowing . . . They want rain
without thunder and lightning. They want the ocean without
the awful roar of its many waters."

— Frederick Douglass

THE UNITED STATES, within this formidable year of 1975, is a rich,
benevolent, sophisticated, murderous, well-mannered and exquisite
social order. There is time and money and resources to conciliate us
all: seminars for the dead man, sociologists for the damned, psy-
choanalysis for the indignant, prison cells for those — too few —
who will not break and buckle in the requisite positions of capitulation, self-cancellation or surrender.

In many societies, the only method of control is frank repression.
In this society, ten decades of experience in counter-revolutionary
rule have trained our leaders in the best of ways to undermine revolt. Physical threat and massive presence of police are used here
only as a last resort: above all in those sections of the cities, or in
relation to those portions of the population, where our hypocritical
pretense of abhorrence at the use of force is temporarily erased by
biological discrimination. In general, methods of direct repression
are not necessary.

In most cases, what we do instead is not to suppress but to divert
the revolutionary instincts of our children. We do it by the use of
words and the co-option of catch phrases. We do it by the designation of a sanctioned counterculture. We do it through those technological devices which I have described above. Certain of these
transformations do, within strict limits, introduce a sense of heightened openness and independence; yet the limits are such as to

leave sacrosanct all basic elements of privilege and exploitation. At best these substitutes create a broader spectrum of potential channels for arriving at the same familiar harbors.

In the face of it all, no matter what they read, think and believe, still I hear friends — teachers in public school — speaking in surprised or even outraged tones over the sudden pressure brought to bear upon an innovative or "experimental" school that seemed for just a little while to be moving onward to some sort of new and promising "wide-open" freedom. Kids were going to probe into the actions of their School Board, examine operations of the power-apparatus of big business, scrutinize the Congress and Department of Defense, analyze the offerings of press and T.V., take sides with the powerless against the rich and strong. When it does not end like this at all, they seem astonished and come out in numbers to protest the great deception that they were so willingly led into.

How many years, how many hours, how many self-invited disappointments will it take before these people can achieve a posture of intelligent rebellion? Public schools are not intended to lead children into avenues of ethics, candor or dissent. Kids within these schools are not expected to come even close to speculations of this kind. They are intended to think *about*, not *into*. They are intended to "imagine a rebellion" built of tape-recorded interviews with the preacher, the police chief or the secretary to the members of the City Council; of impotent mornings spent on walking tours at local factories and public libraries, radio and T.V. stations; of glass-protected bus trips to a nearby ghetto. They are intended to conceive themselves to be free people by the exercise of unimportant liberties and semblances of ineffective option. The goal is not that they *be* potent, but that they never get the chance to recognize their impotence head-on.

Every few years, as we have seen, a school pops up which seems to be less candidly deceptive than the old-time institution. Whether because, in a particular case, a principal sees reason to confront the ordinary expectations of the public school, or because it is believed in certain situations that some forms of innovative freedom will assist in letting off hot air, or else because of absence of consistent supervision in a large bureaucracy, it is a fact that *certain* schools and *certain* teachers sometimes will do *certain* things that seem to be experimental or progressive. Yet it is dishonest, in the wake of all we know and understand, to act as if we do not recognize quite well the reason for existence of the public school.

The school, which is administered and financed by decision of elected politicians, or else of bureaucrats selected by them, is expected to develop, nurture and reward a series of well-broken, homogeneous generations. Its obligation, prior to all other jobs, is to train another generation every time which will be prepared to make the same decisions as the one that came before: proud of its country, unquestioning of its motives, antagonistic to all foreign ideologies, well-protected against ethical considerations other than those of an attractive and self-deprecating kind which serve to decorate its overall self-interest. School does not exist to foster ethics or upheaval. It exists to stabilize the status quo. It exists to train a population which is subject to the power of such instruments of mass-persuasion as the social order has at hand. It exists to get its citizens prepared for moral compromise. It exists to get its citizens prepared to make peace with the ethical imperfections of their rulers. It exists to reconcile its children, in advance, to the inhuman posture of their nation in the world, to an accepted culture of excess in their own homes, to a life of self-awarded anaesthesia in the face of misery on every side.

The man who sits down to an ample piece of beef, who smiles with appetite and nods with satisfaction in recognition of his own good fortune, must not be allowed to dream from this day on that he can dine in moral isolation or in philosophic quarantine. Right by his table stand those starving millions whom he has chosen, with benign delight, to disavow. For him, for others like him, it may be the cell-divisions and the years of self-deceit have done their work too well. It is not in the stars for him to interrupt his meal, put down his fork and knife, wipe off that smile of sleek and cogent satisfaction from his flesh-embedded brow. He lives, and has so lived for years, surrounded by headwaiters. Their task is, first, to spare him from the need to look for too long on the unaesthetic rib cage of the poor — then, if he must, to reassure him that the life within the cage is not worth weeping over. We are victims of a desperate fraud if we believe that we can turn the tables in this land without the price of powerful confrontation and upheaval.

This point is not a pedagogic point alone. It is, by now, a well-implanted North American delusion. The liberal myth is that the wars can cease, the poor can sleep, the schools can prosper and the children of the poor can learn, aspire and thrive, while we who have for these long years enjoyed the proceeds of their hunger, segregation, fear, need suffer nothing. It is not so. We cannot continue with our theater-evenings, garden clubs and tea if we would like to redirect priorities and salvage dying children. The passive, tranquil and protected lives rich people lead depend on strongly armed police, well-demarcated ghettos. The price of liberation for more than a million children in the New York City schools might well be loss of sleep and intervention in the course of peaceful dreams for people fifty miles away. The price of plans to cure ten thousand heroin addicts in the Boston slums might well be a lack of private space for wealthy men and women in the most expensive hospitals and clinics. Art shows, string quartets, luncheon clubs and pleasant dining places might well suffer loss of customers and cash.

These, indeed, may prove to be the least perceptible of payments paid to meet the price of justice. Privileged surgery to serve the few might yield at last to public health and decent food to serve the millions. If we should wish to be quite sure that every mother of a new-born child receives the humane care which she and that young child require, we must expect that there will be no private rooms for anyone at *any* price next year. If we should wish to be quite sure that there will be no family dwelling in a close and crowded tenement-sty, it is also clear that cities like my own cannot allow the rich to occupy the newest plazas and most elegant pavilions built with public funds.

Teachers, then, should not delude themselves about the task ahead. The walls that stand around the unjust world in which the U.S. schools now toil, exist and thrive will not be leveled by the sound of trumpets or by another research project funded by the Carnegie Foundation. There is a terrible yearning in us all for almost any form of warm, placating and believable deception: anything it seems, no matter of what shape or origin, so long as we shall not be forced by our own words to place our bodies on the line, or risk our lives for our beliefs. We turn in desperation to complex technologies (called "systems"), new phantasies of open schools within closed buildings, new phrases ("Discovery," "The Integrated Day") for old deceptions. *What is, in fact, the meaning of alternatives "within the system" if the system is, itself, the primary vehicle of state-control?*

The school that flies the flag and conscientiously serves the interests of that flag cannot serve those of justice. Schools cannot at once both socialize to the values of an oppressor and toil for the liberation and the potency of the oppressed. If innovation is profound, it is subversive. If it is subversive, it is incompatible with the prime responsibilities of public school. It is very tempting to descend upon rare moments of apparent freedom, occasioned in most cases by a situation of inept coordination or of unexpected outcome, and to try to give the system "credit," as it were, for its own slip-up. To do this is, however, to avoid the realistic heart of the whole issue. Harvard gets no credit for Peter Seeger and Thoreau. The Federal Prison System gets no prize for Malcolm X.

In most liberal writings on the transformation of the public schools, there is the quiet and reiterated myth that education can be at once profound, subversive and permitted. Ivan Illich, speaking of Paulo Freire, writes these words: "I do not believe that any government now in power can permit an educational process which follows his principles to be developed." This is the kind of direct statement that we try, in every case, to blur, evade, deny. Freire tells us many times, and in a number of clear ways: We cannot be, at once, "for freedom" and "for socialization." The teacher who decides for freedom in a public school may or may not be able to disguise this provocation in a form that will appear innocuous to supervisors and co-workers. In the long run, however, it is essential that he understand that what he does cannot be tolerated. If it is tolerable, subsidized and publicly endorsed, it is because it is not the real thing.

If it *is* the real thing, then it is essential that he understand that what he does is something that he is not *asked* to do: something as well for which he will be forced to pay a price. Civil disobedience *does* lead to prison. A clear commitment to a pedagogic and political upheaval does, at some point, lead to almost certain and inevitable expulsion from the public schools. Ethical struggle, in an unjust nation, cannot fail to take on the dimensions of a revolutionary labor. No matter how we long to see it in less formidable lines, there is no way to get around the high stakes that are now before us.

In the moment when a teacher sets aside the myth of Neutral Education, he sets aside as well the role of quiet, passive and subservient acolyte of nation, state and social order. To the degree that he elects to stay *within* the public education apparatus, to this degree he undertakes a role which is not "innocent" but tactical in all respects. His function, from this moment on, is to assign connections, to demonstrate the fraudulence of empty options, to undermine the walls of anaesthetic self-protection, to take out low-watt issues and replace them by high-voltage questions, to generate the confidence for insurrectionary actions, to instigate the capability to build up lines of strong and lasting loyalties among like-minded souls — then, too, and at the proper time, to build the readiness for stark and vigorous acts of intervention in the face of pain.

The tenor of the school-reform discussion for at least ten years has been, in its main outlines: therapeutic, Hip, mechanical or "clever." In terms of politics, it has been antiseptic. In terms of confrontation, it has been dishonest. In terms of orientation, it has taken clearance from the universities, cash from the White House, license and decor from The New Republic. The task before us now is to confront ourselves and our co-workers with the implications of our present, devious, non-neutral situation: a situation which amounts too often to a tacit, often criminal collusion with explicit evil. It is our task to force hard issues of this shape and character in terms which cannot be contained, sidestepped, ignored: then to go on, with those who hold our views, to fashion methods of strategic intervention on a scale some of us have not dared to speak of up to now.

"Our educational system," Upton Sinclair wrote within the final pages of *The Goose-step,* "is in the hands of its last organized enemy . . . class greed . . . based upon economic privilege. To slay that monster is to set free all the future." If some of us wish to take a role in liberation of the future he describes, it is too late to talk, debate, discuss — then say it all once more. It is our need to start to do the work to reconstruct the room in which our conscience lives. We must not fool ourselves: nor, least of all, our students and co-workers. Thousands will be out on battle lines for decades. Ten years hence, some of us will no longer be alive.

The weakest form of ethical rebellion, in my own belief, is that which fails to recognize its probable results in terms of enmities created and anxieties be-stirred.

I find the most predictable forms of intellectual retaliation among those tactful, passive, yet well-meaning souls: the Inert Rebels. Those closest to the edge of heart's conversion live in the deepest terror of its possible appeal. There is a whole battalion of such terrified and self-debilitated people here in Cambridge, New York and New Haven, men and women who hold decent views and harbor ethical ideals, yet do not feel the obligation to take action on their own beliefs. They write, converse and lecture honorably on subjects of the kind under discussion here, yet do not choose to live out on the edge of economic, ideological or social risk — and see no reason why they should.

There is one classic method which such men and women use in seeking to dismiss disturbing subject-matter or disturbing views. What people often do, when they are locked within essentially untenable positions, is to solicit evidence which they know well to be available somehow, but which they also know their interlocutor (the author, in this case) will not be able to supply, or not in the *form* which will dismiss the *kind* of question they have had the shrewdness to bring forward. His failure to do so at that moment (or within that book) conveniently permits them to dismiss from mind the fact that they know well the evidence *exists*.

Similar to this is a device by which so many liberal and intimidated people seek to libel an idea, the truth of which they secretly believe, by raising doubts about the *terms* in which it is presented. Thus, for example, we will often hear such people say: "It is a pity. He has a good idea; but he has spoiled it by stating it with so much indignation. He overstates. He is unnecessarily intense . . . He is too hostile, or too moralistic, or too unforgiving . . ." They may be right within the substance of their condemnation; yet it is remarkable that they are able, by this means, to hide from mind the troubling idea that — if for just one moment they are willing to dismiss the *manner* of the writer's presentation — they may be deeply threatened by the truth he has to bear.   In other words, beyond their quarrel with the way he chooses to condemn, they are aware that he is honest in this condemnation.   Somewhere at the distant edge of truth and fear, they also recognize one other painful fact: *They are the objects of his condemnation.*

This is a book which, in a number of respects, "contains itself" or, better said, "contains the very terms by which it can be either criticized or else received as condemnation."   It is not going to be painless, therefore, for an ethical reader to dismiss the challenge that this labor poses to his own career.   In "school-terms," I can be still more precise: This book is not a call for ten more years of pedagogic games, of sandals, smiles and amusing teachers without passions, principles or lesson-plans.   It is a call, instead, for tactics, plans, scenarios of clear and conscious and intentional subversion of the public schools.   The object of this book is not amelioration but sophisticated and prepared rebellion.   Nor can an honorable person soothe his conscience with the old excuse that I refuse to tell him just exactly *what to do.*   Demolition workers are not asked to be good architects as well.   Nor, in any field, have we the right to ask this kind of dual labor in a single hour or a single work.

I have now in preparation, and would like to see in print within another year, a book of "details" — technical, pragmatic, tactical — for people working to confront the process of indoctrination as they face it, day to day, within the U.S. public schools.   The book, however, is not meant to be a substitute for independent or autonomous imaginations working out their own strategic plans.   In the long run, words that come from an old union-labor organizing song still stand and hold: "You've got to go and join up on your own."   People in Sioux City, San Antonio and San Diego can begin to guess, and blueprint, what they need to do, and how, with whom, by what preliminary stages and with what reliable co-workers.   If these people do not make the first preliminary choices on their own, they cannot hope to find the answer in a book by someone else.

This final word.

If, and when, a teacher does take action, and at length should be expelled from public school, it is important that he understand that this is not (unless he wishes) the last chapter of his work and struggle in the lives of children. In some ways, it proves much the reverse. Ejection, in itself — if not perceived in naïve fashion — can be a powerful weapon to expose the public process of indoctrination for its real intent. Rebels in religious history, as numerous paintings and church sculpture can attest, are noted far more often in the act of leaving churches, with robes flying and a look of terror in their eyes, than in the action of respectful entrance. Children learn a great deal more, in my belief, out of the recognition of the price that must be paid by those whom public schools cannot contain, or do not dare to keep, than from ten thousand lessons on Thoreau or Malcolm X.

None of the above, of course, diminishes the high risk which is constantly at stake for any teacher who does not step back, in fear and hesitation, from the question which this book repeatedly presents. It is, moreover, a much greater risk, I know, for those who are my elders, by as much as twenty-five or thirty years and have, therefore, a deeper, more intense, time-ratified investment in the present structure of credentials and rewards. It is, therefore, no easy thing to ask or undertake; yet it is the only honest plea that I can make.

Those who share even a fraction of the viewpoints offered in this book cannot hope to get away unscathed by those whose values and complacence they endanger or condemn. Power knows where its own interest lies; so too do those machineries that serve and strengthen power. School indoctrination is the keystone of a mighty archway in this land. It will not be removed without grave consequences for the structure it supports. Nor will it be taken out without the kind of struggle and the kind of sacrifice that great events and serious human transformations always call for.

Exiles

EXILES

"The form of witness may vary . . . Witness itself, however, is an indispensable element of revolutionary action . . . All authentic . . . witness involves the daring to run risks . . ."
— Paulo Freire

I HAVE SPOKEN several times of Paulo Freire.

Freire is a Christian Marxist, of a gentle, strong, deeply reflective character, who worked for years teaching of "word and praxis" in the poorest sections of Northeast Brazil. After the C.I.A. contrived the overthrow of a "permissive" (semi-democratic) government in 1964, in order to install the strong dictatorship which has remained in power ever since, Freire was thrown into prison, but was freed at length by intercession of the Catholic Church. Already viewed by many as the most distinguished educator in the Third World, Freire found asylum first in Chile, then in Mexico, then — too briefly — here in Massachusetts. For most of one year he lived in a relatively poor neighborhood of Cambridge. Each Sunday afternoon, for many weeks, I used to visit him.

We would sit and talk and drink strong black Brazilian coffee for long hours. During those months he supervised translation of two of his books, led independent seminars and taught at Harvard also. Nonetheless, he did not win an offer of professorship. Harvard, during those years, held spaces open for such men as Galbraith, Moynihan and Kissinger; yet even the Harvard School of Education could not find room for Paulo Freire.

One day, January 1970, he packed his books and papers once again.

The last time that we spoke was just before he handed in his boarding pass to step onto a plane for Switzerland. We stood together just beside the Air France Gate within the International Departure Lounge. Throughout the time that I had known him during the preceding fall, Freire had held back always in our conversations, limiting his words to academic terms and intellectual considerations. Now, as we stood and spoke before he left for what I knew would be at least a year, and probably the full five years, of silence, distance and occasionally perhaps some slender airmail envelope from Switzerland, he stopped, "stopped everything" somehow, like a movie stopping, and he held me strongly by the arms, the way that people do sometimes in South America to say good-bye, and used a kind of language he had never used before, and chose a set of words that he had never spoken.

He said to me: "Jonathan, you are a product of this country and an object of its processes of preparation, as much as any adult that you know — or any child whom you serve as teacher. You must not think that you can do the kinds of things that we have talked about this year unless you are prepared to pay a serious price." Then he said, at last, right there within the modern airport, with all its bells and lights and piped-in music, flight announcements and expensive-looking travelers with their passports and their tickets all around, but as if with hesitation about speaking to me, or anyone, this way: "A young man is going to have to die in certain ways in order to become the kind of man he needs to be." Then he was through the gate and down the tunnel to Geneva.

As I drove back into the city, it was with a sense of loneliness that I have almost never felt before, except perhaps when I was quite young. In part, it was because I simply would *miss* Frèire. He is one of the kindest men on earth and, like my father, a man who took me seriously and spoke to me, at times that counted, in a voice that made me braver, not more cautious. Yet also it was because the way he spoke made me feel less of an affinity to the city that I knew, and therefore less protected by it, than I felt before. The lights along the river did not seem to belong to me now so much as it had seemed at other times; and when I came home to my apartment in the city, walled like that of many other people of my age and my ideas with words and photographs of certain people I admire or revere, I felt a deepened and more deepened sense of fear. In the days that followed, I began to write the first few pages of this book.

I do not feel awkward, though I did for years, to speak of my affection for some of those older people whom I trust and love. The faces and words along the walls of my apartment became more real and more like mandates for me in those hours. I think the reverence that we feel for men and women who have been true teachers, and the way *that* love can change our lives, our vision, our perception of all things we know, and open up new areas of freedom and imagination we have never felt, after certain periods of loneliness that we have never undergone — that this is, in the long run, what education *is,* and nothing else *but* this.

Many young people do not like to think that they will need the consolation or the borrowed strength of older men and women. In part, this is because they may not know the kinds of people I now have in mind. If they do, they have often been afraid to open up their hearts for fear of being disappointed. Yet there have been many who, in struggle with themselves, were not reluctant to take strength and courage from those who have gone before. When Cesar Chavez started to fast, in very great pain he looked up to the photograph of Gandhi. When Gandhi went to prison in South Africa in 1908, he read the words of Thoreau and Saint Francis. When Dr. King began his lonely hours in Montgomery Jail, he turned for strength to writings left by Gandhi.

It may be that discipleship like this is, in the last event, the only thing that can empower a person to live by his beliefs. If there is not the reassurance of this love, I do not know if we will ever find the will to overcome the dangers and the admonitions that are placed before us. Those dangers, of course, are, in large part, for real; and all those admonitions on the part of our own folks are not deluded or co-optive in their goals. Our folks remember much that we forget. Many have risked their lives, careers and friendships in the years since World War Two. More will be obliged to take those risks within the years ahead. There is a price to pay, and a great struggle of the body and the spirit to be undertaken. I see no way in which a serious man or woman can escape the implications of these words.

Notes

NOTES

page

Epigraph is quoted from *Erik H. Erikson, The Growth of His Work,* by Robert Coles; Atlantic-Little, Brown, 1970. See page 39.

I. *Deceptions of the Nineteen Sixties*

2   Joao Coutinho is quoted from his Preface to Paulo Freire's article, "Cultural Action for Freedom," published in pamphlet form by the *Harvard Educational Review* and the Center for the Study of Development and Social Change, 1970. See page vi.

3   Horace Mann is quoted from *The Great School Legend,* by Colin Greer; Viking Press, 1973. See page 75. The original source for this quotation is Mann's "Seventh Annual Report of the Secretary of the Board," Boston, 1844.

For a carefully drawn historical analysis of how the U.S. system of education works as agent of class-stratification, see "How the School System is Rigged for Failure," by Paul Lauter and Florence Howe, *New York Review of Books,* June 18, 1970.

4   Jules Henry is quoted from *Culture Against Man;* Vintage Books, 1965. See pages 283 and 291.

John Kenneth Galbraith's views are paraphrased from *The New Industrial State;* Signet Books, 1968. See page 326.

II. *Straightforward Lies*

7   Quotation at head of Chapter II is taken from *World Geography,* by John H. Bradley; Ginn and Co. (Xerox Corp.), 1971. See page 426.

For an equally evasive student text on the same subject, see *Communist China,* by Donald W. Oliver and Fred M. Newmann; American Education Publications (Xerox Corp.), 1972.

9   For an excellent example of a textbook that disguises U.S. profit-motive in South America, see *Changing Latin America;* American Education Publications (Xerox Corp.), 1969.

John Kenneth Galbraith is quoted from *The New Industrial State.* See page 302.

Nixon passage is quoted from dust-jacket copy: *Richard Nixon,* by Helen D. Olds; Putnam, 1970.

10   It *is* possible to reject the Pledge. For news of a successful court case, see "Yes for Standing Silent," *New York Times,* November 19, 1972. See also, "New Move Underway to Rewrite 'The Pledge,' " *Boston Globe,* January 10, 1971. For an account of one student who had courage to refuse the Flag Pledge and

won vindication in the courts, see "Girl's Flag-Carrying Called 'Illegal,' 'Bizarre,' " *Boston Globe,* November 18, 1970. A much more recent case, involving the refusal of a teacher, is documented in an excellent article, "A Teacher's Right to Shun Pledge to the Flag," *New York Times,* February 18, 1974.

12 Forty thousand infant deaths attributed to absence of appropriate prenatal, pediatric and obstetric care each year: Statistics are those of H.E.W., as quoted in the *Boston Globe,* January 17, 1971.

III. *Saying No*

16 Georges Bernanos is quoted from *Tradition of Freedom;* Dennis Dobson, 1950. See page 161.

Quote on obedience is taken from "Curriculum Guide in Character Education," School Document Number 11, 1962. See *Death at an Early Age;* Bantam Books, 1968, page 180.

Jules Henry is quoted from *Jules Henry on Education;* Vintage Books, 1972. See page 154. For Jules Henry's remarks on how schools train us into acquiescence, see also pages 107–116.

19 The death of civil rights leader, Doris Bland, as consequence of carelessness in supervision, is only one of several instances of institutional racism in Boston's medical profession. For additional documentation, see "A Matter of Life and Death," *Ramparts,* April 1973.

22 The *New York Times* article mentioned here is quoted in *The American Serfs,* by Paul Good; Ballantine Books, 1968. See page 151.

Testimony of witnesses quoted on this page: See *Let Them Eat Promises,* by Nick Kotz; Prentice-Hall, 1969, page 106.

26 An eloquent example of the power to transcend inhibition and to SAY NO is Michael Ferber's statement "A Time to Say No," presented at the Arlington Street Church, Boston, at the time of his conviction for civil disobedience in refusal to accept induction to the U.S. Army for intended service in Vietnam. First published in *Resistance,* June 15, 1968, the speech is now printed in *The New Left: A Documentary History,* by Massimo Teodori; Bobbs-Merrill, 1969.

IV. *No Connections*

27 Marcus Raskin demonstrates how the Myth of No Connections, once allowed to enter our thoughts in school, proceeds to color more and more of our perceptions:

> In the schools, reality is presented as a series of discrete events and harsh specialized courses which are not even pasted together . . . Likewise, in the media one is presented with the 'news' . . . in discrete unrelated ways.

See *Being and Doing;* Random House, 1971, pages 156–157.

30 For readers who adhere still to the myth of a large, free-flowing and amorphous middle class, in which there might be neither victim nor oppressor, several recent books and documents will be instructive. For statistics on class-levels in the U.S., see *The Politics of History,* by Howard Zinn; Beacon Press, 1971. For a conclusive analysis of class structure in the U.S., see "The Working Class

Majority," by Andrew Levison, *The New Yorker*, September 2, 1974. See also *The Myth of the Middle Class*, by Richard Parker; Liveright, 1972.

32, 33   Leo Tolstoi is quoted from *The Kingdom of God Is Within You;* Noonday Press, 1961. See pages 294, 324, 349–350 and 356–358.

34   For more information on the business practices of slumlord Maurice Gordon, see *Boston Globe,* May 2 and 3, 1971.

35   Robert Coles is quoted from two sources: *The Geography of Faith;* Beacon Press, 1971, page 99; and "Dialogue Underground: II," *New York Review of Books,* March 25, 1971.

V. *Progress*

38   Albert Camus is quoted from *The Rebel;* Vintage Books, 1956. See page 194.

Two recent publications for classroom use which lead the student to a false impression of inevitable progress are: *Profile USA: The Census and its Meaning*, by Donald W. Oliver and Fred M. Newmann; American Education Publications (Xerox Corp.),1971; and *Race and Education: Integration and Community Control*, by John C. Baker; American Education Publications (Xerox Corp.), 1971.

40   Ghandi is quoted from *Ghandi's Truth*, by Erik Erikson; W. W. Norton, 1969. See page 170.

45   For evidence of deterioration in health conditions and nutrition of the poor, numerous documents exist in records of the Senate Select Committee on Nutrition and Human Needs. For evidence of increase in hunger, see "Senators Begin Review of Hunger," *Boston Globe*, June 19, 1974. For dramatic demonstration of the lack of progress in the areas of health care, education, malnutrition in the Northern slums, see "Rage Permeates All Facets of Life in the South Bronx, *New York Times*, January 17, 1973. For more recent and explicit evidence on the same subject, see "Hunger Crisis," published in *Fellowship* magazine, January–February 1975. (See also footnote for page 121).

The press, though dominated by the Myth of Progress, occasionally allows a piece which offers startling evidence of deterioration to reach print. Such articles as "Ghetto Life Gets Worse Since '60s," *Boston Globe*, April 16, 1972, and Homer Bigart's series "Hunger in America," *New York Times*, February 16–20, 1969, are rare. It is far more common to find evidence of efforts to withhold the facts, or else the vague and uncommitted article which lists statistics but refuses to make the obvious conclusions. See "Nixon-Negro Feud Spells Danger," *Boston Globe*, January 4, 1970.

VI. *Sunday Afternoon Neurosis*

51   Richard Means is quoted from *The Ethical Imperative;* Doubleday, 1969. See pages 146–147.

Rose H. Agree and Norman J. Ackerman confront the role of death within a child's education in their essay, "Why Children Must Mourn," from *Teacher*, October 1972.

John S. Mann is quoted from an unpublished paper presented to the John Dewey

page

Society, March 19, 1973, in Minneapolis, Minnesota. The essay is titled "In-equality and Education: A Critique of Liberal Pedagogy."

53 George Orwell is quoted from *In Front Of Your Nose*, volume 4 of *The Collected Essays, Journalism and Letters of George Orwell*, edited by Sonia Orwell and Ian Angus; Harcourt, Brace and World, 1968. See page 136.

Reference to Pentagon experts is quoted from *Lawrence and Oppenheimer*, by Nuel Pharr Davis; Simon and Schuster, 1968. See page 247.

54 For courtroom discussion of the use of the word "waste," and the phrase "a very negative emotional reaction," see the *New York Times*, February 23, 1971.

For additional quotations from the unnamed soldier at My Lai, see "It Wasn't Any Big Deal, Sir," *Boston Globe*, March 31, 1971.

Cesar Chavez is quoted from "Profiles: Organizer" (Part II), *The New Yorker*, June 28, 1969.

Records of a generation educated into anaesthesia in the face of horror have flooded U.S. newspapers through the past ten years. Articles such as "Soldier Boasts After Shooting Child in the Neck," *Boston Globe*, May 26, 1970, and "War is an Abstraction to Naval Gunners off North Viet," *Washington Post*, June 28, 1972, are so common now as to be constant witness to our state of anaesthesia. The American press has found it easier to analyze, and to describe, the terminology and weaponry of war than to portray the havoc they produce. See "Let's Say It Right," *New York Times*, January 11, 1970, and "The B-52 — One of History's Most Indiscriminate and Destructive Weapons," *Boston Globe*, May 31, 1971.

56 Robert Jay Lifton is quoted from *Boundaries;* Vintage Books, 1970. See page 32.

Paul Goodman is quoted from *Growing Up Absurd;* Vintage Books, 1970. See page 72 and chapter on "An Apparently Closed Room."

57 For reference to Lawrence Kohlberg's system of morality levels, see *Moral Education/Five Lectures*, edited by Nancy and Theodore Sizer; Harvard University Press, 1970, pages 57–83. An outline of this system appears as well in an American Education Publications booklet for use in the public schools, titled *Moral Reasoning*, by Alan Lockwood; 1972.

61 Paulo Freire is quoted from *Pedagogy of the Oppressed;* Herder and Herder, 1972. See page 31.

Jane Addams has this to say about the "appropriate grade level" syndrome:

> It was not until years afterward that I came upon Tolstoi's phrase 'the snare of preparation,' which he insists we spread before the feet of young people, hopelessly entangling them in a curious inactivity at the very period of life when they are longing to construct the world anew and to conform it to their own ideals.

See "The Snare of Preparation," by Peter Clecak, *American Scholar*, Autumn 1969.

VII. *Great Men and Women*

63 Helen Keller is quoted here from *The Little Red White and Blue Book*, by Johnny (Appleseed) Rossen; Grove Press, 1969. See page 84. This book is a

collection of quotations from a number of distinguished men and women who
are canonized in U.S. history. The irreverent tone of the quotations chosen
from our "Founding Fathers" makes this book a small but useful instrument for
change.

The same quotation appears, in its original context, in *Helen Keller: Her
Socialist Years,* edited by Philip Foner; International Publishers, 1967. See
page 84.

64, 65   Henry David Thoreau is quoted from *Walden and Civil Disobedience;* Washington Square Press, 1968. See pages 7, 55, 344, 346 and 351.

67   The passage on Helen Keller quoted here is a pastiche of standard biographical
works on Keller now present in the public schools.

67, 68, 69   Helen Keller is quoted from *Helen Keller: Her Socialist Years.* See pages
31, 43, 55, 56, 75 and 84.

70   Edgar Friedenberg is quoted from *The Vanishing Adolescent;* Dell, 1972. See
page 76.

71   Robert Coles is quoted from his work on Erik Erikson. See page 339.

VIII. *First Person*

74   Erik Erikson is quoted from his essay, "The Problem of Ego Identity," in
Identity and the Life Cycle, volume I, number 1 of *Psychological Issues;* International Universities Press, 1959. See page 129. This paper was originally
published in the *Journal of the American Psychoanalytic Association,* volume
IV, 1956. The essay has been recently revised as "Identity Confusion in Life
History and Case History," chapter 4 of *Identity: Youth and Crisis;* Norton,
1968. See page 173.

Henry David Thoreau is quoted from *Walden and Civil Disobedience.* See
page 1.

76   The assignment for term-papers is found in *Uptaught,* by Ken Macrorie; Hay-
den Book Co., 1970. See page 70.

In a remarkable example of scholarly abdication of the self, Richard Sennet and
Jonathan Cobb discuss what they see as the inability of an alienated working
class to "say I" — only to state their own conclusions in this essay in the very
language they deplore. See "They Never Say 'I,' " *Boston Globe,* December
15, 1972.

79   Truman Nelson is paraphrased here from *The Sin of the Prophet;* Little, Brown,
1952. See page 450.

IX. *Impotence*

84   Kenneth Keniston is quoted from his essay "Escape from Alienation," reprinted in *Contemporary Moral Issues,* edited by Harry K. Girvetz; Wads-
worth Publishing Co., 1968. See page 562.

86   St. John 16:24.

91, 92   This account of a reporter's classroom visit is presented in the piece, "PS 27
in New York's Southeast Bronx," by Nina McCain, *Boston Globe,* March 22,
1970.

page

94 Robert Coles is quoted from his work on Erik Erikson. See page 362.

Howard Zinn elaborates on Fake Humblehood in these terms:

> What I am criticizing here is not the modesty which scholars might justifiably have about the impact of their work, but the idea that such impact should not be their purpose.

See *The Politics of History,* page 308.

X. *Enemies of Revolution*

95 For the quotation at the head of chapter X, see the contents page of *Life,* May 29, 1970.

Lawrence Kohlberg is quoted from his essay, "Education for Justice," Ernest Burton lecture on Moral Education, Harvard University, April 23, 1968.

George Counts is quoted from *Dare the School Build a New Social Order?;* John Day Company, 1969. See page 27.

96 Several articles which illustrate the pretense of free options have been published in the past five years:

"The Elementary School of the Future," *American Teacher,* January 1974.
"The Informal Class . . ." by Charles E. Silberman, *Boston Globe,* March 21, 1971.
"Revolution in the Classroom," by James Worsham, *Boston Globe,* January 14, 1973.

97 John Mann is quoted from his paper, "The Student Rights Strategy," published in *Theory Into Practice,* volume X, number 5, December 1971.

Paul Goodman is paraphrased here from *Utopian Essays and Practical Proposals;* Random House, 1962. See page 5.

98 For an examination of Rousseau's idea of the concept "open education," see "The Appearance of Freedom," *New Schools Exchange Newsletter,* October 15, 1973.

99 John Kenneth Galbraith is quoted from *The New Industrial State.* See page 326.

100 Paulo Freire is quoted from an unpublished paper, "The Role of the Social Worker in the Process of Change," 1970.

101 Huston Smith elaborates on the theme suggested by the words of Gide in his article, "Two Kinds of Teaching," *The Key Reporter,* Summer 1973.

For an effective refutation of the possibilities for non-political or "neutral" education, see "The American Public School as a Political Entity." This is an unpublished paper by Eugene Mulcahy; copies available from the Shanti School, 480 Asylum Street, Hartford, Connecticut 06103.

102 For multiple examples of false options offered in the schools today by means of "educational technologies," see the following two items: "Good Morning Class . . . My Name is Bzzz Vzz, Crackle," by Michael Seltzer and Howard Krager, *New Schools Exchange Newsletter,* February 28, 1974, and the Annual Catalogue published by Selective Education Equipment, Inc., Brighton, Massachusetts.

104 According to the 1973 *Digest of Educational Statistics*, 49.3 million elementary and secondary students were enrolled in the U.S. public schools in 1972.

XI. *Nonstop Forward Motion*

106 George Counts is quoted from *Dare the School Build a New Social Order?* See page 7.

108 In an interview with Cesar Chavez, published in *Fellowship* magazine, September 1973, Jim Forest writes: "Several years ago a study indicated that the average period of activism for war protesters was five months. Their resistance was taken up like an intense hobby, completely consuming for a time, then abandoned to a kind of attic for one's past."

One prominent example is provided by Ray Mungo, once a leader of student activism at Boston University. Mungo has since retreated from urban life to a Vermont farm, and searches his "attic" only periodically to dredge up source material for publication. See "If Mr. Thoreau Calls, Tell Him I've Left the Country," *Atlantic Monthly*, May 1970.

110 Soren Kierkegaard's words are quoted from the title of his book, *Purity of Heart Is to Will One Thing;* Harper and Row, 1956.

111, 112 Rodger Hurley is quoted from *Poverty and Mental Retardation;* Random House, 1969. See pages 45–46, 58–59 and 62. See also review in *Boston Globe*, January 17, 1970: "Views on Poverty and Retardation," by John Kosa.

XII. *Extremes and Oppositions*

116 John Mann is quoted from his paper, "Inequality and Education: A Critique of Liberal Pedagogy."

Henry David Thoreau is quoted from *Walden and Civil Disobedience*. See page 245.

118 Textbook quotation on the Civil War is taken from *Our America;* Allyn and Bacon, 1955. The passage here is cited in *Death at an Early Age*, page 63.

The N.E.A. guidebook referred to here is titled *Discipline in the Classroom;* National Education Association, 1969. See page 39. See also: *Controlling Classroom Misbehavior*, N.E.A., 1973.

120 "Injustice is the right word to use," writes Dom Helder Camara, Archbishop of Recife. For this brilliant attack on word-evasions, see "The Fetters of Injustice," *Post American*, February–March, 1974 (a publication of The People's Christian Coalition.)

121 Testimony of physicians offered here is taken from *The American Serfs*, by Paul Good. See pages 12, 44 and 45. This book, which received only one brief season of attention at the time that it appeared, is one of the most powerful and well-documented studies of the subject I have seen. Along with the books by Rodger Hurley and Nick Kotz, cited above, *The American Serfs* ought to be required reading for every high school student in the nation. Instead, as often happens with those books that threaten our complacence most, it is by now almost impossible to find.

page

123 The passage on "the principles of conflict resolution" is quoted from *Challenges for the 1970's;* published by Congressional Quarterly, January 1970. See page 151.

The Xerox publication quoted here is titled *Cases and Controversy,* by Donald W. Oliver and Fred M. Newmann; American Education Publications (Xerox Corp.), 1972. See page 7.

123, 124 Other publications which provide advice on the teaching of "conflict resolution" in the schools:

Teaching Public Issues in the High School, by Oliver Shaver; Houghton Mifflin, 1966.
Values Clarification, by Simon, Howe and Kirschenbaum; Hart Publishing Co., 1972.
Taking a Stand, by Donald W. Oliver and Fred M. Newmann; American Education Publications (Xerox Corp.), 1972. The subtitle, "A Guide to Clear Discussion of Public Issues," says more of the publication's true intent than does its pretentious title.

126 Herbert Marcuse is quoted from his essay, "Repressive Tolerance," which appears in *Critique of Pure Tolerance,* edited by Robert P. Wolff; Beacon Press, 1969. See page 98.

Marcus Raskin writes with precision on this point:

> The prophetic task is most needed in the middle classes . . . They are the ones who say that very little can be different just because of the nature of man. Avoidance of extremes and moderation in all things is their political and intellectual advice. Fearing false prophecy, they shore up that tradition in the universities and in the churches.

See *Being and Doing,* page 401.

In a comparable vein, one hundred years before, William Lloyd Garrison — when told by friends that he was "all on fire" — gave them the memorable response: "I have need to be all on fire, for I have mountains of ice about me to melt." See *The Politics of History,* page 147.

XIII. *Ethics*

129 For a cold, unhesitant example of "the charm of realistic cynicism," see the article: "Social Responsibility Called Good Business," *Boston Globe,* May 24, 1974.

134 For documentation of starvation-level statistics, see notes for pages 45, 111 and 121. See also *The American Serfs,* by Paul Good, page 8.

135 Proverbs 29:18

XIV. *Research*

138 Soren Kierkegaard is quoted from *Purity of Heart Is to Will One Thing.* See pages 126–127.

The article by Daniel Moynihan referred to on this page is: "Politics as the Art of the Impossible," *American Scholar,* Autumn 1969.

139 Boss Tweed is quoted from "The Lessons of 1968," by George McGovern, *Harper's Magazine*, January 1970.

140 For a clear example of the kind of meaningless and futile student project I have here in mind, see the research recommended at the end of *The Progressive Era*, by Donald W. Oliver and Fred M. Newmann; American Education Publications (Xerox Corp.), 1972.

145 Several recent articles describe researchers busily involved in — and happily rewarded for — the self-perpetuating process of delay: "Poverty May Be Good For You," *Time*, June 21, 1971, and "School Researchers Grumble at Fate," *Boston Globe*, March 4, 1973.

146 The interview with Moynihan referred to here is titled "Pat Moynihan: 'Too Much!' and 'Too Little!,' " *New York Times Magazine*, November 2, 1969.

147 For detailed statistics on moneys expended per child through the Aid to Dependent Children program, see *Statistical Abstract of the U.S., 1973*, pages 309–311. Figures listed were compiled by the U.S. Social and Rehabilitation Service, Public Assistance Statistics, for 1970. (A.F.D.C. figures change from one city to another. In Boston or New York City the child, as of 1970, would receive approximately $2.50 for all needs per day.)

XV. *The Examination of Dissent*

149 Charles Hampden-Turner is quoted from *Radical Man;* Doubleday, 1971. See page 447.

150 Kenneth Keniston is quoted from *The Uncommitted;* Dell, 1965. See page 101.

The other books to which reference has been made are:
The Agony of the American Left, by Christopher Lasch; Alfred A. Knopf, 1969.
A Prophetic Minority, by Jack Newfield; New American Library, 1966.
Young Radicals, by Kenneth Keniston; Harcourt, Brace and World, 1968.

In February 1974, a group at the University of Massachusetts, Amherst campus, began "a survey of those who were the agents of change" during the 1960s. This undertaking — still in its "first stage" — involves an attempt to determine just who such people were."
Above is quoted from a questionnaire received by the author in February 1974.

151 "A Sane Look at Dissent," by S. J. Micciche, *Boston Globe*, May 24, 1970.

For account of medical conference and discussion of Vietnam, see "Anti-War Doctors, Students Scorned by Medical Society," *Boston Globe*, May 28, 1970.

154 John D. Rockefeller III is quoted from "Youth and the Establishment . . . Can They Work Together?", *Boston Globe*, January 2, 1971.

155 "Jason Epstein: Martin Mayer's Ocean Hill," *New York Review of Books*, March 13, 1969.

"The Good Old Days," by Christopher Lasch, *New York Review of Books*, February 10, 1972.

See also Willard Gaylin's review of Robert Liston's *Dissent in America*, *New York Times Book Review*, May 23, 1971.

page
156, 157 *Challenges for the 1970's.* See pages 11 and 87.

XVI. *The Obligations of the Reader and the Writer of this Book*

159 In reference to truth as a function of "right deeds" rather than "right words," Erich Fromm writes:

> Some people have no freedom to choose the good because their character structure has lost the capacity to act in accordance with the good.

See *Heart of Man;* Harper and Row, 1968, page 131.

Alfred North Whitehead is paraphrased here from *The Aims of Education;* Macmillan-Free Press, 1967. See page 2.

160 For an effective discussion of Inert Concern, in a text primarily for teachers, see *Education and Social Problems,* by Carl Weinberg; Macmillan-Free Press, 1971, page 234.

Paulo Freire is quoted from *Pedagogy of the Oppressed.* See pages 57, 75 and 76.

165 Henry David Thoreau is quoted from *Walden and Civil Disobedience.* See page 348.

For a grotesque defense of the virtues of Inert Concern, see "The Grace of Doing Nothing," by H. Richard Niebuhr in *Contemporary Moral Issues,* page 461:

> It is when we stand aside from . . . conflict . . . when we seem to be condemned to doing nothing, that our moral problems become greatest. How shall we do nothing? . . . We pass resolutions, aware that we are doing nothing; we summon up righteous indignation and still do nothing; we write letters to congressmen and secretaries, asking others to act while we do nothing. Yet is it really that we are doing nothing? There are, after all, various ways of being inactive . . . Some kinds of inactivity, if not all, may be highly productive . . .

Soren Kierkegaard is quoted from *Purity of Heart Is to Will One Thing.* See page 179.

XVII. *Colleges and Universities*

170 For quotation at head of chapter XVII, see *Harvard Class of 1958, 15th Anniversary Report;* Crimson Printing Company, 1973, page 34.

177, 178 Upton Sinclair, Charles Sumner and Ralph Waldo Emerson are all quoted from *The Goose-step,* by Upton Sinclair; A.M.S. Press, 1970. See pages 21, 25, 63, 65, 68, 89, 90, 94, 168 and 182.

178 For information on the corporations that control the policies of Harvard University, see *How Harvard Rules,* first published in 1969, available now from New England Free Press, Boston.

XVIII. *Inexorable Decisions*

181 Frederick Douglass is quoted from *The Life and Writings of Frederick Douglass,* edited by Philip Foner; International Publishers, 1950. See page 104 of volume II.

page

184　According to the 1973 *Digest of Educational Statistics*, 1,128,996 elementary and secondary students were enrolled in New York City's public schools during 1972.

185　Ivan Illich is quoted here from prefatory matter (hardcover edition) of *Pedagogy of the Oppressed*, by Paulo Freire.

Freire's thesis here is developed in his paper, "The Role of the Social Worker in the Process of Change." Specific quotations are from correspondence with the author.

Exiles

186　Upton Sinclair is quoted from *The Goose-step*. See page 478.

193　Paulo Freire is quoted from *Pedagogy of the Oppressed*. See page 177.

ACKNOWLEDGMENTS

This book has been read and criticized by several hundred people in its Mexican edition and in multiple versions here in the U.S. I can thank only a few of those who have helped me the most. First, among people from five nations who assembled with me during summer 1974, in Cuernavaca: Margaret Bearlin, Jim Bishop, Mara Taub, Willie Sordill, Mary Jean Walter, David Strachan, Sara Kerr. I also offer thanks to Sylvia Cleveland, Bill Waller, David Koehler, Mike Meyer, Leonard Solo, Truman Nelson, Dorothy and Larry Olds, Alice and George Papcun, Charles Hampden-Turner, Eric Bentley, Carl Brandt, Paul Sweezey, Rob Cowley, Henry Mayer, Michael Katz, Joel Spring, Ruick Rolland, Michael Lerner, Fred and Robin Staab, Margo Hammond, David Clements, Terry Doran, Eric Davin, Richard Walter, Robert Lifton and Steve Mann.

For help in gaining access to financial aid, and for other deeper kinds of help as well: Leslie Dunbar, Edward Meade, Charles Brown, Jerome Bruner, Mario Fantini, Archibald MacLeish and the Trustees of the Guggenheim Foundation. I do not believe that many people in the large foundations could agree with much of what I have to say within this book. Yet individuals in both the Ford and Field Foundations have been willing to award me limited support to get this writing done. I have tried, wherever possible, to share these funds with my co-workers.

For judgment, patience, loyalty and the limitless expenditure of time, I thank, above all, Barbara Kozol, Yvonne Ruelas, Frances and John Maher, Ruth Wald, Kenneth Keniston, Doris Benaron, Megan Marshall and Beth Taylor.

Deepest thanks belong to my mother and my father.

It is unusual for a writer of my age and my beliefs to be able to remain so close to his own family and to share with them so many hours of encouragement and mutual trust. I have no adequate way to thank my mother and my father for the love and perseverance which have made my life both strong and hopeful in this period of ten years.